ENERGY-EFFICIENT AND ENVIRONMENTAL LANDSCAPING

CUT YOUR UTILITY BILLS BY UP TO 30 PERCENT AND CREATE A NATURAL, HEALTHY YARD

ANNE SIMON MOFFAT, MARC SCHILER,
AND THE STAFF OF GREEN LIVING

Library of Congress Cataloging in Publication Data

Green Living
Energy-efficient and environmental landscaping: cut your utility bills by up to 30 percent and create a natural, healthy yard / Green Living, Anne Simon Moffat, and Marc Schiler.
Includes index.
1. Landscaping — Environmental aspects. 2. Environmental protection.

ISBN 0-9638784-0-9
CIP 93-72535

First Edition

10 9 8 7 6 5 4 3 2 1

Printed in the United States of America

712.6
MOFFAT

Grateful acknowledgment is made for permission to reprint the following: From Brooklyn Botanical Gardens' *The Environmental Gardener* © 1992: "The Lazy Gardener's Guide to Recycling Yard Waste" by Robert Kourik; "An Environmental Gardener's Guide to Pest Management," by Craig Hollingsworth and Karen Iodine; "Where to Get Native Plants," by Janet Marinelli. "Creating a Natural-Looking Garden," by Darrel Morrison is from Brooklyn Botanical Gardens' *Gardening with Wildflowers and Native Plants* © 1989. "Mature Tree Care" and "New Tree Planting" are by the International Society of Arboriculture © 1991. "Natural Lawn Care," by Warren Schultz © *Garbage* 1990. Parts of the "Backyard Wildlife Habitat" by the National Wildlife Federation © 1991 were adapted with permission. The sidebar on changing a conventional landscape to a water-efficient one is reprinted with permission from "Dry Times" by Kent Martin © *Organic Gardening* 1988. The accompanying illustration is reprinted with permission from Elissa Rosenberg.

Illustrations by Diane Zampino and Diane Divenere

Book design and cover by Glenn Richardson

Cover photo credits: Steve Martino for the southwest landscape, the South Florida Water Management District for the hot, humid landscape, and Karen Bussolini for the remaining photos.

Printed on recycled paper.

This book is available at quantity discounts for bulk purchases or fund raising.

Appropriate Solutions Press
Dover Road Box 39
South Newfane, Vermont 05351
(802) 348-7441

Contents

Acknowledgments

To those publishers who have granted us permission to reprint articles: Thank you. I'm especially grateful to Barbara Pesch of the Brooklyn Botanical Gardens who gave us permission to reprint four articles (noted on the copyright page). I highly recommend Brooklyn Botanical Gardens' publications for anyone who wants to further explore the world of gardening and landscaping.

I appreciate the help of John Behm of the National Wildlife Federation for permission to use "Backyard Wildlife Habitat." Although our chapter on wildlife landscaping is substantially different from "Backyard Wildlife Habitat," we did rely heavily on material from the National Wildlife Federation.

Several thank-yous to Carol Abbott of the International Society of Arboriculture for permission to reprint "Mature Tree Care" and "New Tree Planting." The International Society of Arboriculture is a nonprofit organization supporting tree-care research and preservation around the world. It can be reached at P.O. Box GG, Savoy, IL 61874.

I appreciate the photo help of Steve Martino and Karen Bussolini. Steve, an award-winning landscape architect working from Phoenix, Arizona, designed the Southwest landscape pictured on the cover. Karen Bussolini, based in Kent, Connecticut, specializes in garden and architectural photography.

Special thanks to Doug Welsh, horticulturist at the Texas Agricultural Extension Service and coauthor of *Xeriscape Gardening*. Doug generously read through the chapter on water-efficient landscaping and sent some excellent photos.

A number of people have contributed to this new edition. Most significant are Glenn Richardson for his layout and design work, Margaret Wimberger for her proofreading, copy-editing, and general counsel, and Diane Divenere for her illustrations. Less involved but helpful contributors were Joe Glickman for editoral advice, Lynne Weinstein for her photo knowledge, and Elissa Rosenberg for her illustrations. Text scanning by Dave Caputo of Radical Solutions in Amherst, Massachusetts was a huge time saver.

Introduction

If you're not sure what energy-efficient and environmental landscaping is, you're not alone. During the year that I researched and prepared this manuscript, I was often asked: "What's the book about?" My answer was usually met with an *un*knowing nod or the response, "What's that?"

Perhaps a shrewder man would have taken the hint and moved on. Instead, the blank looks convinced me that this book was needed. This country has 40 million acres of yard. Most of those yards waste water, are sprayed with chemicals (over 200 million pounds of lawn chemicals alone last year), and can't support wildlife. Only a small percentage are designed with indoor comfort in mind.

The difference between an energy-efficient, water-conserving, non-toxic landscape and a conventional one is the difference between working with nature and fighting it. Not surprisingly, working with nature has its advantages: It can save thousands of dollars in utility bills, greatly reduce yard maintenance, increase your enjoyment of your property, and lessen your negative impact on the earth.

How Can Landscaping Do All That?

If you've ever relaxed in the shade of an oak on a hot day or hurried across an open field to escape a biting wind, you've experienced how the landscape can alter the climate. On the same day, at the same time, at only slightly different locations, landscaping can change the temperature by 20-25° F.

Harnessing the effects of plants and landforms can keep you cooler in the summer and warmer in the winter. (You can even do both on the same property.) Using appropriate plants can also practically eliminate the need to water your yard. It requires some planning, some background on how plants and weather work, and some knowledge of which plants will work best for your needs. But it doesn't take a Ph.D. in horticulture: If you can follow a recipe, you can put nature to work for you.

How Much Money Can This Book Save You?

Since we don't know the particulars of your property and how well insulated your house is, it's impossible to say exactly. According to the U.S. Department of Energy, energy-efficient landscaping can save up to 30 percent on your heating bills. For a home in, say, Dayton, Ohio, with a $1,000 yearly heating bill, that translates into $300 saved per year. If your house is well insulated and you live in a mild area, you'll save less. But it's also possible to save even more: A study of a poorly insulated house in a cold windy area showed windbreaks of trees cut heating costs 40 percent.

Landscaping can have an even greater cooling effect. Tests in Florida documented a 50 percent reduction in air-conditioning costs for a variety of houses. Savings for scantily insulated mobile homes can easily reach 75 percent—or in some cases, the need for air conditioning has been eliminated. In a hot climate, it's common to spend over $500 a year for air-conditioning. Cutting that in half saves $250, each year. Naturally, your savings potential is less if your house already sits in a grove of palm trees.

In many areas of the country, the yard is responsible for 50 percent of household water consumption. By taking a cue from nature and creating a landscape that fits its region and particular location, you can lower your outdoor watering needs by 80 percent while reducing yard maintenance. (If you value your time, include that as money saved.) Changing a conventionally landscaped suburban property in Santa Fe or Boston to a water-efficient one can save over $400 in water bills during a dry summer. Other areas of the country may have lower water rates, but even at half those rates you'll save a chunk of change.

You may not be able to take full advantage of all the suggestions in this book and save over $700 (tax-free) a year. Or you might have to wait for some plants to mature to reap full benefits. (If this is the case, we've provided interim suggestions that give almost immediate, albeit somewhat reduced, results. We've also included a list of fast-growing plant species in Appendix F). Regardless, most people can save at least a few hundred of dollars a year by properly reworking their yard.

Energy-efficient landscaping also improves the value of your house. Buyers are willing to pay more for a house with low utility bills. And tasteful landscaping (we've given design guidelines and suggestions) will increase the overall worth of your property. According to a National Gardening Association survey cited in *Kiplinger's Personal Finance Magazine*, a well-designed and maintained landscape adds anywhere from 7 to 15 percent to the resale value of your home. Other professional sources cite that home values increase by as much as 25 percent after landscaping.

Saving More Than Just Money

Controlling the temperature with plants is always preferable to using air conditioners and furnaces. Burning oil, gas, or wood pollutes, contributes to global warming, and depletes precious resources. Air conditioners leak ozone-depleting chemicals and increase demand at power plants.

Plants not only keep you comfortable without creating pollution, they actually clean the air by absorbing carbon dioxide, the largest contributor to global warming. Planting new trees can help us with our carbon dioxide problems, but it won't be enough. It's been estimated that in order to accommodate our global carbon dioxide emissions, all the world's deforested areas would have to be replanted. Since that seems highly unlikely, we need to plant trees at the same time that we reduce carbon dioxide emissions. Energy-efficient landscaping does both.

In addition to conserving resources, an environmentally friendly landscape shouldn't use toxic chemicals on the lawn. It should use plants native to your region and recycle organic waste for fertilizer. An ecofriendly landscape should also be an area where wildlife can thrive. This book shows you how to create just that.

For those who need it, it also includes some landscaping basics, such as how to prune a hedge and how to transplant a tree. *Energy-Efficient and Environmental Landscaping* tells you how to design a pleasing and functional landscape. Everything is explained assuming the reader has no previous landscaping experience. Landscape designers, architects, and planners can also benefit from our user-friendly format that provides easy reference and a good refresher course. Building-design professionals will find our appendices and bibliography helpful sources for more detailed information.

Our goal is to help lower the harmful impact our properties make on the environment and our savings accounts. So dig in and enjoy.

MARSHALL GLICKMAN
Editor

PUBLISHER'S NOTE

After the oil crisis in the 1970s, a number of articles and books were published on energy-efficient landscaping. The best of the books was *Landscape Design That Saves Energy* by Anne Simon Moffat and Marc Schiler (William Morrow, 1981). *Landscape Design That Saves Energy* went through a couple of printings, was a popular Book-of-the-Month-Club selection, and received acclaim from a variety of publications, such as *The New York Times* and the *Country Journal*. In their recent book, *The Naturally Elegant Home* (Little Brown, 1992), noted garden and landscape writers Janet Marinelli and Robert Kourik referred to *Landscape Design That Saves Energy* as "still the best work on the topic."

Alas, by the time Marinelli and Kourik's book was published, *Landscape Design That Saves Energy* was out-of-print—along with the rest of the books on the topic (with the exception of one technical volume on energy-efficient site design). Apparently, as the oil crisis receded into the back of American minds and the price of oil and gas dropped, the interest in saving energy waned.

Now that most of us are more environmentally conscious and interested in saving money, we felt it was a particularly appropriate time to reissue, in an updated and revised form, a book that should never have gone out-of-print in the first place. The basic information contained in *Landscape Design That Saves Energy* is as valuable today as it was thirteen years ago. We've edited the book to make it more user-friendly, eliminated the references that were no longer relevant, and added material on environmental landscaping that simply wasn't available until recently. *Energy-Efficient and Environmental Landscaping* includes the latest in energy-efficient, water-conserving, and environmentally conscious landscaping.

Energy-Efficient Landscaping

CHAPTER ONE

Why Energy-Efficient Landscaping Makes Sense

Landscaping for energy efficiency is hardly a new idea. The earliest house builders used plants to modify the climate as well as for structural materials. They knew that during the day the ground temperature in a forest is much cooler than at the top of the tree canopy and that at midday a vine-covered wall is always cooler than a bare wall. A home sheltered on its upwind side by an evergreen windbreak uses less fuel in winter, and a mature, deciduous tree shading a roof and southern wall offers great comfort in the summer.

Knowledge of the local climate and an excellent understanding of building materials and the landscape contributed to the exceptional success of early architecture. With elementary technology and resources, primitive societies designed homes that stayed comfortable even in hostile climates. Builders frequently used the landscape to improve microclimate, that is, the local climate on a small site.

Natives of the hot, humid South Pacific, for instance, constructed open homes of bamboo and palm leaves to take advantage of available cooling breezes. In North America, the Powhattan Indians in Virginia always put their buildings under trees to help shed snow and rain, and the nomadic Omaha Indians of the Great Plains abandoned their wooden abodes in the winter for tents set up in wooded ravines, which offered better protection from chilling winds.

In New England, the early settlers built snug houses, well oriented to the sun, with strategically placed windbreaks of evergreens. In the Southwest, thick-walled haciendas with protected patios were landscaped with cacti and other drought-resistant succulents outdoors while in court yard spaces, leafier species offered some shade and retained valuable moisture.

After the invention of mechanical home heating and cooling systems, builders' respect for the natural environment waned. When oil is cheap and you don't have to chop wood to keep warm, it's easy to forget the art of natural heating and cooling. Practically no one worried that wasting energy would hurt the environment and deplete resources.

For about a century, contemporary architecture largely ignored climatic design. Builders focused on construction costs, just about ignoring operating expenses. Building inefficiencies were masked by cheap fuel.

Skyrocketing oil prices in the 1970s made us recognize that modern building design didn't take advantage of natural elements. Our ongoing environmental problems continue to remind us of that ignorance. Automobile inefficiencies get a lot of press, but the impact of poor housing is more enduring. Gas-guzzling cars will have vanished from the roads long before our current housing is replaced by more energy-efficient structures.

America has responded to the need for more energy efficiency with technology: insulation, solar hot-water heaters, argon-filled window panes. They're all good inventions, but they shouldn't replace the simpler energy-saving techniques our ancestors used. Landscaping remains one of the most basic but neglected methods for conserving energy.

We now know more than ever how to use plants to save energy. Computer simulations and new methods for quantifying the energy-saving potential of landscaping have allowed us to refine techniques that precisely measure the ability of various planting schemes to protect buildings from temperature extremes. (Numerical results of some of this research are in Appendix E.) The practice of energy-efficient landscaping has evolved from an imprecise, common-sense art into a science.

We're not implying that energy-efficient landscaping is a substitute for proper insulation, storm windows, and tight construction. But for a modest additional investment it offers much more energy savings for your dollar than many touted devices now on the market.

The most compelling reason for using energy-efficient landscape design is cost. Landscaping offers one of the most inexpensive, flexible forms of investing in energy efficiency and differs from most other conservation strategies by requiring no large initial financial investment. Your home landscape can be developed gradually as funds are available. Also, a single general strategy can both conserve heat in the winter and reduce the need for air conditioning during summer. Most mechanical systems require separate sets of equipment for heating and cooling. That means two financial commitments and two maintenance routines. Landscaping is one of the very few general strategies to offer climate control year-round.

The economic merits of designing the landscape can be illustrated by contrasting two different planting strategies for cooling. One requires a large financial investment and the second, a minimal one.

Trees are an excellent defense against excessive heat buildup, especially when they shade southern or western facades. They can transform an unbearably hot patio or inside living area into a pleasant refuge. A tree with a light leaf canopy, such as honey locust (*Gleditsia triacanthos*), larch (*Larix decidua*), or eucalyptus, can control the sun's heat inside a home better than a lightly colored plastic coating on a window or a fully drawn white Venetian blind. A dense tree that throws a heavy shade, such as oak (*Quercus* species) or maple (*Acer* species), will temper heat buildup better than a reflective coating on glass. An average full-sized deciduous tree evaporates 100 gallons of water during a sunny summer day, which uses up about 660,000 British thermal units (BTUs) of energy and cools outside a home as well as five average (10,000-BTU) air conditioners. Shading by foliage can lower the interior temperature of a lightly constructed building such as a garage by as much as 20 degrees Fahrenheit. It can also cut in half the time a building is uncomfortably warm. Not surprisingly, the effects of shading by foliage inside a heavier, better-insulated structure are less dramatic and vary depending on the construction materials.

A rapid solution to the problem of a hot room with a southern or western exposure can be provided by planting a single, fifteen-foot deciduous shade tree such as red maple (*Acer rubrum*) at a total cost of about $800 (prices vary considerably, depending upon location). This tree has a four-inch trunk and rootball forty inches in diameter, weighs more than 1,000, pounds and usually requires professional moving and

Landscaping effects of summer temperatures on a house in a temperate climate

planting. If your needs are not that pressing or your budget not that generous, buy an inexpensive 5 to 6 foot shade tree for $60, three or four specimens of a fast-growing vine for $40, and materials to build a trellis. Planting the tree isn't hard, and the fast-growing vine, such as select *clematis* species or Virginia creeper (*Parthenocissus quinquefolia*) will provide almost immediate shade. After about six years the smaller tree will have caught up with the 15 footer and offer the same benefits. Researchers in southern Florida calculated a four-year payback period for the full cost of a contractor-installed energy-conserving landscape. If you do the work yourself, you can get net savings after the first season.

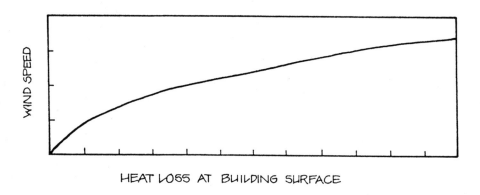

Wind speed vs. heat loss

The mechanical alternatives, such as an air conditioner or thermal windows, are more expensive. None are as aesthetically pleasing.

The economic benefits of using landscape design to conserve heat in cold climates are similarly compelling. Heat loss at a building's surface is proportional to the square of the wind velocity rushing past it. For example, if wind speed doubles, heat loss quadruples; if wind speed increases five times, heat loss is multiplied twenty-five times. Wind increases the heat load on a building by increasing the heat loss of already warmed air and by blowing in cold air, which needs to be heated. Windbreaks, consisting of dense rows of trees such as evergreens, deflect wind over the structure and decrease its heat loss. Recent studies of identical buildings on similar sites have shown that the proper placement of a shelterbelt for one home reduced its winter fuel consumption by up to 33 percent.

In certain situations, plants must be removed from grounds to achieve an energy-efficient design. For example, low-growing trees and shrubs that block desirable winter sunshine or poorly placed windbreaks that cause heat-dissipating wind turbulence should be cut down.

Cost isn't the only benefit of energy-efficient landscaping. No other energy system is self-regulating. Trees are in full bloom exactly when you need foliage for summer shading. And like considerate friends, the leaves go away when you need the sun's heat. Plants even cooperate with our needs in their yearly variations. In cold springs the leaves arrive later, and in Indian summers they last longer. Even allowing for occasional pruning and other care, plants require less attention and expense than mechanical devices do. And what they need, you can usually do yourself—no need to call a repairperson. Plants don't wear out. In fact, most trees get more valuable and beautiful with age.

The environmental advantages of modifying temperature with landscaping has already been mentioned in the introduction. Even if you've only scanned the headlines, you know that the less oil and coal we have to burn to keep comfortable the better, and planting more trees is always a plus for our oxygen supply. For those concerned about the Mideast or trade deficits, consider that we can implement a landscaping conservation strategy with totally domestic resources.

Your energy-efficient landscape should be well planned. Arbitrarily planting trees can actually increase your utility bills. Many people ignore planning and an overall landscape concept because they think only in terms of specific shrubs or trees. They fall in love with a wind-break of blue spruce (*Picea pungens*) or a shading flowering cherry (*Prunus cerasifera*), rush out to buy them, and put them in the ground without considering how they might be used in the total landscape.

The result can be a hodgepodge of nursery plants—hard to manage, disappointing to look at, and uncomfortable to live with. We've provided guidance to avoid this problem.

Obviously, the size of your building site and aesthetic considerations determine the number of energy-saving landscape strategies you may use. Usually it's not possible to implement all of our suggestions for a particular climate, but everyone can select landscape suggestions most appropriate for their situation.

CHAPTER TWO

Putting Nature to Work: The Basic Principles

An important goal of good building design—whether it's architecture, landscape planning, or interior decoration—is to create a space that naturally maintains an ideal temperature. Since interior decoration has only a minor impact on indoor temperatures and architectural changes are expensive, landscaping for energy efficiency is a practical way to make your house better suited for climate control.

The first step to designing a landscape that tempers the climate is to understand the forces that affect temperature and your comfort.

THE PHYSICS OF COMFORT: A PRIMER

Four factors affect our comfort: the energy contained in objects that radiate heat, the temperature of the air, air movement, and humidity. Precise definitions will help explain why each matters to our comfort.

Heat

Heat, which is a form of energy, is distinguished from temperture, which is a measure of how much energy is stored. For example, two freshly poured cups of tea, one half-full and the other filled to the brim, are the same temperature, but the full one contains more heat energy. Different materials require different amounts of energy to be raised to

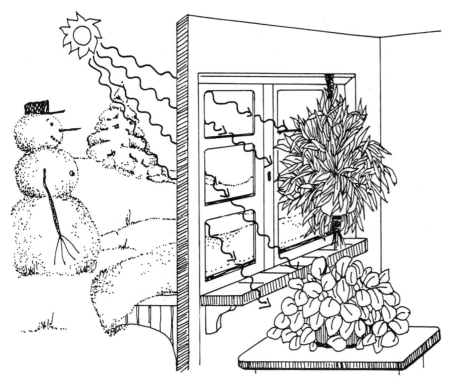

Radiant solar energy warming a room in winter

the same temperature.

"Specific heat" refers to the energy needed to raise a given weight of a substance by one degree Fahrenheit. The higher a material's specific heat, the more energy it takes to reach a certain temperature, the more heat it holds, and the longer it takes to cool down. Air, for instance, has an extremely low specific heat and heats up rapidly; metals such as gold and lead have higher specific heats. Water has a very high specific heat; it takes a lot of energy to reach a certain temperature, is an excellent reservoir of heat, and releases substantial heat when cooling down. This is why lakes and oceans have a pronounced effect on climate. They heat up and cool down slowly and moderate extremes of temperature.

Heat always travels from warmer to cooler substances, attempting to remove temperature differences. Heat energy can be transferred by four methods: radiation, conduction, convection, and latent heat (also called changes of state).

Radiation

Radiation transfers heat in space from object to object. It requires no contact between the object emanating the heat and the receiving substance. It can even take place in a complete vacuum.

Radiation is the heat you feel when you stand in front of a fireplace or lie on a beach and soak up the sun's rays. Radiant heat can be collected from the sun independent of the air temperature. A sun-filled room collects radiant heat and warmth through a window, even in midwinter. Conversely, at night, heat energy that has been absorbed during the day will be reradiated back into the sky and lost, if it is not blocked. In arid regions the cloudless nights have the potential for substantial radiational cooling—except in cities where the low-lying smog often prevents it.

Radiation can be blocked by opaque barriers such as walls, heavy drapes, and plants with dense foliage, or it can be filtered by translucent objects such as clouds, light shades, or vines on trellises.

RADIATION

Conduction

Whereas radiation is heat transfer without touching, conduction is heat transfer by direct contact. Touching a hot iron or an electric-stove coil gives a quick, painful lesson on the power of conduction. It is conduction of heat away from your body that causes you to shiver after a plunge into a cold swimming pool. Blocking conduction is more difficult than blocking radiation and requires specialized insulating materials, such as fiberglass, which has air cells that inhibit heat transfer.

CONDUCTION

Convection

Convection is similar to conduction, but it conveys heat by the movement of liquid or gas—most notably air and water. It is a form of mixing and occurs because most materials expand and rise when heated. Smoke from a fire drifts upward because warmed air rises. If you stand over a gravity-feed, hot-air grate, the warm air currents transfer heat to your feet via convection. This mode of heat transfer can be blocked by physical barriers that inhibit the movement of air and other fluids.

CONVECTION

Latent heat

Heat can be transferred through a change of state, also called latent heat. Latent heat refers to the amount of heat absorbed when a substance melts from a solid to a liquid or evaporates from a liquid to a gas. Changes of state consume vast quantities of energy. For example, it takes 180 BTUs of heat energy to heat 1 pound of water from freezing to boiling.* It takes an additional 1,000 BTUs to evaporate the same pound of water into steam, without increasing the temperature of the steam at all. The enormous capacity of water for latent heat explains why a filled teapot cooking over a red-hot burner doesn't explode. The energy of the flame is used to convert water into steam. This principle also explains an important aspect of the human body's system for temperature regulation. The body releases excess heat by perspiring, and the evaporation of the sweat uses up and draws away large amounts of heat energy from the body.

Latent heat is also responsible for the air-conditioning influence of plants. Plants protect themselves from overheating by processing excess heat from the sun into evaporating water. This is called transpiration and is roughly equivalent to our perspiring. As mentioned above, converting water from liquid to gas uses a tremendous amount of energy. Since plants have the capacity to draw on and evaporate huge amounts of water, they can also absorb a large amount of heat from the air. This process lowers the ambient air temperature and increases humidity.

LATENT HEAT TRANSFER

* The definition of a British thermal unit (BTU) is the amount of heat energy needed to heat 1 pound of water 1 degree Fahrenheit. Therefore, it takes 212°-32° or 180 BTUs to heat a pound of water from freezing (32° F) to boiling (212° F).

In a single sunny summer day an acre of turf can transfer more than 45.3 million BTUs of energy, enough to evaporate about 5,430 gallons of water. Ten square feet of grass can return half a ton of water to the atmosphere in the course of a growing season, transferring a great deal of energy. Temperatures over grassy surfaces are about 10 to 14 degrees cooler than temperatures over exposed soil because grass evaporates water and transfers the air's heat energy into the latent heat of water vapor. Clearly, plants can do this only if they have a good water supply.

Once you have a basic understanding of heat, temperature, and heat transfer, the other factors contributing to comfort—humidity and air movement—are easier to understand.

RELATIVE HUMIDITY

Relative humidity is the ratio of the actual amount of moisture in the air to the maximum amount the air could hold at a given temperature. As humidity increases, it approaches the saturation point, the point at which the air can hold no more moisture and precipitation occurs.

As humidity increases, it becomes harder to add more water to the air. It is more difficult to evaporate sweat—and unload excess body heat—in humid environments because the air is already approaching its saturation point. That's why you feel less comfortable in humid environments.

When a relative humidity of 60 percent or more accompanies a temperature above 80° F., it feels muggy. In an arid, desert climate, the same temperature would not be uncomfortable because body heat could easily be transferred into the air through sweating and evaporation. On the other hand, high humidity at low temperatures accentuates the impact of cold because it increases heat loss and gives an unpleasant, raw feeling. When the air temperature is much lower than body temperature, conduction takes over. The air's specific heat is higher when moist, and it rapidly draws heat away from the body.

AIR MOVEMENTS

Air movements—winds and breezes—also contribute significantly to comfort, mainly by increasing heat transfer. In hot, humid climates, air movements are desirable because they increase evaporation and heat loss, but in hot, arid climates, winds may carry away precious water. Winds in cold weather are unpleasant and even dangerous because they carry away heat. The notorious wind-chill factor describes how air movements accelerate heat loss. For example, at 0°,

Wind-Chill Factor

| Wind Speed, mph | Actual Temperature (°F) | | | | | | | | | | | |
	50	40	30	20	10	0	-10	-20	-30	-40	-50	-60
	Perceived Air Temperature (°F)											
Calm	50	40	30	20	10	0	-10	-20	-30	-40	-50	-60
5	48	37	27	16	6	-5	-15	-26	-36	-47	-57	-68
10	40	28	16	4	-9	-21	-33	-46	-58	-70	-83	-95
15	36	22	9	-5	-18	-36	-45	-58	-72	-85	-99	-112
20	32	18	4	-10	-25	-39	-53	-67	-82	-96	-110	-124
25	30	16	0	-15	-29	-44	-59	-74	-88	-104	-118	-133
30	28	13	-2	-18	-33	-48	-63	-79	-94	-109	-125	-140
35	27	11	-4	-20	-35	-49	-67	-82	-98	-113	-129	-145
40	26	10	-6	-21	-37	-53	-69	-85	-100	-116	-132	-148

Wind speeds in excess of 40 mph have little additional chilling effect.

if the air is still, a casual, well-clothed hiker need not worry about frostbite. But at 20° F, if a gusty 40-mile-per-hour wind is blowing, cautions should be taken to guard against excessive heat loss from the body's extremities, which may lead to frostbite.

Understanding the basic mechanics of heat transfer and how they affect our comfort helps clarify how landscaping can be used to modify climate. The following sections show how the major forces that generate climate—sun, wind, and water—can be tempered by landscaping.

SUN

The sun is the greatest single force affecting climate. Each year the earth makes its orbit around the sun in an elliptical path while rotating on its own axis from west to east, making the sun appear to move from east to west. Knowledge of these two types of motion enables us to predict the sun's "position" in the sky. This allows us to use the sun's energy to our advantage. When it's warm, we want to block the sun's radiant energy from entering living areas. When it's cool, we want to bring all available radiation into our home.

Before designing an energy-efficient landscape, we need to know the sun's path—the arc it travels in the sky. The solar path has two components: its absolute height in the sky, measured by the altitude angle; and the distance it travels on its path between the eastern

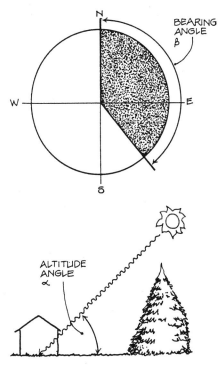

EXPLANATION OF BEARING AND ALTITUDE ANGLES

BEARING ANGLE β

ALTITUDE ANGLE α

ELEVATION

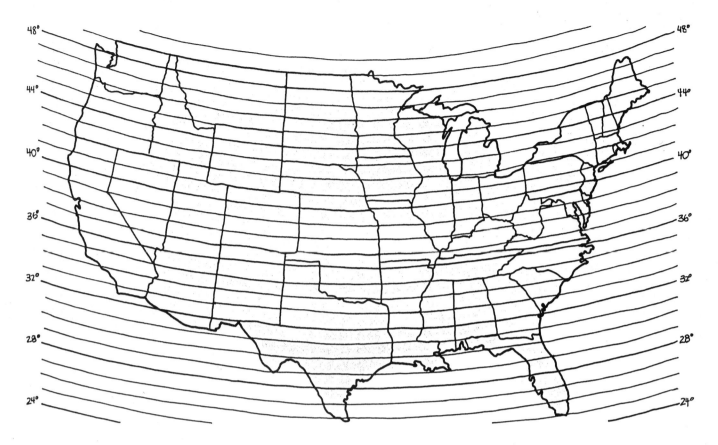

The latitudes of North America

sunrise and the western sunset, called the bearing angle. All positions in the solar hemisphere can be described by these two measurements. The bearing angle in this book is defined in reference to due north because most people learn to read maps from this perspective. (Note, however, that in some disciplines, including architecture and some branches of engineering, it is customary to measure bearing angles from due south.)

To determine the solar path and its variation with changing seasons where you live, first find the approximate latitude for your region on the map of the United States above. Then turn to Appendix C for the charts on solar position, and look at the figures on the table for your approximate latitude. They chart the path of the sun over different latitudes at each of the four seasons. The data for June, March/September, and December are indicated because they represent the periods of the sun's longest, highest arc (summer solstice), the midpoint of its travels (fall and spring equinox), and its shortest, lowest arc (winter solstice).

The following example shows how the solar-path charts are read for 40° N latitude, a line that traverses the North American continent across areas near New York City, Philadelphia, Pittsburgh, Columbus, Indianapolis, Springfield, Illinois, Denver, Salt Lake City, and Mendocino, California.

The first column under the monthly headings refers to daylight

JUNE 22

time	altitude angle	bearing angle
5:00 am	4.23	62.69
6:00 am	14.82	71.62
7:00 am	25.95	80.25
8:00 am	37.38	89.28
9:00 am	48.82	99.81
10:00 am	59.81	114.17
11:00 am	69.16	138.11
12:00 pm	73.44	180.00
1:00 pm	69.16	221.88
2:00 pm	59.81	245.82
3:00 pm	48.82	260.19
4:00 pm	37.38	270.71
5:00 pm	25.95	279.74
6:00 pm	14.82	288.37
7:00 pm	4.23	297.30

MARCH 21, SEPTEMBER 24

time	altitude angle	bearing angle
6:00 am	0	90.00
7:00 am	11.17	100.08
8:00 am	22.24	110.67
9:00 am	32.48	123.04
10:00 am	41.21	138.34
11:00 am	47.34	157.54
12:00 pm	49.59	180.00
1:00 pm	47.34	202.45
2:00 pm	41.21	221.65
3:00 pm	32.48	236.95
4:00 pm	22.24	249.32
5:00 pm	11.17	259.91
6:00 pm	0	270.00

DECEMBER 22

time	altitude angle	bearing angle
8:00 am	5.48	127.04
9:00 am	13.95	138.05
10:00 am	20.66	150.64
11:00 am	25.03	164.80
12:00 pm	26.55	180.00
1:00 pm	25.03	195.19
2:00 pm	20.66	209.35
3:00 pm	13.95	221.94
4:00 pm	5.48	232.95

time, from the approximate time of sunrise for that season to the time of sunset.

The second column describes the altitude angle, or height of the sun in the sky, at a given time. The sun is always highest at noon.

The third column indicates the angle of the sun with respect to due north at different times of day. Notice that the sun is always due south (180° away from north) at noon.

Also note that daylight savings time artificially shifts the clock by one hour. The sun rises one hour "later" than the value in the table, reaches its zenith at 1:00 P.M., and sets one hour later than the value in the table.

At latitude 40° N, in June, the sun rises at a bearing angle of 62.69° (northeast), sets at 297.30° (northwest), and reaches a maximum altitude angle of 73.44°; in March and September the sun rises at an angle of 90° (due east), sets at 270° (due west), and reaches a maximum altitude angle of 49.59°; in December the sun rises at 127.04° (southeast), sets at 232.95° (southwest) and creeps across the sky to reach only the low altitude angle of 26.55°.

Notice the change in the length and height of the sun's arc through the seasons. The longest, highest arc is on the first day of summer, June 22, when the sun rises north of east and sets north of west. The lowest, shortest arc is on the first day of winter, December 22, when the sun rises south of east and sets south of west.

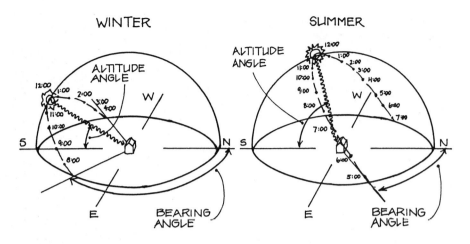

WINTER

SUMMER

Sun's path across the sky at 40° N latitude

SHADING MASK/SOLAR PROJECTION FOR 40° N LATITUDE

Radial lines are bearing angles. Concentric circles are altitude angles.

Roman numerals are months.
I = January
II = February

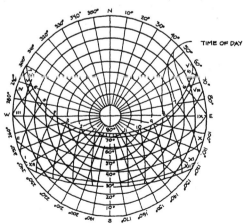

Use the tables in Appendix C to compare the solar-path charts for different latitudes. You'll notice that the seasonal changes in the sun's arc are most striking as you travel away from the equator. As you travel north, the period of daylight increases dramatically in the summer, until you reach the extreme of midnight sun in the arctic. In northern regions the summer sun rises farther to the northeast and sets farther to the northwest. In the winter the sun's shorter path originates farther southeast and sets farther southwest, barely rising over the horizon.

But in the extreme north, no matter the length of its arc, the sun never climbs very high into the sky. One must travel south, toward the equator and into the tropics, to witness the sun directly overhead.

Solar-projection maps such as the one shown observe the earth from a point in the sky and offer an excellent method for studying the sun's altitude and bearing angle during daylight throughout the year.

The effect of the sun's heat on a building depends on both the sun's position in the sky and the intensity of its light. The intensity of radiant energy reaching the earth depends on a number of variables, including the presence of clouds, smog, and, most important, the density and thickness of the atmosphere. During winter the sun is lower in the sky than it is during the summer, and radiant heat must pass through a larger slice of the atmosphere to reach the earth than it does during summer. The longer trip through the atmosphere diminishes the sun's intensity. That is why the winter sun is generally weaker than the summer sun. However, if you use proper building design and landscaping, the winter sun can still contribute valuable radiant energy, despite its diminished intensity.

As light and heat in the form of solar radiation penetrate the atmosphere to the earth, a variety of effects may occur. A fraction is reflected back into space from high clouds; part is scattered into the sky as it strikes small particles in the atmosphere; and part is absorbed and reradiated by the gases in the atmosphere. The remaining radiation penetrates to the earth's surface where it is either absorbed or reflected by the ground, buildings, plants, and animals. Absorbed radiation heats the objects, which can then reradiate the heat. Reflected radiation is not absorbed and is bounced back into the immediate atmosphere. In nature, most surfaces absorb some radiation and reflect another portion.

CONTROLLING THE SUN'S HEAT WITH PLANTS

To stay comfortable during warm weather, it's necessary to control both absorbed and reflected radiation. This can be done by filtering or completely blocking the sun's heat or by reducing reflected radiation. Trees, shrubs, grasses, and other ground covers work well for both. They offer climate control in tropical regions, where the sun is almost always oppressive, and in temperate regions, where solar heat requires only seasonal control.

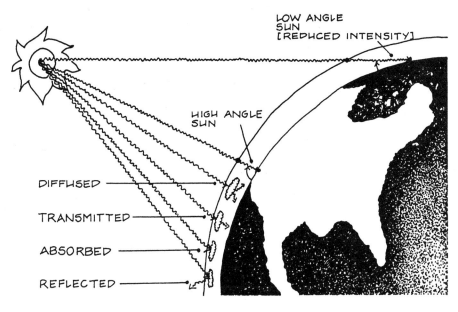

Earth's atmosphere and its effects on solar intensity

Plants interact with solar radiation in two ways to influence microclimates. They block the sun (create shade) and absorb heat. This absorbed heat is used to evaporate the plant's stored water (this is a plant's mechanism for handling excess heat—roughly its equivalent of sweating). This conversion of captured sunlight into vaporized water increases relative humidity rather than air temperature. In very dry air, plants may actually lower ambient air temperature if they have sufficient water to evaporate. The remaining captured radiation is used for photosynthesis and to heat the plants.

The Best Plants for Blocking the Sun

Some plants can almost completely block the sun's rays. The chart in Appendix E describes the effectiveness of various trees at intercepting sun. Species such as Norway maple (*Acer platanoides*), red ash (*Fraxinus pennsylvanica*), and the small-leafed European linden (*Tilia cordata*), which have dense foliage, multiple leaf layers, or a dense canopy, can absorb and block 75 percent of the sun's energy (and 95 percent of its light). Plants with open, loose foliage, including vines and trees such as honey locust (*Gleditsia triacanthos*) and pin oak (*Quercus palustris*) achieve more modest filtration of solar energy. One advantage of vines is that they offer shade soon after planting, while trees take longer to mature.

In temperate climates deciduous plants in full leaf are generally the best interceptors of direct solar radiation. They offer their strongest sun-blocking potential in summer, and in winter, when their leaves have been shed, they allow in the much desired sunshine. When evaluating plants as sun filters, consider the species' shape as well as its density. Each plant casts a distinctive shadow, which may be round,

REFLECTION, ABSORPTION, AND TRANSMISSION

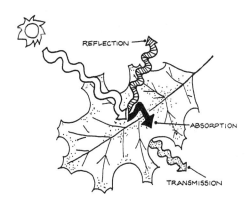

oval, pyramidal, or columnar in form. In Appendix F, tree shape is described in the "Comments" column. Consider the form of the area to be protected before selecting plants to cast shade.

Plants with coarse surfaces reflect the sun's heat best. The multi-faceted surfaces of leaves are much better at reducing reflection than the light, smooth surfaces of manmade pavements or building materials. Dark plants with smaller leaf surfaces such as conifers (*Pinus* species, for example) or plants with pubescent, fuzzy surfaces, such as select elm (*Ulmus* species), greatly reduce reflection. Vines growing up walls or trellises and ground covers such as grass, pachysandra, or ice plant (*Mesembryanthzemum*) also buffer against unwanted reflection.

By blocking or filtering direct or reflected sunlight, plants can powerfully temper local climates. In the daytime, the ground temperature in a forest may be as much as 25° F. cooler than at the top of the tree canopy. At night the foliage prevents reradiation into the sky, and the temperature at the forest floor will be warmer than the temperature at the canopy.

At midday, a vine-covered wall is always cooler than a bare wall. Dramatic proof of how plants cast shade and relieve the sun's impact was gathered by researchers in California's Imperial Valley, who found that bare-surface ground temperatures ranging from 136° F. to 152° F. cooled an average of 36° F. only five minutes after shadows from overhead foliage appeared.

WIND

The sun provides the energy that drives atmospheric motion, better know as wind. Winds start blowing when warm air rises as it expands and cooled air sinks as it contracts. From this simple beginning, the behavior of winds becomes extremely complex. Breezes are usually refreshing and desirable, but as we all know, when velocity increases, winds can be unpleasant and even destructive.

Winds are grouped into three categories: local and regional persistent winds; global persistent winds, such as the trade winds of the tropics; and maverick winds, such as cyclones, tornadoes, and hurricanes. Local persistent winds—the sea breeze, the land breeze, the mountain wind, and the valley wind—greatly influence our comfort and can be controlled with careful landscape design.

Air flows in much the same way as water: Cold air settles to the lowest level, and hot air rises. It will flow over, under, and around anchored objects and will be bent, bounced, and resisted by obstructions such as buildings, fences, hills, valleys, and plants. Air movements, like water, exert pressure against any surface that inhibits their flow.

Sculpting the Wind with Plants

Whenever the wind flows over a solid barrier, there is increased pressure upwind (where the wind blows from) and a protected, low-pressure area immediately downwind or to leeward (where the wind blows to). However, the low-pressure area pulls the boundary layer of air flowing over the barrier into it. Thus, the lee side of a slope receives protection and contains a pocket of relatively still, quiet air. But this protected region has a limited range because the low pressure region sucks wind back into place.

In contrast, a pierced barrier allows some wind to penetrate, resulting in less pressure differential between the upwind and the downwind sides. This penetrable windbreak has less wind reduction near it, but the overall calming effect extends farther beyond it. The suction immediately behind this penetrable windbreak is less than that produced by a solid barrier, and the acceleration of wind back to its original speed is more gradual.

A windbreak of trees acts as such a penetrable barrier. These windbreaks are most effective when placed perpendicular to the prevailing wind.

Blocking Cold Winds

As already noted, heat loss from a building's surface is proportional to the square of the wind velocity (e.g., if wind speed doubles, heat loss quadruples; if wind speed increases five times, heat loss is multiplied twenty-five times). Wind increases heat loss by convection and by adding to the volume of cool air blown into a building, which then needs to be heated. Therefore, a carefully situated windbreak of trees and shrubs can be a powerful energy saver in climates with cool periods.

Because the quality of wind protection depends on the penetrability, height, and width of the plants used, no one plant species can be recommended for all situations. It depends on your property and your microclimate.

The effect of solid and penetrable windbreaks on airflow

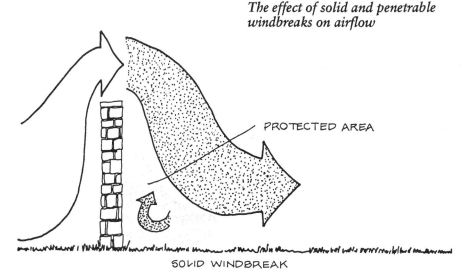

PROTECTED AREA

SOLID WINDBREAK

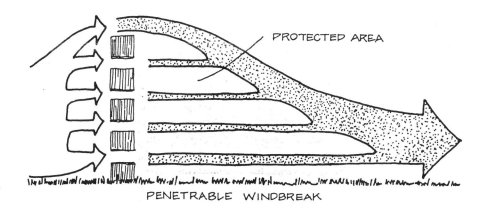

PROTECTED AREA

PENETRABLE WINDBREAK

The effect of shelterbelt on wind velocity

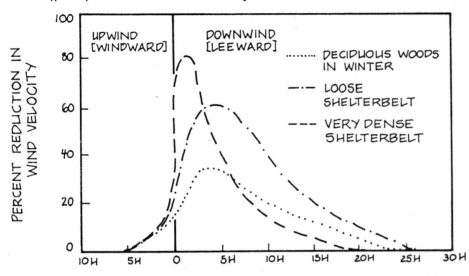

The more penetrable the windbreak, the more modest wind reduction to leeward, but the farther be-hind the windbreak this modest protection extends. Dense, coniferous evergreens are usually recommended for cold climates because they branch to the ground and provide effective wind control year-round. Spruce trees make excellent wind blocks, as do white pine. Spruce offers more protection, but white pine grows faster.

In general, wind speed is reduced for a distance of two to five times the height of the barrier upwind of an obstruction, and up to fifteen times the height downwind. The maximum wind protection downwind from a barrier is found within five times the height of the barrier. That means a 25-foot-high windbreak provides the most effective protection 125 feet downwind.

Wind velocity is cut up to 80 percent directly downwind of a dense screen planting such as spruce *(Picea* species) or fir *(Abies* species) trees. For example, a windbreak of dense, 20-foot Austrian pine (*Pinus nigra*) cuts a 12-mile-per-hour wind velocity to 3 miles per hour. Taking into account the wind-chill effect, on a 20° F. day, that means the difference between what feels like below-zero temperatures and an almost imperceptible cooling breeze (similar to the breeze generated by walking).

A loose barrier of Lombard poplar trees (*Populus nigra* cv. "Italica") in full foliage reduces leeward wind velocity by only 40 percent. In general, a leafless deciduous tree has only 60 percent of the wind-blocking ability of its full-foliage potential. Irregular windbreaks that have some foliage density throughout their height are most effective at breaking up the airstream over them. Therefore, a mixture of plant species and sizes offers better wind control.

The lower wind velocities on both sides of windbreaks attracts precipitation. This means that small snowdrifts may be formed upwind and large snowdrifts downwind of a windbreak. Plant barriers affect snowdrifts in the same way that they influence air movements. The downwind drifts near a solid barrier are deep and do not extend a great distance from the barrier. In contrast, the downwind drifts near a penetrable windbreak are shallow and extend farther. Solid barriers produce drifts on both sides, whereas more open plantings keep the

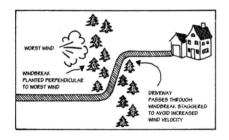

Avoiding accelerated winds when an opening is necessary in a windbreak.

drift on the downwind side. The greater the velocity of the wind, the closer the drift to the barrier itself. A well-designed windbreak will slow the velocity of the wind and cause snow to be deposited before it reaches a path or driveway. In snowy climates, try to avoid putting windbreaks close to driveways and walkways— place them at least as far away as the height of the windbreak.

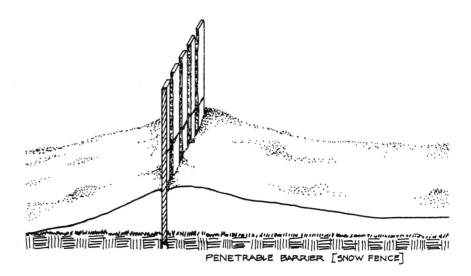

PENETRABLE BARRIER [SNOW FENCE]

Plants that provide protection from wind to leeward may also produce a pocket of cold beneath them. Planting groups of trees for wind control and permitting the accumulation of snow and undisturbed litter beneath them insulates the ground. This means the ground warms slowly on a sunny day, which ensures that snow thaws later and more evenly in the spring. Spring perennials, such as early flowering bulbs, planted beneath such windbreaks will be well insulated against wind and extreme temperatures, but will bloom later in the spring.

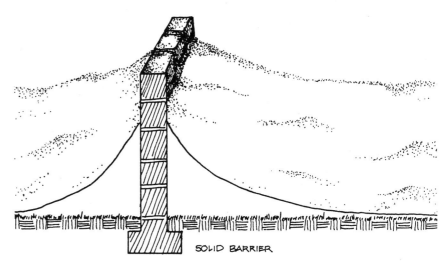

SOLID BARRIER

Varying effects of windbreak density on snow deposit

It is important to recognize that at a break in a wind barrier, high pressure is released and the wind velocity increases above its open field velocity. This is known as the Venturi effect. For example, just past the edge of a moderately dense shelterbelt, wind speed is increased 10 percent above its velocity in an open field. Also, because foliage serves as a direct block to the passage of air, air movements directly beneath the leaf canopy may be accelerated. Therefore, careful placement of a windbreak is essential, and poorly placed windbreaks should be removed. Their growth should be carefully monitored to prevent the development of scrawny bare spots near the ground that encourage the acceleration of wind. If you want trees with high canopies for a windbreak, fill in the bare spots beneath them with shrubs and bushes.

The Venturi effect may also be used to blow parking areas, walkways, and roadways clear of snow. Alternatively, plantings may be designed to channel winds and cause desirable snowdrifts and deposits on ski trails and toboggan runs.

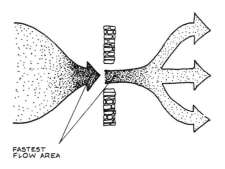

FASTEST FLOW AREA

VENTURI EFFECT

Plants that block wind may also prevent heat loss by adding a layer of insulating air around a building. A hedge of yew (*Taxus* species) or privet (*Ligustrum* species) adjacent to a wall will provide a pocket of dead-air space, insulating against heat loss.

Using Cooling Winds

Plant barriers can do more than just obstruct, filter, and deflect winds; they can also channel and accelerate desirable breezes into defined areas. This strategy is helpful in warm climates when cooling breezes are needed. A funnel of trees or tall hedges that guides the prevailing winds can provide constant natural air-conditioning. Because of the Venturi effect, as the funnel narrows, wind velocity increases, and so does your pleasant breeze. A large scoop that narrows can increase the velocity of prevailing winds that are light and steady but would otherwise be ineffectual. If the narrowest end of the funnel is covered by a breezeway or a tree with a high canopy, the effect improves. Also, since cooler winds flow downhill, dense evergreens planted on a slope may trap and hold cold air, creating cool spaces upwind of the barrier.

The Size of Your Windbreak

The size of your windbreak depends on the size of your house. Ideally, it should be higher than the area of the house you want to protect. To be most effective, your wind barrier should extend fifty feet wider than the area you are shielding, since wind speed picks up at the edges of a wind block. If your property is too small to allow this, make the windbreak as wide as you can and move it closer to your house.

The maximum length of a wind shadow from a windbreak is created by a barrier eleven to twelve times its height, but unless you plan to put your windbreak far from the house, maximizing that protected area isn't necessary.

Planting Your Windbreak

If the wind by your house is powerful, we recommend that you plant a variety of tree sizes and species—some fast-growing and some slower. A strong, tall windbreak needs to have well-anchored roots. That means planting young trees and choosing species that will grow well in your soil. The young trees you plant for long-term wind protection should not be staked. This will allow them to develop a root system that can handle high winds. If the wind on your property is so powerful that you must stake the young trees or they'll uproot, stake them loosely.

While you're waiting for small trees to grow, a fence and fast-

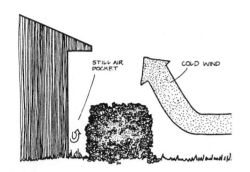

STILL AIR POCKET   COLD WIND

AN INSULATING HEDGE

growing trees and shrubs can give immediate wind protection. Be prepared to lose a few fast-growing trees to the wind and to take them away when they hinder your ideal maturing windbreak plantings. A windbreak fence should be louvered to increase the length of its wind shadow. Another option for an instant windbreak is to use polyethylene netting specifically designed for blocking the wind. Made of tightly knitted threads, the netting can be easily attached to any kind of fence post. It comes in 3 1/2- or 6-foot widths and lengths of 25 or 50 feet. If you're ambitious and creative, you could use the polyethylene netting to build large wind barriers.

For most people, space will restrict windbreaks to one or two rows of trees. Gordon Heisler of the USDA Forest Service recommends "a spacing of 6 feet on center or even closer for pines, spruces, and fir; and 3 or 4 feet for columnar species such as *aborvitae*." Close spacing means faster results because crowns will close together more quickly.

If you have the space, a second row of trees is ideal. Spacing of 10 to 12 feet between rows is ideal for evergreens. Staggering the trees in the rows so they aren't stacked directly behind one another will increase the windbreak's effectiveness. A free-form, natural-looking arrangement can also be effective, as long as there are no gaps in the barrier.

Planning for Wind Control Around Your House

Effective wind controls demand careful analysis of the direction and strength of the prevailing winds during different seasons. Don't try to predict the wind situation around your home from information your neighbor has collected. Identical homes on adjacent lots can experience very different air movements. In addition to the prevailing winds there will be odd pockets of erratic wind in courtyards and between buildings.

To find out the direction of prevailing local winds on your property, tie strips of cloth on several posts, 5 or 6 feet up. Anchor the posts at all compass points and at any suspected odd wind pockets. It's best to study and chart the wind movements for at least several weeks each season (sample chart shown in chapter 13). This information will guide your landscaping plans (covered in detail in chapter 13). In northern areas, wind patterns around buildings may also be traced by watching the way snow is deposited. Make your first observation after a fresh snow on a calm day. Later, observe the shift in snow patterns after the wind has blown channels and paths. Note where the ground is bare and where the snow has piled in drifts. A third method for determining wind patterns is to study smoke released from a chimney, small fire (check with your town's ordinances before building one), or barbecue.

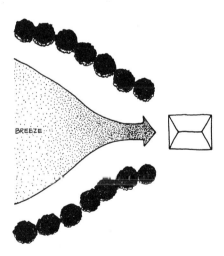

CHANNELING COOL BREEZES IN WARM CLIMATES

Before planting trees or shrubs, check whether the species you've selected can withstand your region's strongest storm forces. In heavy storms, trees can blow into buildings. Dead wood and weak or unbalanced branches are vulnerable to strong winds. It is prudent to plant softwood trees a safe distance from outdoor living areas and buildings. Generally, fast-growing trees such as pine (*Pinus* species) and larch (*Larix* species) have soft woods and are weaker. Silver maples (*Acer saccharinum*), cottonwoods, poplars (*Populus* species), and willows (*Salix* species) are especially susceptible to breakage.

WATER

Moisture is the third most important feature that establishes a microclimate. Water is the best reservoir of heat energy and is a great equalizer. As already noted, water has a high specific heat, which means it's slow to warm up and cool off and consumes large amounts of energy when it evaporates into a gaseous state. Water tempers the extremes of climate.

When sunlight strikes water at a low angle, the light is reflected. However, when the sun's rays strike water at high solar angles, much of the radiant energy is captured and stored by the water. That means large bodies of water act as giant solar storage tanks, retaining valuable energy and releasing it slowly. The ameliorating effect of water helps make ocean and lake properties so pleasant. Conversely, the absence of water in the Great Plains and desert regions explains their extreme temperature fluctuations.

Large surfaces of water also temper extremes of climate by encouraging evaporation and the transfer of radiant energy into latent heat. As evaporation takes place, energy is drawn from the surrounding air, temperature drops, and humidity increases. Even small amounts of water, including ponds, pools, and fountains, can offer climate control by providing a base for evaporation. In general, the larger the body of water is, the greater its influence on climate.

Temperature differences between water and ground also generate convection air currents, resulting in the familiar offshore breezes that provide relief in hot

Solar radiation being captured and stored by a body of water

REFLECTION

ABSORPTION

HEAT BUILDUP

climates. During the day, the sun warms the land and the land warms the air over it. This warm air rises, and cool, heavier air rushes in off the sea to take its place. At night, if the land cools down sufficiently, the process is reversed: The sea, retaining much of its daytime warmth, heats the air over it, which rises and is replaced by heavier, cooler air blowing off the land. Thus, breezes flow from over a body of water onto shore during the day and evening, and off the land and onto water late at night and in the early morning.

Along coastlines, the sea breeze and its nocturnal equivalent appear with clocklike regularity along coastlines. It is a dependable, valuable friend, especially in the tropics and subtropics, and carries poetic names: the *virazon* of Chile, the *datoo* of Gibraltar, the *imbat* of Morocco, the *ponente* of Italy, the *kapalilua* of Hawaii, or the "doctor" of various English-speaking tropical regions. In temperate regions, sea breezes tend to be seasonal, appearing in the warmer weather of late spring and summer. The well-known San Francisco summer fog is brought in by such a breeze. Thanks to these refreshing winds off the Pacific, San Franciscans work and sleep in the comfortable 60s° F. in July, while ninety miles northeast and inland, in the breezeless oven of the Sacramento Valley, temperatures soar to 110° F. Seasonal sea breezes spring up habitually between ten and eleven o'clock in the morning and start to subside at about four in the afternoon. By seven or eight o'clock at night they have died out. Then the land breeze freshens, and the sequence is repeated. This natural airflow pattern over large bodies of water may be used for natural ventilation and energy conservation.

Water in the form of snow is a good insulator. Snow piled on a

Offshore and onshore breezes generated by convection

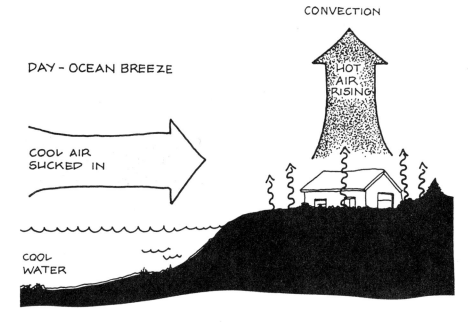

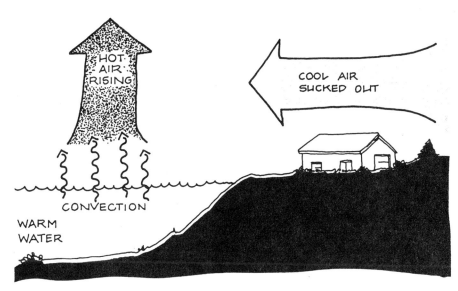

roof prevents heat loss by convection and reduces heating costs. Similarly, when snow is piled against a northern or windy wall, it protects against wind chill, reducing residential heat loss. Shrubbery helps to trap snow in preferred locations.

Plants and Water

It's no accident that classic gardens incorporate pools, fountains, or other bodies of water in their design. The various ways in which energy is exchanged among water, plants, and air can be manipulated to improve microclimates. All plants, especially trees, harness the cycles of water evaporation and energy exchange. Trees tap into so much water that they can be like small lakes and ponds—absorbing heat and evaporating water. The result is the same: lower ambient temperatures and increased humidity.

Obviously, if plants are to cool the microclimate by evaporation, they must have leaves and access to water. Desert plants expose a minimum of leaf surface to protect themselves from excessive evaporation and water loss. Such plants still offer the benefit of shade, but they can't be used to temper extreme heat by evaporating water.

Plants may alter microclimates by intercepting precipitation. Only 60 percent of the rain falling on a pine-forest canopy and 80 percent of the rain falling on a hardwood forest reaches the ground. In general, softwoods (conifers) are more effective precipitation barriers than hardwoods. Softwoods have leaves with a great number of sharp angles and trap water droplets in their numerous cavities. Because trees intercept and slow down water movement, they also help to control surface-water runoff and soil erosion.

Trees, vines, and shrubs can also be used to control moisture retention and humidity. Plants with high canopies lose water to the air. But because these same plants filter solar radiation and inhibit windflow, they also reduce evaporation from the vegetation and earth beneath. This results in an environment of controlled humidity and temperature on the forest floor. The relatively high humidity and low evaporation rate stabilize temperature, keeping it lower than that of the surrounding air during summer days and preventing it from dropping greatly at night. A vine-covered trellis, gazebo, or pavilion in the garden will produce a similarly controlled environment.

LANDFORMS

Landforms, including hills, valleys, and deserts, influence climate and comfort by altering the swirling flow of the atmosphere. Mountain ranges are among the most dynamic determinants of local and regional weather. At the very largest scale, continental mountain ranges divert air masses, affect the flow of moisture-laden air, assist in trapping and condensing moisture, and block or accentuate the effects of sun.

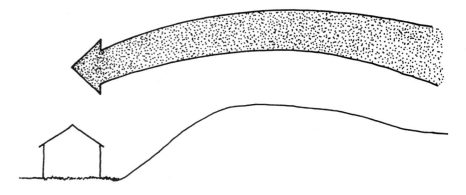

Landforms don't need to be mountain-size to affect climate. Berms—small, manmade mounds of earth—can block low sun, provide a better orientation for utilizing solar radiation, obstruct or channel winds, and offer insulation. They can also provide privacy and noise control. Small hollows can also shape microclimates. Berms and hollows are especially valuable for enhancing the comfort of outdoor living areas.

Berm deflecting breezes

Planting on Landforms

The comfort of outdoor living spaces can easily be enhanced by adding vegetation to a landform. Plants must be carefully selected for the artificial warm and cool pockets created by manmade landforms. They may have to withstand climatic conditions that are atypical for the area. A well-designed berm planted with trees, shrubs, and ground covers can be very attractive, and if it is carefully located, it can modify extremes of climate, provide privacy, and, in certain cases, reduce noise levels by as much as 80 percent.

Berms can also be used as insulators. Soil retains heat and changes temperature gradually. For dirt-cheap insulation, build a berm against concrete and stone walls. Six inches of earth will insulate from wide daily swings in air temperature; that's why basements are cool on sultry summer days and warmer than you'd expect on frigid winter nights. At greater depths, soil temperatures respond only to seasonal changes, and this change occurs after a considerable delay. The magnitude of the seasonal temperature changes decreases rapidly as soil depth increases. For example, in the Minneapolis-St. Paul area, where winters are frigid and summers are warm, the temperature of soil 15 to 24 feet below the surface remains near 50° F. year-round, only 18° less than comfortable room temperature. This is why underground houses can be practical in areas of extreme daily or seasonal temperature change.

The soil layer on berms used for insulation must be thick and kept dry, since wet soil drains energy. Earth banked against a wall can be attractive when landscaped with ground covers, flowers, and shrubbery. Because the tops of berms tend to be dry, species must be carefully selected. Another option is to mold small water-holding pockets into the soil around each specimen.

Two cautions before building soil insulating berms: Don't build them against any wooden sections of your house. Underground wood provides a breeding site for termites, carpenter ants, and other insects that cause structural damage. Second, if you build the sides of berms too steep, they will erode or wash away and can be hazardous to small children (who might fall off).

NOTES ABOUT MANMADE MATERIALS
Color

Color influences a material's response to radiant energy. Light colors tend to reflect heat and reduce an object's heat gain; dark materials absorb energy and get hot. Summer air temperatures immediately above paved blacktop can easily be more than 20° F. higher than at nearby shaded areas of grass. In hot climates, driveways should be light-colored and not too close to the house. If you do use blacktop, place it on the north side of the house. In cold climates, blacktop is perfect for absorbing the sun and melting snow.

If you live in a hot area, painting your roof white can save a substantial amount of cooling energy. A study done by the Center for Building Science at Lawrence Berkeley Laboratories found that by having its roof painted white, a house in Sacramento, California, increased its ability to reflect solar radiation fourfold. They found the home used 40 percent less cooling energy during the summer after it was painted.

Composition

Although color influences an object's response to heat, even more important is what the object is made of. We've seen homeowners and town planning boards make the mistake of installing bright green artificial turf where grass should be. Granted, artificial turf will save some maintenance for a little while, but it certainly won't be pleasant. A study at Chicago's Cominsky Park in mid-August showed that when afternoon grass temperatures were 85° F., artificial turf was 160° F.

Earth-based materials, such as, stone, brick, clay, and masonry store heat and will reradiate it after everything else has cooled down. If you live in the Southwest where the days are hot and the nights cool, this can be used to your advantage. If you live in Florida, you want to avoid stone and brick too close the house—especially on the southern side.

A house in Sacramento, California, used 40 percent less cooling energy the summer after its roof was painted white.

CHAPTER THREE

Energy-Efficient Landscaping for Cool Climates

The cool regions of the United States, including the northern reaches of New England and the north-central states along the Canadian border, are known for cool summers and roaring winter snowstorms. As anyone who's lived there can tell you, biting cold spells, with temperatures plummeting well below 0° F., can last for days and weeks at a time.

In most of the region, harsh winters extend from October to late April or early May and are relieved by comfortable summers. During the summer and autumn, humidity tends to be high in the evening and early morning. In general, the area receives plenty of snow, rain, and hail. Sunshine is possible during at least half of all daylight hours—much less than in the rest of the country. There is also tremendous seasonal variation in the availability of sunshine: In winter the sun skirts the horizon for only eight hours; in midsummer there are sixteen hours of daylight.

Winds are a serious liability, since they increase heat loss and can be enhanced by the region's many hills, valleys, lakes, and coastal influences. Northern cities with skyscrapers are especially affected, since the canyonlike architecture of urban centers promotes adverse wind turbulence. When wind strikes the surface of a building, its velocity is transformed into pressure, about half of which flows down the building to the bottom. When an escape route is found, such as the corner of a tall building, the pressure is transformed back into wind velocity, which accelerates heat transfer. These air movements account for the icy cold winds along Chicago's Lake Shore Drive in winter and the tremendous heating costs of the area's buildings. Skyscrapers help to funnel the wintry blasts traveling south over Lake Michigan into Chicago's busines district.

The colonial settlers in this cool region constructed houses for a severe climate. New England abounds with saltbox and Cape Cod-style houses that were built to let the sun in and keep the cold out. These designs can be improved on by the addition of weatherstripping, insulation, and efficient windows. Ideally, new houses should be compact and clustered together to minimize exposure to winds and heat loss. Windows should face south whenever possible, be minimized to the east or west, and avoided to the north. Super-efficient low-E (low-emissivity) windows should be used whenever possible. Air locks and vestibules for doors are ideal.

Building sites should be carefully selected for maximum solar exposure and protection from winter winds. Building a house on a south-facing slope gives maximum sun exposure while using the earth to protect you from the chilly north. In drier areas of the cool region, home builders can evade excessive cold and wind by copying the conservation strategy used by North Dakota Indians and building living areas underground.

Landscaping, including the use of windbreaks and plant-covered berms, was recognized by our ancestors in this rugged region as an important contributor to energy-efficient design. It can reduce heating needs by as much as 30 percent.

SUN

The chilly climate of the northern regions of the United States is relatively easy to design landscapes for. The need to minimize heating loads outweighs all other considerations and streamlines the design process. In areas such as Minneapolis-St. Paul, which has hot summers, it is necessary to pay some attention to moderating the summer heat (if this is true of your area, consult the chapter for temperate climates). But for most of the cool region the goal is simple: Welcome in the sun.

The best way to achieve this is as follows: Along the face of your home, carve out a swathe, from the southeast to the southwest, that is clear of all sun-blocking obstructions. In midwinter about 85 percent of the total solar energy is collected between 9:00 a.m. and 3:00 p.m., when the sun travels from a bearing angle of about 150° (southeast) to 210° (southwest). During this six-hour period the sun traverses a

AIRFLOWS IN URBAN ENVIRONS

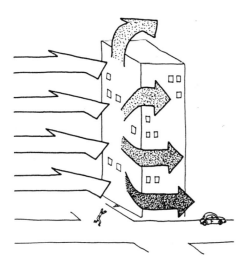

short, low arc in the sky, going from an altitude angle of about 15° at 9 a.m. to a "high" noon altitude angle of only 20°. This crescent of sky should be kept free of all tall plants and trees. When the sun is low in the sky, its warming impact is highest (although still modest) on vertical south-facing wall surfaces and windows. For this reason these walls and windows should have unobstructed access to the sun. Be cautioned that because the low winter sun casts especially long shadows, moderately distant objects that are due south may partially shade your house, blocking some of the sun's radiant energy.

To the east, north, and west—that is, outside of the winter sun's arc—landscape with thick plantings of trees, shrubs, and hedges. During winter, the early-morning and late-afternoon sun is so low in the sky that it offers no appreciable radiant heat, and therefore there is no harm in blocking it. During midsummer, when the sun rises at about 5 a.m., the plants will screen the sun and discourage premature, early-morning awakenings.

If you haven't already installed your driveway or patio, place it near the south wall of your house. The driveway will absorb the heat from the sun during the day and reradiate it back toward the house at night for added warmth.

If you live in a cool region that has occasional summer heat spells and would benefit from shade, plant a high-crowned deciduous tree close to the south face of your home. It will not screen the low winter sun but will offer desirable summer shade.

Area to be kept clear of vegetation

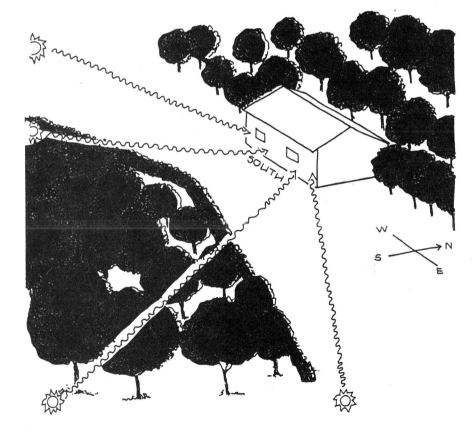

WIND

An old adage says that wood warms you three ways: once when you cut it, again when you carry it home, and finally, when you burn it. We've added a fourth way: Windbreaks of trees, shrubs, and wooden fences provide valuable protection from heat-stealing winds. Landscapers in the cool region will get the greatest energy-saving return by investing in plant designs that deflect cold winds. If you have a limited budget, focus your resources on wind control. Cold blasts of air sweeping south from Canada or off the Great Lakes are a menace. Winds use convection currents to blow away a home's precious heat without even entering the structure. In addition, cold air seeps into a home via cracks and ill-fitting doors and windows and needs to be warmed up, putting further demands on the building's heating system. The prevailing direction of these frigid winds must be determined before any plans are made to divert them up and over a structure. Use the techniques described in chapter 2 and chapter 13 to determine wind direction.

Rows of tall trees planted in stands that are wider than the mature height of the trees provide excellent shields from unwanted winds. These windbreaks provide the greatest protection if they are planted perpendicular to the direction of the wind. Single trees scattered loosely are useless as windbreaks and may even impair home energy conservation, since they can cause local air turbulence as wind blows through a maze of slim obstructions.

Recall from chapter 2 that a solid screen barrier offers impressive protection from wind immediately downwind, but that beyond five times the height of the solid barrier, the protection falls off rapidly. This is because a pocket of negative pressure is created downwind, drawing winds back down and into place. A loose barrier offers more modest protection downwind, but its effectiveness extends a greater distance—up to fifteen times the height of the barrier.

Therefore, if you want to cut winter winds dramatically over a short distance, plant windbreaks of dense evergreens such as pine (*Pinus* species) and spruce (*Picea* species) close to the home. They offer excellent shelter from strong winds for a distance of up to five tree lengths downwind of the barrier, with maximum protection at a distance of two to three tree lengths. However, this strategy for blocking winter winds also blocks sun and is appropriate only if the winds blow from the northeast, north, or northwest, where there is no fear of obstructing the sun's precious radiant heat.

Windbreak: wider than tall

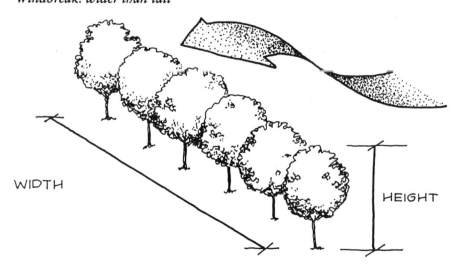

WIDTH

HEIGHT

If you need to calm winds over a distance greater than five times the height of the windbreak, or if you require wind protection from the south, plant a loose barrier of conifers or deciduous trees some distance south of your home. It will protect from wind yet still allow exposure to sun.

Before planting a windbreak to the south, determine the maximum height of such a windbreak or the distance it should be placed from your home. This calculation will prevent you from creating a windbreak that is too tall and blocks the winter sun. First, look up the altitude angle of the sun during the winter solstice (December 22) in your area, and its tangent, from the tables in Appendices C and D. The variables can be determined by the equation:

$$\begin{matrix} \text{tangent of altitude} \\ \text{angle of sun during} \\ \text{midwinter solstice} \end{matrix} = \frac{\text{maximum height of windbreak}}{\text{distance of windbreak from house}}$$

For example, if you live in Butte, Montana (latitude 46° N.), where the midwinter sun rises to a maximum altitude angle of 20.55°, and you want to plant a windbreak 100 feet from the south face of your home, the trees selected should grow no taller than 37 feet. Or:

$$\tan (20.55) = \frac{x}{100}$$

$$.37 = \frac{x}{100}$$

$$x = 37 \text{ ft.}$$

For example, a loose windbreak of American mountain ash (*Sorbus americana*) or tree lilac (*Syringa reticulata* var. *japonica*) planted 100 feet from the south face and growing to a maximum height of 30 feet will offer your home reasonably good wind protection and modest protection up to fifteen times the height of the wind-break—without obstructing the low winter sun.

Wind protection downwind of dense and loose shelterbelts

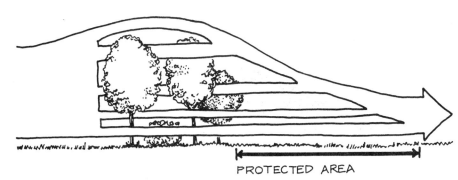

The following summarizes the guidelines for planting windbreaks. Tall, *dense* barriers of evergreens and deciduous trees offer profound but short-range protection from winds and should be placed close to the home along its northern side. Most homes derive great benefit from generous landscaping to the north, and all energy-saving landscape designs in cool regions should begin with windbreaks planted to the north. *Loose* barriers of evergreens or deciduous trees offer more modest wind protection

Noon winter sun angle for Butte, Montana (from table for 46° N. latitude) α = 20.55° (β = 180° or due south)

$$\tan\alpha = \frac{\text{Height of Barrier}}{\text{Distance to House}}$$

$\tan\alpha$ = .374 (from Appendix D)

$$\frac{\text{Height of Barrier}}{\text{Distance to House}} = .374 \text{ or about } 1/3$$

Therefore:
Choose a tree that will not grow taller than 1/3 the distance to the house, or conversely, plant the tree three times as far from the house as the expected mature tree height.

Example: A 37′ tree should be at least 100′ south of the house.

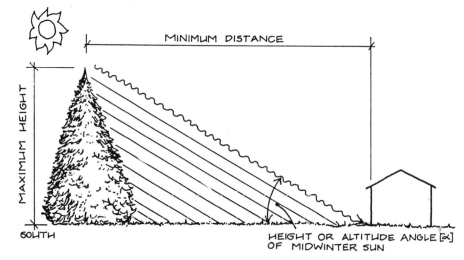

Calculation of tree placement to allow winter sun to reach house

MINIMUM DISTANCE

MAXIMUM HEIGHT

SOUTH

HEIGHT OR ALTITUDE ANGLE [α] OF MIDWINTER SUN

over a distance of up to fifteen times the height of the windbreak and should be placed 100 to 300 feet from the home. This type of barrier can be positioned anywhere without fear of totally blocking the sun.

Fast-growing trees such as white pine (*Pinus strobus*) are appropriate for starting windbreaks, but they have the drawback of being relatively soft woods and vulnerable to breakage in high winds. However, they do provide an environment appropriate for later, secondary hardwood growth. With time and patience you will see the transition of a forestation pattern from softwoods to hardwoods.

The virtues of each of these growth types are combined by planting a double shelterbelt, consisting of a windbreak of fast-growing softwoods some distance from the home that will slow down winds, and a second one of slower-growing hardwoods within their shadow. Eventually, the hardwoods will replace the softwoods.

WATER

As discussed in chapter 2, it takes a great deal of energy to change the temperature of water, therefore lakes and other large bodies of water change temperature slowly. They also absorb and retain some of the sun's energy, acting as giant solar-energy storage tanks. As winter approaches, the temperatures of large lakes remain higher than the ambient air temperature. On the other hand, shoreline areas are cooler in summer than inland areas are. This explains in part why northern communities near large bodies of water such as Duluth, Minnesota, have milder climates than inland areas at comparable latitudes such as Bemidji, Minnesota.

Unfortunately, small pools and ponds that can be easily added to a landscape plan do not offer an appreciable ameliorating effect on climate. They simply do not hold enough heat to significantly alter the microclimate around a home. In fact, certain cautions should be taken so that they do not make your home less comfortable. For example, never construct a pond that is upwind of living areas. This situation will bring raw winds into the home, especially in spring, when the water temperature is colder than the air. Unshielded bodies of water to the west are also undesirable because they reflect glare into the home during the winter months, when the sun is low in the sky. Low-growing deciduous shrubs planted between the water and your home can filter light reflected off ponds.

LANDFORMS

Artificially built-up landforms can be a major design asset in cool regions because they can divert unwanted winds away from buildings and, when placed close to a home, insulate against sharp temperature drops. If possible, place berms immediately next to your house to gain the full insulation value of the earth. A berm separated from your house by a small air pocket will also deflect the wind. In cool regions of the United States the most energy-efficient home designs take advantage of landforms by building underground and landscaping on the roof or along a wall of the structure.

The only cool area where building underground is an inappropriate strategy is in regions of pema-frost, such as Alaska. An attempt at an underground home in this region will yield disastrous results. Once you have made the extraordinary effort of cutting through the ground for construction, the heat generated within the structure would melt the permafrost, settling the home farther into the ground—usually unevenly.

Berm against home

COLD WIND

If you build a conventional home fully above ground in the cool region, don't site it in a valley bottom. Cold air runs downhill and forms a pool in the valley. Similarly, don't place berms around a structure on the downhill side, as this catches cold air flowing downslope and creates a pocket of it.

SPECIAL LANDSCAPING STRATEGIES

Using Vines, Shrubs, and Groundcovers: Woody shrubs that hold snow against a wall also insulate against heat loss by trapping heat inside the structure and discouraging convective heat losses. Hardy vines such as American bittersweet (*Celastrus scandens*) or

Virginia creeper (*Parthenocissus quinquefolia*) will offer modest insulation against convective heat losses as well, by pocketing a still layer of air between the wall and the vine.

Evergreen vines that also grow as ground covers, such as English ivy (*Hedera Helix*), are especially valuable landscape materials because they offer a splash of green during prolonged winters. Bricks, slate, and pavement are also appropriate ground covers on the south side because they absorb the sun's heat, giving an extra measure of warmth to an outdoor living area and making it comfortable for a few more weeks in the spring and autumn. This is especially valuable in cool regions where summers are brief.

Low-growing shrubs and ground covers are favored landscape materials in cool regions because ice and wind often ruin species that aspire to be tall; most species that thrive in the colder regions have learned to huddle together in a low profile.

In the northern regions of the United States the use of alpine plants in rock gardens results in attractive and colorful settings, especially to the south of a building, where there is the need to use low-growing species. Delicate-looking alpine plants can withstand the harsh stresses of the cool region, even in the rocky screes above the treeline. Successful rock gardens capture the character and feel of a mountain scene, with spots of delicate flowers, including select primrose (*Primula* species), anemone and phlox species, and ground covers set among boulders and less massive rocks. Never underestimate the attractiveness and value of select native wildflowers and grasses in the development of a garden.

Rock Gardens

Creating an artistic natural rock garden requires careful designing. Haphazard planning has produced too many rock piles that masquerade as gardens. Always prepare a planting plan before purchasing a single species and locate plants in a pleasing arrangement according to

their culture requirements, and blossoming schedules. The first step is to become familiar with a plant's color, time of bloom, size, and growth habits. In a naturalistic garden, planting in formal rows or geometrical patterns should be avoided. Irregular plant groupings strengthen the desired natural effect. Rugged trees that withstand subzero temperatures, including jack pine (*Pinus Banksiana*), red pine (*Pinus resinosa*), Scots pine (*Pinus sylvestris*), and Norway spruce (*Picea Abies*), can offer an ideal backdrop to the decate-looking rock gardens. Select birch (*Betula* species) and the eastern sycamore (*Platanus occidentalis*), even when leafless, offer interesting color and form. There is an ample choice of deciduous and evergreen species that furnish constant color and mass, providing individual ornaments and privacy screens to northern landscapes throughout the year while protecting homes by guiding cold winds away from living areas.

Plant Suggestions

The following are suggestions for plant species that survive in the cooler regions of the United States. Not all of the species grow throughout the region. Check with your local Extension agent or nursery to determine a plant's growing pattern in your area. Please note that some species grow quite slowly here.

Tall Deciduous Trees
(growing to a height greater than 35 feet)

Acer platanoides cultivars (Norway maple)

Acer rubrum (red maple, scarlet maple, swamp maple)

Acer saccharinum (silver maple)

Acer saccharum (sugar maple, rock maple)

Aesculus X carnea cv. "Briotti" (ruby horse chestnut)

Betula papyrifera (canoe birch, paper birch, white birch)

Betula pendula cultivars (European white birch)

Cladrastis lutea (American yellowwood)

Fraxinus pennsylvanica lanceolata (green ash)

Gleditsia triacanthos (honey locust)

Nyssa sylvatica (black tupelo, blackgum, sour gum, pepperidge)

Platanus occidentalis (eastern sycamore)

Quercus alba (white oak)

Quercus rubra (northern red oak)

Quercus coccinea (scarlet oak)

Salix alba var. *tristis* (golden weepin willow)

Tilia americana (American linden, basswood)

Tilia cordata (little leaf linden)

Tilia tomentosa (silver linden)

Short and Medium Deciduous Trees
(growing to a height less than 35 feet)

Acer ginnala (Amur maple)

Amelanchier canadensis (shadblow, downy serviceberry)

Amelanchier grandiflora (apple serviceberry)

Crataegus mollis (downy hawthorn)

Elaeagnus angustifolia (Russian olive, oleaster)

Malus species (crab apple)

Morus alba (white mulberry)

Phellodendron amurense (Amur cork tree)

Prunus X blireiana (Blireiana plum, purpleleaf plum)

Prunus cerasifera (cherry plum)

Sorbus americana (American mountain ash)

Sorbus aucuparia (European mountain ash, rowan tree)

Sorbus decora (showy mountain ash)

Syringa reticulata var. *japonica* (Japanese tree lilac)

Ulmus pumila (Siberian elm)

Tall Evergreen Trees
(growing to a height greater than 35 feet)

Abies balsamea (balsam fir)

Abies concolor (white fir, concolor fir)
Picea Abies, also called *Picea excelsa*
and cultivars (Norway spruce)
Picea glauca cv. "*Densata*" (Black
Hills spruce)
Picea pungens (Colorado spruce)
Pinus Banksiana (jackpine, gray pine,
scrub pine)
Pinus resinosa (red pine, Norway pine)
Pinus strobus (eastern white pine)
Pinus sylvestris (Scotch pine, Scots pine)
Pseudotsuga Menziesii, also called
*Pseudotsuga taxifolia, Pseudotsuga
Douglasii* (Douglas fir)
Tsuga canadensis cultivars (Canada
hemlock)

Short and Medium Evergreen Trees
(growing to a height of less than 35 feet)

Picea Abies cultivars (Norway spruce)
Tsuga canadensis cultivars (Canada
hemlock)

Deciduous Windbreaks, Hedges, and Borders

Berberis Thunbergii cultivars (Japanese
barberry)
Caragana arborescens (Siberian pea tree)
Elaeagnus angustifolia (wild olive,
Russian olive, silverberry)
Elaeagnus commutata (silverberry)
Ligustrum amurense (Amur privet)
Lonicera species (honeysuckle)
Prunus tomentosa (Manchu or
Nanking cherry)
Symphoricarpos albus var. *laevigatus,*
also called *Symphoricarpos
racemosis* (snowberry)
Syringa vulgaris hybrids (French
hybrid lilacs)

Evergreen Windbreaks, Hedges, and Borders

Juniperus chinensis cultivars (Chinese
juniper)
Juniperus virginiana cultivars (eastern
red cedar)
Thuja occidentalis (American arborvitae)

Deciduous Shrubs

Cornus alba cv. "*Sibirica*" (Siberian
dogwood)
Potentilla fruticosa (bush cinquefoil)
Spiraea latifolia (meadowsweet)
Viburnum trilobum, also called *Viburnum
americanum* (American cranberry
bush)

Evergreen Shrubs

Chamaecyparis pisifera cultivars
(Sawara false cypress)
Euonymus Fortunei cultivars (winter
creeper)
Juniperus communis cultivars
(common juniper)
Pinus aristata (bristlecone pine,
hickory pine)
Pinus cembra (Swiss stone pine)
Pinus Mugo, also called *Pinus montana*
(mugo pine, Swiss mountain pine)
Rhododendron maximum (rosebay
rhododendron, great laurel)

Deciduous Vines

Celastrus scandens (American
bittersweet)
Clematis hybrids (hybrid clematis)
Humulus japonicus, also called *Humulus
scandens* (Japanese hop)
Parthenocissus quinquefolia (Virginia
creeper)
Parthenocissus tricuspidata (Boston Ivy)
Polygonum Aubertii (silver-fleece vine,
silver-lace vine)
Vitis riparia (riverbank grape)

Evergreen Vines

Hedera Helix cultivars (English ivy)

Ground Covers

Aegopodium Podagraria cv. "*variegatum*"
(silver-edge bishop's weed,
silveredge goutweed)
Ajuga reptans cultivars (bugleweed,
carpet bugle)
Androsace sarmentosa (rock jasmine)
Antennaria dioica (everlasting,
pussy's toes)

Arctostaphylos uva-ursi (bearberry, kinnikinnick)
Hedera Helix cultivars (English ivy)
Juniperus horizontalis cv. "Wiltonii" (Wilton carpet juniper)
Saxifraga species (rock foils)
Sedum species (stonecrop, live-forever)
Thymus praecox subsp. *arcticus* (mother-of-thyme)
Vinca minor (common periwinkle, trailing myrtle, creeping myrtle)

CHAPTER FOUR

Energy-Efficient Landscaping for Hot, Arid Climates

Hot, arid regions are characterized by wide daily fluctuations in temperature. During the day, the hot sun parches the earth of moisture. At night a clear, cloudless sky permits heat to reradiate into space, and the ground temperature plummets. A daytime temperature of more than 100° F. can drop to 65° F. within hours.

The cool season lasts from November to March or April, with January temperatures ranging from 30° to 40° F. minimum to 60° to 70° F. maximum. The summers are extremely hot; average maximum temperatures above 100° F. are common, and minimum temperatures during this season average 70° to 80° F. The region is one of the sunniest in the United States and has little precipitation, usually between 1 and 10 inches per year.

Hot winds are regarded as plagues in this region. They carry away precious moisture and bring dust and sand. Furnacelike blasts add a hard edge to arid environments, dehydrating skin and scorching eyes. The winds of drought, such as Southern California's Santa Ana, are often given proper names, like personal enemies. The few cool winds that blow here are treasured and should be funneled into living areas.

Keeping a home cool during the day and warm at night are the goals of energy-efficient landscaping in this region. Successful home and landscape designs here temper and equalize extremes of temperature by discouraging hot winds and retaining any available moisture. Economical use of plants and water can help to accomplish these goals.

As indicated in chapter 2, day-to-night temperature fluctuations can be ameliorated within buildings by the use of heavy construction materials, which absorb and release heat slowly. Adobe or stone walls that are chilled at night will help keep you cool during the day. After a day in the sun the stone walls will radiate heat, but this can be mitigated by simply opening some windows. Any external areas paved with asphalt, concrete or stone, which absorb and reradiate heat, should be minimized, shaded, avoided to the south, and located downwind of and as far as possible from dwellings and related outdoor living areas. The ideal house design for arid climates has few doors and windows opening to the outside. Instead, most windows would face an internal courtyard or patio, where care has been taken to reduce heat buildup, dehydration, and glare.

Shading on west, north and east exposures

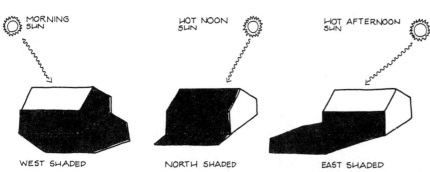

The ideal house would also offer protection from blowing dust. Any living areas that are outside the walls, including patios or balconies, would be located east or north of the house. An eastern location benefits from late-afternoon shadows, and the northern from midday shadows. Unfortunately, this shading effect is minimal in the summer, when it is needed most, and maximized in the winter, when overheating and the need for shading is less severe.

The ability of plants to lower temperatures via latent heat depends on the local availability of water. Plants are better than fountains or pools for evaporative temperature control because plants also cast shade, control reflection, and usually provide usable space underneath. Plants, especially trees, may also tap hidden sources of moisture, producing masses of foliage and edible fruits. Certain trees have roots that can penetrate more than 100 feet into the subsoil and rocky substrata in their search for subterranean springs. Drought-resistant trees such as the almond (*Prunus dulcis*) can survive and flourish in apparently waterless conditions. Olives (*Olea europaea*) and carobs (*Ceratonia Siliqua*) can be planted in clefts of rocks where no soil is obvious; their roots will penetrate deep into a hillside, seeking water.

From an environmental perspective, plants are always preferable to air conditioners for temperature control. Air conditioners leak ozone-depleting chemicals and create more demand for themselves because their operation generates heat just outside their casing. Plants not only cool without creating pollution, they also clean the air by absorbing carbon dioxide (the largest contributor to global warming). If you do use air conditioners, shade them. Their metal frames heat up, putting added pressure on the machine. Trees, shrubs, and vines offer appropriate sun screens.

How much you save from energy-conserving landscaping depends on your house and property. If some of our recommendations have already been implemented (either naturally or planned), then obviously our suggestions will have less of an impact on your air-conditioning bills. Careful landscaping should still mean substantial savings, however. Fifty percent savings have been documented on a large variety of houses. In some cases, such as mobile homes, proper landscaping can totally eliminate the need for air conditioning.

SUN

In hot, arid regions, uncontrolled radiant energy during the hot months is the greatest liability to home energy consumption. Landscapes should be designed to subdue the effects of the summer sun, which arches high into the sky and is almost directly overhead during midday.

An investment in landscaping on the southern exposure will yield the maximum energy-saving benefits in this region. If you have a limited budget, focus your resources here. The goal is to block the rays of the sun as it reaches its zenith directly overhead. Tall, high-crowned trees planted close to the home are best. Palm trees are often chosen for this solar control. However, some palm species such as the Mexican Washington palm (*Washingtonia robusta*), present a fire hazard in arid regions because they store dead leaves at the crown and along the trunk. These leaves should be removed regularly. Also, care must be given to retrieving the fruit borne by the palms. Tall, columnar Eucalyptus species that require little moisture, such as the desert gum (*Eucalyptus rudis*), may also be used as sun screens.

Another strategy for shading south-facing roofs, walls, or windows is the use of trellises. The slatwork on these structures can be angled to block summer sun and permit winter sun to penetrate. Trellises covered with thick vines cast additional shade. Coral

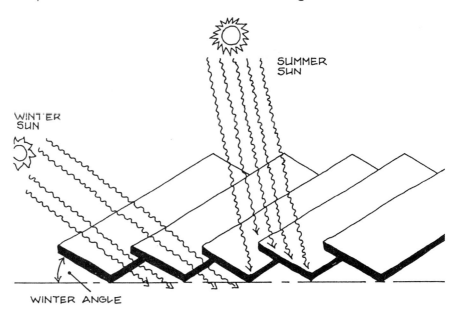

Trellis with slats at solar control angle

vine (*Antignon leptopus*) and cat's claw vine (*Macfadyena Unguis-cati*) are species that thrive with little moisture. Reflected glare on southern exposures can be controlled by planting drought-resistant ground covers, including Sprenger asparagus (*Asparagus Sprengeri*), select juniper, ceanothus, sedum species, and ground morning glory (*Convolvulus mauritanicus*). Grass is an extremely poor choice for ground cover here because it requires more water per square foot than any other ordinary landscape material as well as large amounts of fertilizer. The ground covers mentioned above will cut glare as effectively as grass does and require far less energy-intensive maintenance. Of course, in heavily trafficked areas, few ground covers endure as well as grass does. If you do plant grass in this region, use a low-water species (see the chapters on water-efficient landscaping and organic lawn care).

On the eastern face of your home you can control the sun by planting bushes or low trees such as honey mesquite (*Prosopis glandulosa*) or desert willow (*Chilopsis linearis*). In regions where water is rationed, many species of low-growing cactus such as prickly pear (*Opuntia littoralis*) planted close to the home are appropriate. In general, species with light foliage or a loose structure are desirable to the east. They hinder early-morning heat buildup but permit the pleasant dawn light to filter in.

To the west, landscaping is needed for protection from the low but torrid late-afternoon sun. Low trees with dense foliage, such as California live oak (*Quercus agrifolia*) and fan palms (*Palmaceae chamaerops*), or thick bushes, including thorny elaeagnus (*Elaeagnus pungens*) and sweet bay (*Laurus nobilis*), will effectively block the sun if planted close to the home. Low-growing cacti, including prickly pear and organpipe (*Lemaireocereus thurberi*), can accomplish the same goal if planted adjacent to the structure. Western exposures are also vulnerable to harsh glare and benefit from verdant expanses to cut reflection. Choose drought-resistant ground covers such as stonecrop (*Sedum* species). If water is extremely scarce, divide the yard into sections of planted ground cover and nonreflecting natural materials such as wood chips. This design adds color and texture to a yard or patio, does not reflect heat or light, conserves moisture, and relieves the severity of a desertlike landscape.

Since sun rarely appears on the north face, landscaping here has minimal value for controlling heat radiation. Bushes planted to the

Cacti casting shade on eastern or western exposure

LOW SUN
[MORNING & EVENING]

northwest and north may be desirable for blocking unwanted mid-summer sun shortly before sunset and reflected light or hot winds. If there are no hot winds from the north, short plantings such as California privet (*Ligustrum ovalifolium*) or tamarisk (*Tamarix parviflora*) at a distance of 10 feet or more from the house are appropriate. They reduce glare and heat reflected from the ground, cut off the mid-summer evening sun, yet allow the house to reradiate heat toward the sky during the night.

WIND

The guidelines for controlling winds are simple. Hot, dry winds must be channeled away from living areas, using bushes, palms, cacti, evergreen trees, or manmade screens or baffles. Windbreaks should be planted perpendicular to the prevailing winds. Entrances and windows should receive extra protection from hot blasts. If your site is blessed by cool, moisture-laden breezes from a specific direction, landscape to funnel them into living areas. The Venturi effect (see chapter 2) can enhance such breezes.

Hedge protecting home entrance from hot wind

HOT WIND

WATER

Evaporative cooling from plants, pools, or fountains can provide ideal air conditioning. But areas that suffer from drought should also have landscape designs that enclose the water source, prevent moisture loss, and provide natural recycling of water. This can be accomplished by limiting plantings to an internal atrium or fully enclosed courtyard, or by having only indoor plants, and by making special efforts to envelop all sources of moisture outside a home. For example, exposed pools and fountains should be shaded, and walls or closed fences should be built to contain the cool air resulting from the evaporative process and direct it into living areas. Trellises or canopies can partially enclose or cover water sources and help to contain the valuable cool, moisture-laden air. Submersible electric pumps no bigger than a fist can recirculate the same water over and over without the need for costly pipe connections to house plumbing; they make shaded fountains a relatively inexpensive proposition. If it is impossible to enclose the source of water, at least place it upwind from the home so that humidified

Bird's eye view (plan) of pool upwind of house

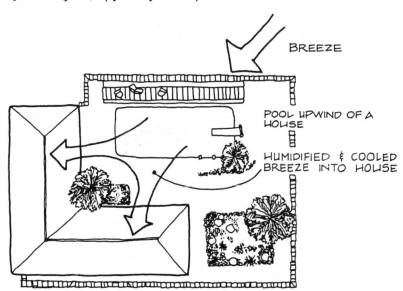

BREEZE

POOL UPWIND OF A HOUSE

HUMIDIFIED & COOLED BREEZE INTO HOUSE

breezes pass through the living areas.

In this region, pools that contribute pleasantly to cooled, humidified air can also be the source of unwanted glare, especially when they are west of a living room. The reflection of the low, late-afternoon sun off the water can be broken by a hedge or windbreak.

SPECIAL PLANTING STRATEGIES

How Houseplants Can Help:
In arid regions, more than in any other climate, houseplants improve the internal environment and can limit energy consumption. They are extremely effective humidifiers and air coolers and, with a minimum of care, are far more reliable than appliances. Because the air is always arid, houseplants help to maintain a healthful climate year-round. (Houseplants are not recommended in hot, humid areas, where added moisture in the air is a liability.) Place houseplants in a sunny window to reap the double benefit of shade and added humidity.

Outside Living Areas: Plants make the outdoors an inviting alternative to indoor, air-conditioned spaces. The most productive planting strategy for hot, arid areas is the design of an enclosed garden or atrium. During the summer, high-crowned trees such as palms cast shade immediately below them. Low shrubs, flowers, and ground covers cool the air further by evaporating water. Because cooled air falls, this valuable commodity is retained and protected within the confines of the atrium. Enclosed atriums also offer protection from moisture-stealing hot winds and are the ideal location for fountains or manmade pools. Precious moisture is recycled in enclosed landscape designs.

If your home was not designed with an enclosed courtyard, build an enclosure around a selected outdoor living area. Put walls around your swimming pool, fountains, or reflecting ponds, and build trellises over at least part of the area. Minimize paved areas and landscape with drought-resistant species. Your reward is a protected, climate-controlled area that needs only a modest volume of water to replenish daily losses to evaporation. The atrium or courtyard may even support plant life not indigenous to hot, arid regions.

Using Native Species: Outside the atrium walls, however, where species must withstand low humidity, limited irrigation, poor soil, and extremes of temperature, only native species endure. This is not a serious constraint for landscape designers. There is a great wealth of flowering and nonflowering plants to choose from; some of the most beautiful flowering plants thrive here, providing a display possible in cooler climates only under glass. Dry gardens can generate high drama with plantings of ocotillo (*Fouquieria splendens*), yucca, century plants (select *Agave* species), tamarisk, Jerusalem thorn (*Parkinsonia aculeata*), fan palms, cacti, and other succulents. But more important than the plant varieties is the way in which they are used. Restraint is the key. Use open space between plantings, and don't crowd plants together. Gray gravel, raked earth, and other materials that reflect little light can separate plants. Some plants can thrive in containers. This kind of landscape might look strange if each plant is a different species, but by keeping the palette simple and by planting in great drifts, you can achieve a unified look.

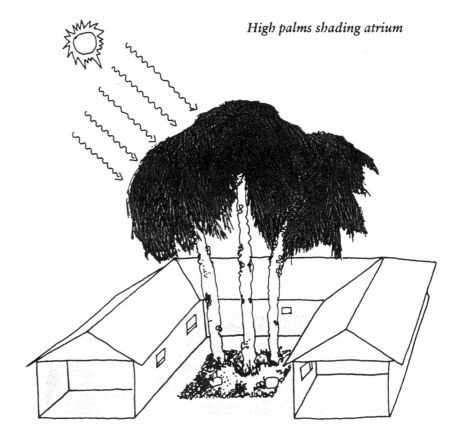

High palms shading atrium

For Novice Arid-Region Landscapers: Gardeners new to this area should be cautioned that most native species thrive with little moisture. Some novice landscapers have drowned their gardens with an overabundance of attention and water. Excessive irrigation wastes water and energy. Some species, such as the California live oak (*Quercus agrifolia*), succumb to excess watering.

Gardeners in arid regions must abandon the horticultural designs characteristic of the temperate regions if they wish to adhere to a plan of energy conservation. Economy in watering is usually necessary and desired. Hand-watering is best done at windless times—during night or early-morning hours—to reduce evaporation. Drip irrigation, which involves delivering water to individual plants through a system of narrow tubes or porous tubing, may be one of the most efficient methods ever devised for watering flowers, trees, shrubs, vines, and commercial crops. It can cut water use by 20 to 50 percent. Mulching also helps hold water in soil by reducing evaporation. To mulch, cover root areas with such materials as pine needles, composted manure or garden refuse, ground bark, leaves, sawdust, straw, or a dust mulch (see the chapter on water-efficient landscaping for further details).

Transplanting demands watering. Most native plants should be set out in the fall to benefit from winter rains. If your area is suffering from drought, postpone extensive planting. (For more details see the chapter on water-efficient landscaping.)

For Community Areas: Landscape design in arid regions should also attempt to provide shade for necessary paved areas, including parking bays and sidewalks. Asphalt and concrete retain enormous amounts of radiant energy and can easily reach 120° F. when the air temperature is 95° F. Moreover, pavements cool slowly because of their high specific heat. Carefully planted hedges, vines, and trees can transform an unbearably hot walkway or street into a cool, shaded passage.

The benefits of the planting strategies just described were documented in Davis, California, where researchers found that large trees could lower the temperature of a commercial shopping area by at least 10° F., making for happier shoppers and lower air-conditioning bills.

THE RESULTS

The overall appearance of a landscaped site in an arid region differs radically from the manicured lawn and shrub settings found in

Site plan

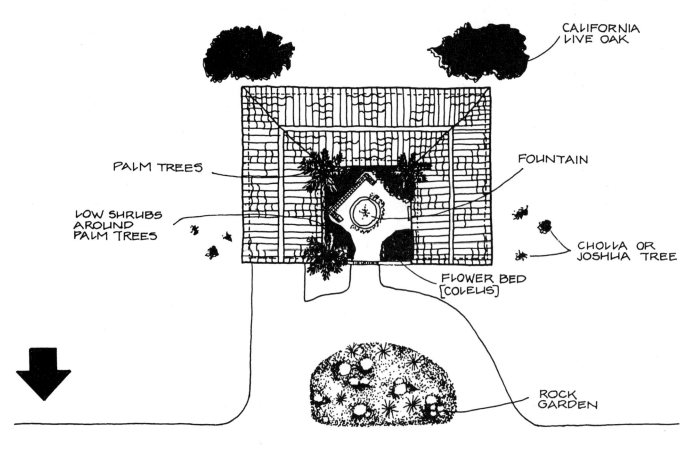

other locales. It is naturalistic in appearance. The land is harsh, and native plants are often sharp and jagged. There is a dramatic seasonal transition in color, from the lush colors of winter and spring, when water is adequate, to the golden browns of summer and fall. Landscaping with native plants recreates and preserves the best of natural desert ecosystems and, at the same time, conserves energy within the home and in the garden. However, landscaping inside a protected courtyard or atrium may produce a small paradise of lush greens, even during dry summers.

Plant Suggestions

The following suggested plants survive in arid or semiarid regions. Not all of the species grow throughout the nation's hot, dry areas, and some tree species may grow only into squat shrubs in the more severe climates. Much depends on the immediate environment and on pruning. Check with your local extension agent or nursery to determine a plant's growing pattern and whether it is appropriate for your location.

Tall Deciduous Trees
(growing to a height greater than 35 feet)

Acer macrophyllum (big-leafed maple, California maple)
Cercidiphyllum japonicum (katsura tree)
Cladrastis lutea (American yellowwood)
Fraxinus velutina var. *glabra* (Modesto ash)
Ginkgo biloba (ginkgo, maidenhair tree)
Gleditsia triacanthos var. *inermis* (thornless honey locust)
Koelreuteria paniculata (golden-rain tree, varnish tree)
Magnolia heptapeta (Yulan magnolia)
Morus alba (white mulberry)
Parkinsonia aculeata (Jerusalem thorn)
Paulownia tomentosa (empress tree, royal paulownia)
Pistacia chinensis (Chinese pistachio)
Platanus racemosa (California plane tree)
Pyrus Calleryana (Callery pear)
Sophora japonica (Japanese pagoda tree, Chinese scholar tree)
Ulmus parvifolia (Chinese elm)
Zelkova serrata (Japanese zelkova)

Short and Medium Deciduous Trees
(growing to heights less than 35 feet)

Albizia julibrissin (silk tree)
Amelanchier X grandiflora (apple serviceberry)
Cercidium floridum (Palo Verde)
Cercis canadensis (eastern redbud)
Cornus florida (flowering dogwood)
Elaeagnus angustifolia (Russian olive)
Lagerstroemia indica (crape myrtle)
Malus baccata (crab apple)
Prosopsis glandulosa, also called *Prolopsis juliflora* (honey mesquite)
Prunus dulcis (almond tree)

Tall Evergreen Trees
(growing to heights greater than 35 feet)

Araucaria heterophylla (Norfolk Island pine)
Cedrus atlantica cv. *"Glauca"* (blue Atlas cedar)
Ceratonia Siliqua (carob tree)
Cupressus arizonica (Arizona cypress)
Eucalyptus polyanthemos (red box gum, silver dollar tree, Australian beech)
Eucalyptus rudis (desert gum)
Magnolia virginiana, also called *Magnolia glauca* (sweet bay)

Pinus canariensis (Canary Island pine)
Pinus Thunbergiana (Japanese black pine)
Quercus agrifolia (California live oak, coast live oak)
Quercus suber (cork oak)
Quercus virginiana (live oak)

Short and Medium Evergreen Trees
(growing to heights less than 35 feet)
Agonis flexuosa (willow myrtle, pepper mint tree, Australia willow myrtle)
Chilopsis linearis (desert willow)
Olea Europaea (common olive)
Pinus halepensis (Aleppo pine)
Pittosporum phillyraeoides (weeping or willow pittosporum)
Pittosporum rhombifolium (diamond-leaf pittosporum, Queensland pittosporum)
Yucca brevifolia (Joshua tree)

Tall Palm Trees
(growing to heights greater than 35 feet)
Arecastrum Romanzoffianum, also called *Cocos plumosa* (queen palm)
Washingtonia filifera (Washington palm, desert fan palm, petticoat palm)
Washingtonia robusta (Mexican Washington palm, thread palm)

Short and Medium Palm Trees
(growing to heights less than 35 feet)
Brahea dulcis (rock palm)
Chamaerops humilis (European fan palm, Mediterranean fan palm)
Phoenix Roebelenii (dwarf date palm, pigmy date palm)
Trachycarpus Fortunei, also called *Irachycarpus excelsus*, Chamaerops excelsa (windmill palm)

Deciduous Windbreaks, Hedges, or Borders
Berberis Thunbergii (Japanese barberry)
Chaenomeles, also called *Cydonia*, species (flowering quince)
Cotoneaster divaricatus (spreading cotoneaster)
Kolkwitzia amabilis (beauty bush)
Ligustrum ovalifolium (California privet)

Lonicera species (honeysuckle)
Symphoricarpos orbiculatus (Indian currant, coralberry)
Tamarix parviflora (tamarisk, salt cedar)

Evergreen Windbreaks, Hedges, or Borders
Berberis Julianae (wintergreen barberry)
Berberis X mentorensis (Mentor barberry)
Elaeagnus pungens (thorny elaeagnus, silverberry)
Euonymus japonica (evergreen euonymus)
Ilex vomitoria (yaupon)
Juniperus chinensis cultivars (Chinese junipers)
Juniperus scopulorum cultivars (Rocky Mountain juniper, Colorado red cedar)
Juniperus virginiana cultivars (eastern red cedar)
Ligustrum japonicum (Japanese privet)
Lonicera nitida (box honeysuckle)
Opuntia littoralis (prickly pear, tuna cactus)
Osmanthus heterophyllus, also called *Osmanthus ilicifolius* (holly osmanthus)
Photinia serrulata (Chinese photinia)
Pyracantha coccinea (fire thorn)

Deciduous Shrubs
Buddleia Davidii (orange-eye butterfly bush)
Calycanthus floridus (strawberry shrub, Carolina allspice)
Deutzia species (deutzia)
Fouquieria splendens (Ocotillo, coach whip, vine cactus)
Hibiscus syriacus (rose of Sharon, shrub althea)
Parkinsonia aculeata (Jerusalem thorn, Mexican Palo Verde)
Philadelphus species (mock orange)
Spiraea species (spirea, bridal wreath)
Tamarix ramosissima, also known as *Tamarix pentandra* (Odessa tamarisk)

Evergreen Shrubs
Abelia X grandiflora (glossy abelia)
Agave attenuata (fox tail agave)
Agave Vilmoriniana (century plant)
Aucuba japonica (Japanese aucuba, Japanese laurel)

Ceanothus species (ceanothus, California lilac, wild lilac)

Coccoloba uvifera (sea grape, shore grape)

Cotoneaster dammeri, also called *Cotoneaster humifusus* (bearberry cotoneaster)

Cotoneaster horizontalis (rock spray, rock cotoneaster)

Euonymus Fortunei (winter creeper)

Euphorbia pulcherrima (poinsettia)

Fatsia japonica, also called *Aralia japonica*, Aralia sieboldii (Japanese fatsia, Formosa rice tree, paper plant)

Ilex X altaclarensis cv. "Wilsonii" (Wilson holly)

Ilex cornuta (Chinese holly)

Juniperus communis (common juniper)

Juniperus conferta (shore juniper)

Juniperus procumbens (Japanese garden juniper)

Juniperus sabina (savin juniper)

Laurus nobilis (sweet bay)

Lemaireocereus Thurberi (organpipe cactus)

Leptospermum scoparium (tea tree, New Zealand tea tree, manuka)

Myrtus communis (myrtle)

Nandina domestica (nandina, Chinese sacred bamboo)

Nerium Oleander (oleander, rosebay)

Nolina Parryi (beargrass)

Pinus aristata (bristlecone pine, hickory pine)

Yucca Whipplei (Candle of the Lord)

Deciduous Vines

Actinidia arguta (bower actinidia, tara vine)

Antigonon leptopus (coral vine)

Campsis X Tagliabuana cv. "Madame Galen" (Madame Galen trumpet vine)

Celastrus scandens (American bittersweet)

Clematis hybrids (hybrid clematis)

Hydrangea anomala, also called *Hydrangea petiolaris* (climbing hydrangea)

Macfadyena Unguis-cati, also known as *Bignonia tweediana* (cat's claw vine)

Polygonum aubertii (silver-fleece vine, silver-lace vine)

Wisteria floribunda cultivars (Japanese wisteria)

Wisteria sinensis, also called *Wisteria chinensis* (Chinese wisteria)

Evergreen Vines

Akebia quinata (five-leaf akebia)

Bignonia capreolata, also called *Anisostichus capreolatus*, or *Doxantha capreolata* (cross vine, trumpet flower)

Bougainvillea hybrids (bougainvillea)

Euonymus Fortunei (common winter creeper)

Jasminum species (jasmine)

Lonicera sempervirens (trumpet honeysuckle)

Ground covers

Aegopodium Podagraria (silver-edge bishop's weed, silver-edge goutweed)

Ajuga reptans (bugleweed, carpet bugle)

Arctostaphylos uva-ursi (bearberry, kinnikinnick)

Asparagus Sprengeri (Sprenger asparagus)

Baccharis pilularis (dwarf coyote bush)

Bougainvillea species (bougainvillea)

Ceanothus gloriosus (Point Reyes ceanothus)

Ceanothus griseus var. *horizontalis* (Carmel creeper)

Ceanothus thyrsiflorus var. *repens* (creeping blue blossom)

Convolvulus mauritanicus (ground morning glory)

Dichondra micrantha, also called *Dichondra repens* (dichondra)

Echinocereus Englemanii (hedgehog cactus)

Euonymus Fortunei (winter creeper)

Juniperus horizontalis cv. "Wiltonii" (Wilton creeping juniper)

Lantana montevidensis (weeping lantana)

Osteospermum fruticosum (trailing African daisy)

Pachysandra terminalis (Japanese pachysandra, Japanese spurge)

Rosmarinus officinalis cv. "Prostratus" (dwarf rosemary)

Sedum species (stonecrop, live-forever)

CHAPTER FIVE

Energy-Efficient Landscaping for Hot, Humid Climates

The hot, humid climate of Florida and the coastal regions of Georgia, South Carolina, and the Gulf States is shaped by maritime tropical air that is heated by the sun and sweeps off the Caribbean and the Gulf of Mexico. An average annual rainfall of sixty inches or more coupled with the presence of undrained lowlands can produce unpleasantly high humidity during most of the year. While this heavy air occasionally explodes with the torrential downpours of a hurricane, most often the hot, humid climates are sultry and slow to change. Moisture-laden air resists wide, daily fluctuations in temperature. This muggy atmosphere magnifies the oppressive effects of heat. For example, the limit of human tolerance (that is, the maximum air temperature at which extended work can be performed) approaches 150° F. in dry air but is reduced to only 90° F. in full humidity.

Despite these drawbacks, the hot, humid region offers a pleasant climate, without the extremes of cold, dryness, and temperature that plague other areas of the United States. This climate also nurtures the greatest profusion of exotic and colorful flora found anywhere in the country. The sun shines on an average of two thirds of all possible daylight hours. During most of the year the average temperature falls within the range of 65 to 85° F.

A hot, humid climate is especially challenging to landscapers seeking to create a comfortable atmosphere. The temperature can't be reduced by evaporation because additional water in the air only adds to the discomfort; long-term heat spells eliminate the possibility of using thick construction materials (as is done in hot, arid regions) to transform extremes of climate into a comfortable middle range within a building; and no construction material exists that filters humidity to a desirable level and still permits adequate airflow.

Avoiding heat storage and promoting ventilation to dissipate humidity are the two key goals of energy-efficient design in this region. Here the best-planned buildings use a two-stage or slotted roof, minimize interior walls, have elongated shapes with a high surface area, and raise floors off the ground. Such designs draw in cooler, heavier air through the ground floor or basement and release warmer, lighter air via roof vents, creating a constant light breeze indoors. Galleries around a building, floor-to-ceiling windows, and jalousies can enhance air movement. Homes in the humid subtropics also have lightly constructed walls of pale shades, to lessen heat retention.

Landscaping can further reduce the retention of heat and humidity by shading windows, walls, roofs, and air conditioners and by channeling cool breezes into living areas. However, landscape materials must be carefully selected and placed, since heavy plantings can have the undesirable effect of generating unwanted excess humidity or blocking desirable light winds. In fact, some established plantings may have to be removed to enhance comfort.

At its best, landscaping also increases comfort by expanding the use of outdoor living areas. Many designers in this region suggest planning grounds to increase time spent living outside. Outdoor areas, if properly shaded, screened, and ventilated, can be comfortable year-round. The exotic and colorful plants that grow profusely in various parts of this region, including Chinese hibiscus (*Hibiscus rosa-sinensis*), the common camellia (*Camellia japonica*), southern magnolia (*Magnolia grandiflora*), the bird of paradise plant (*Strelitzia reginae*), and shrimp plant (*Justicia Brandegeana*), can shelter and decorate trellises, pergolas, patios, and gazebos. The creation of a climate-controlled outdoor living area will not only cut fuel bills for air conditioning and dehumidifiers but will also provide a screen from neighbors and from the heat and noise of the street. It will offer an opportunity to enjoy more birds, butterflies, and other wildlife.

An energy-efficient landscape design for a suburban lot can easily reduce air temperatures by 7° F.—and even more if shade falls on paved or unplanted surfaces. Anyone who has visited a well-designed nursery in a hot, humid area knows the value of landscaped grounds. They always offer a cool, colorful, and fragrant refuge.

In the hot, humid region, large-scale planning of housing

developments and business areas reaps extra benefits for individual energy conservation. Valuable site-planning principles for this region include positioning traffic thoroughfares to channel desirable breezes, dispersion of structures to allow maximum wind circulation, and the planting of canopy shade trees along property lines.

Walkways to centrally located community facilities should be tree-shaded. And if pedestrian access to such facilities are convenient and comfortable, it will reduce car traffic, thus eliminating another source of heat. It was once common to use large shade trees in public areas. In Oaxaca, Mexico, in the sixteenth century, there was a famous five-hundred-year-old Montezuma cypress in a central market that could purportedly shade one thousand people. Today, unfortunately, the air conditioner substitutes high technology for simple, careful design.

SUN

A home nestled in a grove of high-canopied palm trees uses the ideal technique for providing shade from oppressive sun. During the morning and evening hours, when the low sun casts long shadows, distant palms will shade the eastern and western walls. At midday, when the high tropical sun is immediately overhead, palms planted close to the home will shade the roof. Such high-crowned plants provide shade while allowing cooling breezes to reach the home.

However, few are privileged to have access to this ideal natural site. In hot, humid regions, your challenge is to use plants to provide shade, while avoiding the undesirable effects of extra humidity pro-

Benefits of placing home in a palm grove

duced by heavy plantings. Overly dense plantings block cooling breezes and trap humidity in a pocket of dead air.

If you're considering installing solar-energy panels on your roof, first weigh the advantage of building shade canopies, which diminish the cost of air conditioning, against the need for unobstructed solar collectors, which reduce the cost of heating water. A good solution is to shade most of the roof and to place the collectors on the remaining unshaded area. However, since solar collectors must be placed in the proper position, it is often wiser to simply

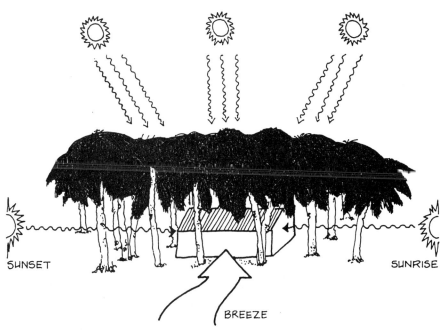

SUNSET

SUNRISE

BREEZE

VENTILATING BREEZES PASS UNOBSTRUCTED UNDER CANOPY

Plan of tree layout

place them on the ground in an unshaded area, even though a pump may be required to recirculate water from the collectors.

Those who don't have the natural solar protection offered by a palm grove can plant a fast-growing light shade tree to the east. Species such as the silk oak (*Grevillea robusta*) or scrub palmetto (*Sabal palmetto*) will filter the early morning sun.

Protecting your home from the high midday sun is the single most important landscape strategy in this region. If you have limited resources for a new landscape design, use them to solve this problem by protecting the southern facade your home. On the south face, high-crowned palms such as Veitchia winin or Sagisi palm (*Heterospathe elata*) planted close to the home will shade the roof from the blazing summer sun during midday. When planting these and similar species, remember that the mature crowns of such palms can be up to twenty feet in diameter, and well-spaced plantings are needed for healthy growth. If several palms are planted some distance from the south face of your home, they will block the lower winter sun during midday. Before planting, decide whether the winter sun is desirable. Palms are ideal sun screens, but they do have some drawbacks: Some have sparse root systems, which may cause them to topple during severe hurricanes; a few have heavy fruits such as coconuts that must be removed at frequent intervals

Mature palms shading southern exposure on summer day

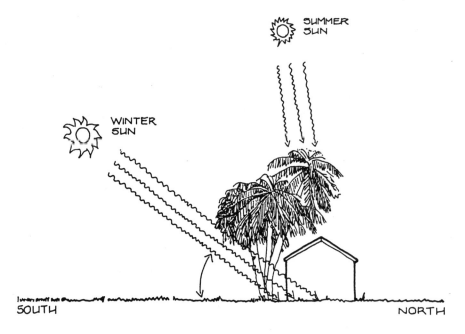

lest they fall and injure passersby; and others develop a dry thatch that can be a fire hazard, especially in hot, humid regions, where roofs may be lightweight and therefore vulnerable to flames.

Another strategy for shading southern windows and walls while permitting the installation of unobstructed solar collectors on roofs is the construction of "eyebrow" trellises attached to the undersides of eaves and covered with deciduous vines such as Virginia creeper (*Parthenocissus quinquefolia*). In winter the leaves fall, allowing the sun's rays to penetrate to the home. Be careful in your selection of vines: Aggressive species with woody stems can invade and damage construction materials; for example, they can enter the cracks in roofing tiles and grow into a home.

To the west a grove of distant, tall palm trees or shorter palms planted closer to the home, or a single large tree such as gumbo-limbo (*Bursera simaruba*), will shade walls and windows from the hot, late-afternoon sun. A trellis covered with a vine such as skyflower (*Thunbergia grandiflora*), with its pendant clusters of large, light-blue flowers, will also accomplish this goal. Some people are reluctant to plant large shade trees or build trellises to the west because they block views of the sunset. Unfortunately, without some shading such views are very expensive to maintain. Air-conditioning is needed to temper the effects of a blazing afternoon sun during the period before sunset. When the sun approaches the horizon, it is perpendicular to the western facade, which absorbs much of the sun's radiant heat. In some areas, especially those close to the sea or with thin soil, it is customary to cover grounds with light-colored coral, stone chips, or other reflective materials. This is a very poor landscape strategy for a western facade because these materials reflect the light and heat of the low-afternoon sun into the home. Ground covers such as artillery ferns (*Pilea microphylla*), asparagus fern (*Asparagus Sprengeri*), the yellow-flowering wedelia (*Wedelia trilobata*), or wandering Jew (*Zebrina pendula*), are far more desirable than coral or stone chips, even if you can only afford to plant them in artistically defined sections of your garden. Their greater cost will be compensated for in part by reduced air-conditioning bills and lessened visual glare.

There is little reason to plant species to the north for sun shading,

Vine-covered trellis shading southern exposure

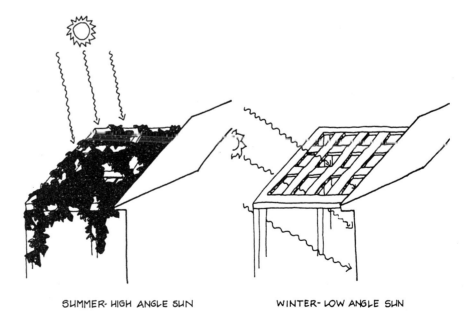

SUMMER· HIGH ANGLE SUN   WINTER· LOW ANGLE SUN

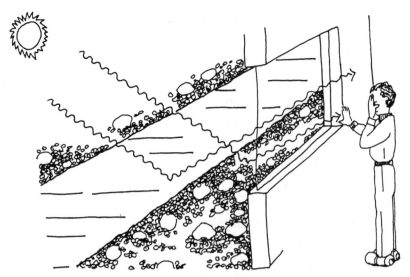

since the sun rarely appears on this facade in the United States. On occasion, however, low-growing species may be of value if planted to the extreme north-west, where they will block the early-evening sun during several weeks of midsummer. Plantings on the north may also be useful for screening reflection and glare but should not block any venti-lating breezes.

Light gravel/pavement reflecting sunlight into home

WIND

In hot, humid regions, cool winds that dispel moisture and promote the evaporation of sweat are treasured. Identify them, understand their behavior and direction, and learn to use them to your advantage.

Testing their flow can be a challenge, since sluggish tropical-air movements can be difficult to detect. Try to investigate their nature by observing a wind sock or piece of yarn nailed to a pole or the pattern of water droplets falling from a fountain or lawn sprinkler. Make these observations over a period of days during each season. Offshore breezes will probably have a predictable, cyclical nature.

Breezes may be managed by designing the landscape to channel breezes into your home or an outdoor living area. Here the Venturi effect (see chapter 2) can be used to your advantage. A narrowing wind scoop that funnels air toward the home can accelerate and increase the cooling impact of a light breeze that would otherwise be ineffective. As we have seen, a trellis or other structure that offers a "roof" to the funnel can further enhance the cooling breeze.

In some hot, humid areas, occasional winter winds that blast out of the north can cause temperatures to plunge, perhaps even to freezing. If this is a problem in your area, the effects of these northern winds can be minimized by planting windbreaks of pines (*Pinus* species), Senegal date palms (*Phoenix reclinata*), or Spanish stopper (*Eugenia foetida*). Windbreaks should be planted perpendicular to the direction of the wind and used only if really necessary.

WATER

From a strictly physical viewpoint, the addition of pools, ponds, or water basins to a hot, humid climate is not a good idea. They in-crease mugginess, attract insects, and cause glare. These disadvantages more than offset any slight drop in ambient temperature the pool offers. Of course, there are other reasons to have a pool or pond. Water brings a garden alive with its reflections, sparkling movement, and soothing sounds, not to mention the immediate joy of jumping in a pool. However, a plan that incorporates ponds, pools, or fountains into the landscape should follow certain guidelines to minimize their potential unpleasant effects.

Tree funnel with covered end for enhancing breeze

To reduce reflected glare into the home, build ponds as far away from your house as possible, and never locate them to the south or west. If a body of water already exists at these points, plant low-growing shrubs or hedges between it and your home to screen reflected light. Try not to place a body of water upwind from the home or patio, because it will only increase humidity in your living areas. If this situation is unavoidable, always shut windows facing the muggy breeze. Don't completely enclose fountains or pools with trellises or walls: They discourage breezes and contain the humid air.

Proper drainage is an important consideration when landscaping in hot, humid areas because still waters encourage the proliferation of mosquitoes and other insects. Mildew, fungus, and musty odors are also more likely to appear if drainage is improper. In the garden, use non-reflecting, permeable paving materials, such as treated wood slabs or brick, to prevent puddles. If irrigation is needed, subsurface or drip systems are preferable to sprinklers.

LANDFORMS

Modest-sized landforms are of little benefit in altering the microclimate in this region, but they shouldn't be ignored. Depressions in the earth may give rise to drainage problems, since water puddles evaporate with difficulty in a hot, humid environment. Siting a new structure on a slight rise in the terrain is advantageous since it often increases the breeze and ventilation effects through the building.

Benefit of placing home on a rise

SPECIAL LANDSCAPING STRATEGIES

Houseplants Houseplants are unlikely to improve the indoor climate in this region because they release moisture into the air, increasing unwanted humidity. If, in your judgment, the psychological advantages of having colorful plants at home outweigh the disadvantage of added mugginess, cultivate houseplants but remove them from direct sunlight to reduce excess evaporation.

Landscaping for Apartments If you live in an apartment or condominium and garden a terrace, you can also landscape to temper your climate. For example, a woman in Houston, Texas, who lives in a small apartment facing north and opening onto a little balcony several floors above the street has devised a high-rise, low-maintenance garden perfectly suited to meet her needs. On the east and west sides of the balcony she planted clematis vines (*Clematis* hybrids) that grow upward from tubs onto a wide-meshed net stretched from her balcony railing to the lower railing of her neighbor's balcony above. In the morning she is greeted with a big dazzling display of blue, pink, and purple clematis blooms. When she returns from work, the handsome foliage screens her from the view of neighbors and reduces the heat and glare of the late-afternoon sun. Vines can cool terraces and adjacent rooms with dappled shade in the heat of summer and—if deciduous types are used—will lose their leaves to admit welcome winter sun.

Vines are not the only plants that help control the microclimate of an urban aerial garden. Some woody plants, including holly (*Ilex* species) and fire thorn (*Pyracantha* species), grow well in containers and can be used to cast shade. Moreover, they have the advantage of being movable, and their position on a balcony may be changed several times during the year to correspond to the changing arc of the sun and related shading needs. Even a tomato plant growing from a plastic tub and trained up a wooden stake can offer helpful shade in addition to its fruit. Before planning a roof or terrace garden, check with a building engineer to determine whether the building can withstand the added weight.

THE RESULTS

The greatest benefit of landscaped grounds in hot, humid climates is the potential for transforming outdoor areas into usable, livable extensions of the home. A well-designed and properly used garden and patio removes heat- and humidity-generating activities such as cooking, cleaning, and eating from the confines of heat-retaining walls. It also maximizes freedom of choice in using outdoor spaces and offers a secluded retreat from everyday pressures.

A mark of good design in hot, humid regions is not only a house that invites you in, but also a garden that invites you out.

The following lists name representative landscape materials appropriate for the hot, humid region. The definitions of shrub, tree, hedge, and ground cover are not inflexible. Much depends on the environment and how the plant is pruned and fed. For example, some trees, such as bottlebrush (*Callistemon citrinus*), can make fine shrubs. Some low-growing shrubs can be used as ground covers.

These lists should be used as helpful guides. Before making a final selection, check with a local nursery or your Extension agent to determine a plant's growth habit in your area.

Site plan of house showing plantings

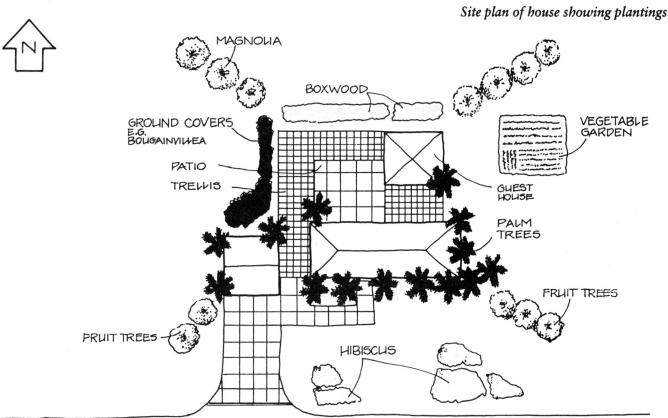

Tall Deciduous Trees
(greater than 35 feet in height)

Bursera simaruba (gumbo-limbo, West Indian birch, also called tourist tree)
Cercidiphyllum japonicum (katsura)
Cladrastis lutea (American yellowwood)
Fraxinus pennsylvanica (red ash, green ash)
Jacaranda mimosifolia (green ebony)
Liquidambar Styraciflua (sweet gum)
Liriodendron Tulipifera (tulip tree)
Nyssa sylvatica (black tupelo, black gum, sour gum, pepperidge)
Paulownia tomentosa (empress tree, royal paulownia)
Pistacia chinensis (Chinese pistachio)
Platanus X acerifolia (London plane tree)
Quercus nigra (water oak)
Quercus palustris (pin oak)
Quercus phellos (willow oak)
Taxodium mucronatum (Montezuma cypress)
Ulmus parvifolia (Chinese elm)

Short and Medium Deciduous Trees
(less than 35 feet in height)

Albizia Julibrissin (silk tree)

Bauhinia variegata (Buddhist bauhinia, mountain ebony, orchid tree)

Cercis canadensis (Eastern redbud)

Chionanthus virginicus (fringe tree)

Cornus florida (flowering dogwood)

Cornus Kousa (Japanese dogwood)

Delonix regia (poinciana regia, poinciana tree, royal flame)

Halesia carolina (Carolina silverbell)

Koelreuteria elegans (Chinese flame tree)

Lagerstroemia indica (crape myrtle)

Magnolia heptapeta (Yulan magnolia)

Magnolia X Loebneri (Merrill magnolia)

Magnolia X Soulangiana (saucer magnolia)

Magnolia stellata (star magnolia)

Morus alba (white mulberry)

Parkinsonia aculeata (Jerusalem thorn)

Prunus X blireiana (blireiana plum, purpleleaf plum)

Prunus cerasifera cv. "*Thundercloud*" (Thundercloud plum)

Sapium sebiferum (Chinese tallow tree)

Tall Evergreen Trees
(greater than 35 feet in height)

Araucaria heterophylla (Norfolk Island Pine)

Calocedrus decurrens, also called *Libocedrus decurrens* (California incense cedar)

Casuarina equisetifolia (horsetail beefwood, Australian pine)

Cedrus Deodara (deodar cedar)

Cupressus sempervirens cv. "*Stricta*" (Italian cypress)

Ficus benjamina (weeping fig, Java fig, weeping Chinese banyan, Benjamin fig)

Grevillea robusta (silk oak)

Magnolia grandiflora (Southern magnolia, bull bay)

Magnolia virginiana, also called *Magnolia glauca* (sweet bay)

Pinus canariensis (Canary Island Pine)

Pinus caribaea (slash pine, swamp pine, Cuban pine)

Quercus Suber (cork oak)

Quercus virginiana (live oak)

Ulmus parvifolia, also called *Ulmus sempervirens* (Chinese evergreen elm)

Short and Medium Evergreen Trees
(less than 35 feet in height)

Bauhinia Blakeana (Hong Kong orchid tree)

Brassaia actinophylla, also called *Schefflera actinophylla* (Australia umbrella tree, Queensland umbrella tree, octopus tree)

Callistemon viminalis (weeping bottlebrush)

Cephalotaxus Harringtonia, also called *Cephalotaxus drupacea* (Japanese plum yew)

Cinnamomum Camphora (camphor tree)

Citrus species (orange, lemon, lime, and grapefruit trees)

Litchi chinensis (lychee, litchi nut)

Manilkara Zapota (sapodilla)

Podocarpus macrophyllus cultivars (yew podocarpus)

Psidium littorale (strawberry guava)

Pyrus Kawakamii (evergreen pear)

Schinus terebinthifolius (Brazilian pepper tree)

Tall Palm Trees
(greater than 35 feet in height)

Arecastrum Romanzoffianum, also called *Cocos plumosa* (queen palm)

Heterospathe elata (Sagisi palm)

Veitchia Winin

Short Palm Trees
(less than 35 feet in height)

Acoelorrhaphe Wrightii, also called *Paurotis Wrightii* (Everglade palm)

Chamaerops humilis (European fan palm, Mediterranean fan palm)

Chrysalidocarpus lutescens, also called *Areca lutescens* (butterfly palm, yellow palm, bamboo palm, Areca palm, cane palm)

Phoenix reclinata (Senegal date palm)

Phoenix Roebelenii, also miscalled *Phoenix loureirii* (dwarf date palm, pigmy date palm)

Ptychosperma Macarthurii (Macarthur palm)

Rhapidophyllum hystrix (needle palm, porcupine palm, blue palmetto)

Rhapis excelsa, also called *Rhapis flabelliformis* (lady palm)

Sabal Palmetto (cabbage palmetto)

Trachycarpus Fortunei, also called *Trachycarpus excelsus, Chamaerops excelsa* (windmill palm)

Deciduous Windbreaks, Hedges, and Borders

Calycanthus floridus (strawberry shrub, Carolina allspice)

Chaenomeles species, also called *Cydonia* (flowering quince)

Hydrangea macrophylla, also called *Hydrangea hortensis* (common bigleaf hydrangea, house hydrangea)

Ligustrum amurense (Amur privet)

Ligustrum ovalifolium (California privet)

Spiraea species (spirea, bridal wreath)

Vitex Agnus-castus (chaste tree)

Evergreen Windbreaks, Hedges, and Borders

Buxus sempervirens (common boxwood)

Coccoloba uvifera, also called *Coccolobis uvifera* (sea grape, shore grape)

Codiaeum variegatum cultivars (croton)

Elaeagnus pungens cultivars (thorny elaeagnus, silverberry)

Eriobotrya japonica (loquat, Japanese plum)

Eugenia foetida (Spanish stopper)

Euonymus japonica cultivars (evergreen euonymous)

Feijoa Sellowiana (pineapple guava)

Gardenia jasminoides cultivars (gardenia, cape jasmine)

Ilex opaca cultivars (American holly)

Ilex vomitoria (yaupon)

Ixora coccinea (flame-of-the-woods, jungle geranium, ixora)

Jasminum humile cv. "Revolutum" (Italian jasmine)

Juniperus virginiana cultivars (eastern red cedar)

Ligustrum japonicum cultivars (Japanese privet)

Lonicera nitida (box honeysuckle)

Myrtus communis cultivars (myrtle)

Nerium Oleander cultivars (oleander)

Osmanthus heterophyllus, also called *Osmanthus ilicifolius* (holly osmanthus)

Photinia serrulata (Chinese photinia)

Pittosporum Tobira (Japanese pittosporum)

Prunus caroliniana (Carolina cherry laurel)

Pyracantha coccinea cultivars (fire thorn)

Thevetia peruviana, also called *Thevetia nereifolia* (yellow oleander)

Viburnum odoratissimum (sweet viburnum)

Viburnum Tinus (laurustinus)

Deciduous Shrubs

Buddleia Davidii (orange-eye butterfly bush)

Cotoneaster divaricatus (spreading cotoneaster)

Deutzia species (deutzia)

Hibiscus Rosa-sinensis cultivars (Chinese hibiscus, rose of China)

Hibiscus syriacus (rose of Sharon, shrub Althea)

Evergreen Shrubs

Abelia X grandiflora (glossy abelia)

Aucuba japonica (Japanese aucuba)

Brunfelsia calycina cv. "Floribunda" (yesterday, today, and tomorrow)

Callistemon citrinus, also called *Callistemon lanceolatus* (lemon bottlebrush)

Camellia japonica cultivars (common camellia)

Camellia sasanqua (sasanqua camellia)

Carissa grandiflora (Natal plum)

Cotoneaster dammeri, also called *Cotoneaster humifusus* (bearberry cotoneaster)

Cotoneaster horizontalis (rock spray, rock cotoneaster)

Cotoneaster lacteus (Parney's red clusterberry)

Euonymus Fortunei cultivars (winter creeper)

Euphorbia pulcherrima (poinsettia)
Fatsia japonica, also called *Aralia japonica, Aralia sieboldii* (Japanese fatsia)
Ilex X altaclarensis cv. "Wilsonii" (Wilson holly)
Ilex aquifolium cultivars (English holly)
Ilex cassine (dahoon, dahoon holly)
Ilex cornuta cultivars (Chinese holly)
Ilex crenata cultivars (Japanese holly)
Juniperus chinensis cultivars (Chinese juniper)
Juniperus communis cultivars (common juniper)
Juniperus conferta (shore juniper)
Juniperus procumbens cultivars (Japanese garden juniper)
Juniperus sabina (savin juniper)
Justicia Brandegeana, also called *Beloperone guttata* (shrimp plant)
Nandina domestica (nandina, Chinese sacred bamboo)
Platycladus orientalis cultivars, also called *Thuya orientalis* (Oriental arborvitae)
Rhododendron evergreen hybrids (evergreen hybrid azalea)
Rhododendron indicum cultivars (Indian azalea)
Tetrapanax papyriferus, also called *Fatsia papyrifera* (ricepaper plant)
Tibouchina Urvilleana, also called *Tibouchina semicandra* and *Pleroma grandiflora* (glory bush)

Deciduous Vines

Actinidia arguta (tara vine, bower actinidia)
Campsis X Tagliabuana (trumpet vine)
Clematis hybrids (hybrid clematis)
Hydrangea anomala subsp. *petiolaris*, also called *Hydrangea petiolaris, Hydrangea scandens* (climbing hydrangea)
Parthenocissus quinquefolia, also called *Ampelopsis quinquefolia* (Virginia creeper, woodbine)
Parthenocissus tricuspidata, also called *Ampelopsis tricuspidata* (Boston ivy, Japanese creeper)

Polygonum Aubertii (silver-fleece vine, silver-lace vine)
Wisteria floribunda cultivars (Japanese wisteria)
Wisteria sinensis, also called *Wisteria chinensis* (Chinese wisteria)

Evergreen Vines

Akebia quinata (semievergreen) (five-leaf akebia)
Bignonia capreolata, also called *Anisostichus capreolatus, Doxantha capreolata* (cross vine, trumpet flower)
Bougainvillea hybrids (bougainvillea)
Ficus pumila (creeping fig)
Gelsemium sempervirens (Carolina jasmine)
Hedera canariensis (Algerian ivy)
Hedera Helix (English ivy)
Justicia Brandegeana, also known as *Beloperone guttata* (shrimp plant)
Lonicera sempervirens cultivars (trumpet honeysuckle)
Thunbergia grandiflora (skyflower, blue trumpet vine, clock vine)
Trachelospermum jasminoides, also called *Rhynchospermum jasminoides* (star jasmine, Confederate jasmine)

Ground Covers

Asparagus Sprengeri (Sprenger asparagus)
Hedera Helix (English ivy)
Pilea microphylla (artillery fern)
Sedum species (stone crop, live-forever)
Wedelia trilobata (wedelia)
Zebrina pendula (wandering Jew)

CHAPTER SIX

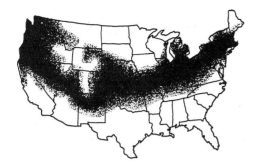

Energy-Efficient Landscaping for Temperate Climates

The essence of temperate-zone weather is change. With each season, temperate climates give you something different—often to extremes. In that sense, the word *temperate* can be misleading. Tropical and polar air masses meet and battle over these regions. The weather runs to extremes, from below-zero icy to subtropical steamy. Cold, snowy winters follow hot, humid summers. Transitional periods can bring destructive storms, mercurial temperature changes, and winds. These winds can drive up the wind-chill factor in winter or take the form of cooling summer breezes.

Temperate regions receive a moderate mix of sunshine and clouds and ample rainfall. Snowfall varies widely, from 20 inches or less annually in some southern and coastal regions to more than 70 inches in the snow belt.

Since temperate in this climate varies greatly, you have to design for both extremes. During winter the goals are to keep the heat in and the cold out by blocking wind and letting all available sunlight penetrate. The summer strategy is to temper the heat by shading the sun and creating cooling breezes. A well-planned and landscaped property can do both.

Houses in the temperate zone should be compact, well insulated, caulked, and weatherstripped for winter comfort. Windows should be efficient low-E (low-emissivity) glass, kept to a minimum on the east and west and avoided on the north. Construction materials should be selected for thermal efficiency. Wood-frame construction is ideal because it allows ample room for insulation. Metals, such as window frames, accentuate heat loss or gain and should be kept to a minimum. Air locks and vestibules can cut heat loss, and porches help cool in the summer.

If you are building, try to select a site that permits exposure to winter sun and offers protection from undesirable winter winds. Un-attached structures such as garages or tool sheds should be positioned to block unwanted winds.

Outdoor living areas with paved or stone surfaces are best located to the south, under a deciduous tree. This will create a pleasant shaded spot in the summer. And in the early spring and late fall, when trees are bare, the same paved area will retain extra warmth from the sun's heat—just when you need it.

Energy-conscious early-American settlers established this proto-type by adapting traditional English houses and reducing living space and window areas, using wood as the building material (instead of the traditional stone or brick) and often placing a massive chimney in the center to store and radiate heat. Judicious design of open porches provided natural ventilation for passive cooling. They also used windbreaks to block brisk northerlies and deciduous trees for summer shade.

The potential rewards for such careful planning are great. In temperate regions as much as 30 percent of a homeowner's heating and cooling costs can be saved through energy-efficient landscaping. Proper planting coupled with routine care can moderate uncomfortable extremes of temperature twenty-four hours a day year-round.

SUN

The most important consideration in designing an energy-efficient landscape design in this zone is taking advantage of the sun's radiant energy—the driving force of all weather systems. In temperate climates sunwise landscaping has two goals: to block or filter summer sun that causes over-heating and to permit all warm-ing winter radiation to reach most living areas. Both goals can be met by choosing the right plants for height, foliage density,

Vegetation for eastern exposure

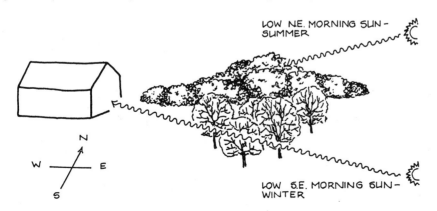

LOW N.E. MORNING SUN—
SUMMER

LOW S.E. MORNING SUN—
WINTER

N
W — E
S

and growing patterns, and by knowing where to place the plants around your home. Dense trees such as Norway maple (*Acer platanoides*) can block as much as 95 percent of the sun's light and 75 percent of its heat. Even a leafless deciduous tree cuts out as much as 25 percent of the sun's energy.

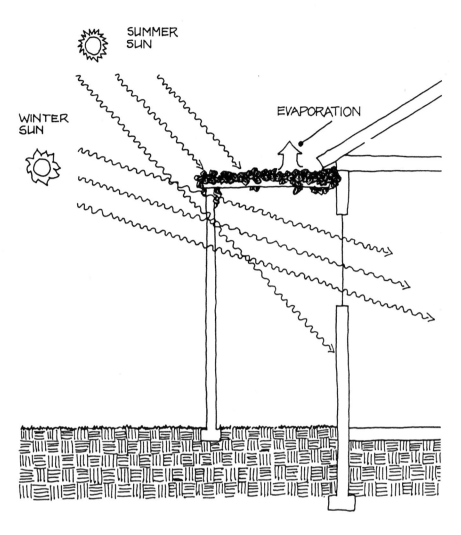

SUMMER SUN

WINTER SUN

EVAPORATION

Vine-covered trellis

The correct positioning of plants is achieved by planting species in harmony with the solar paths (as discussed in chapter 2). For example, throughout the year the sun strikes the east side of a building at a low angle, transmitting little radiant heat. The hours following sunrise are underheated in the winter and occasionally overheated in the summer. Therefore, plants such as low deciduous trees that block or filter the sun only in the summer are desirable on the east and northeast. Since sunlight often provides an early-morning psychological boost, trees that filter rather than block summer sunlight are best. The appropriate model for this situation is a low-density, light, and low-crowned deciduous tree such as dogwood (*Cornus florida*) or some cultivars of Japanese maple (*Acer palmatum*) planted close to the home. An open deciduous shrub of medium height, such as pussy willow (*Salix discolor*) or lilac (*Syringa vulgaris*), is also good for an eastern or northeastern location. Plants that cast light shade outside a window temper the sun's energy more effectively than a lightly colored plastic coating on windows or a fully drawn white venetian blind.

If you live in the northern extremities of the temperate zone, where usually all radiant heat is desirable, or if you are working with a very limited budget, don't plant to block sun on the east. Save landscaping additions for the western and southern facades, where plantings have a greater impact on comfort and energy consumption.

On the south side of a house, the sun's angle varies greatly between summer and winter. The summer sun is very high in the sky at midday and can be cut off by planting a tall, columnar tree with a high crown and dense foliage very close to the house. If this tree is

Benefits of tall narrow trees vs. short wide trees

LOW WINTER SUN

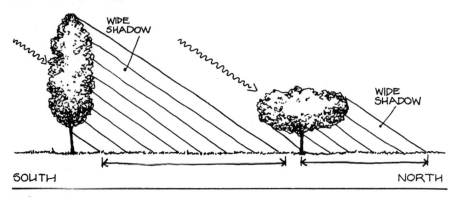

HIGH SUMMER SUN

HIGH SUMMER SUN

A] FOR SHADING GROUND SURFACES, LOW WIDE TREES ARE BEST, BECAUSE TALL NARROW TREES SHADE MORE IN WINTER THAN IN SUMMER, BUT...

B] FOR SHADING BUILDINGS, TALL TREES ARE NECESSARY.

also deciduous, it will not cut off the desirable winter sunlight and warmth. Red maple (*Acer rubrum*) and eastern sycamore (*Platanus occidentalis*) are good species to plant adjacent to southern exposures. Such trees also allow a slight breeze to pass beneath them. Dense trees evaporate great amounts of water vapor, using up latent heat energy, which makes the air cooler. The combination of shade, evaporation, and convection offered by a single mature tree gets rid of as much heat as five 10,000-BTU air conditioners. The right tree is much cheaper and easier to maintain than an air conditioner, doesn't create more pollution or damage the ozone layer, looks better, and increases your property values.

This planting strategy could, however, create problems if you have solar collectors mounted on the roof; they won't work if you've shaded them. If the solar collector is to be used to generate electricity for cooling, you're better off with a tall tree planted close to the south face of the house. If the collector is for hot water, then place it on an unshaded roof area or on unshaded ground on the south side.

An overhang on a roof, arbor, trellis, or pergola covered with deciduous vines such as wisteria or select clematis species can also effectively protect southern exposures from excessive summer sun, simultaneously providing both shade and the cooling effect of evaporation. Dense trees or shrubs planted in southerly positions away from the house are ineffective barriers to summer sun and may be harmful filters of solar radiation in winter. Before planting trees to the south or deciding whether to remove existing ones, determine the maximum height the hedge can be or the distance it should be placed from your home. This calculation will prevent you from having a hedge that is too tall and blocks the winter sun. Begin by looking up the altitude angle of the sun during the winter solstice (December 22) in your area and its tangent from Appendices C and D. The variables can be determined by the equation:

$$\text{tangent of altitude angle of sun during midwinter solstice} = \frac{\text{maximum height to hedge of trees}}{\text{distance of trees from house}}$$

For example, New York City, Philadelphia, Pittsburgh, Columbus, and Denver all lie at about 40° N. latitude, where the midwinter sun rises to a maximum altitude angle of about 26.50°. Thus, if you live in one of those places and want to have a hedge of trees 100 feet from the south face of your home, the trees selected should grow

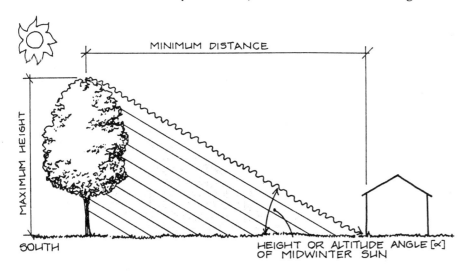

MINIMUM DISTANCE

MAXIMUM HEIGHT

SOUTH

HEIGHT OR ALTITUDE ANGLE [∝] OF MIDWINTER SUN

Noon winter sun angle for Columbus, Ohio (from table for 40° N. latitude) $\alpha = 26.55°$ ($\beta = 180°$ or due south)

$$\tan\alpha = \frac{\text{Height of Barrier}}{\text{Distance to House}}$$

$\tan\alpha = .499$ (from trigonometric tables in Appendix D)

$$\frac{\text{Height of Barrier}}{\text{Distance to House}} = .499 \text{ or about 1/2}$$

Therefore:
Choose a tree that will not grow taller than 1/2 the distance to the house, or plant the tree twice as far from the house as the expected mature tree height.

Example: A 50' tree should be 100' south of the house.

no taller than 50 feet (see illustration and appendices for step-by-step explanation of calculation). A hedge made of Norway maple (*Acer platanoides*) or most fruit trees planted 100 feet from the south face and growing to a maximum height of 50 feet will not block the low winter sun. In this situation, an existing hedge of trees taller than 50 feet should be trimmed.

Western exposures always receive sun at a low angle. The late-afternoon hours are usually too hot in the summer, and in winter the reflection from snow can cause glare. If this presents a problem for your house, you should cut off or reduce the sun in the summer and temper it in the winter. A combination of short, low-crowned evergreens and deciduous plants placed close to your house on the west and northwest will filter the late-afternoon sun in the winter while providing complete screening in the summer. Yews (*Taxus* species), arborvitae (*Thuja occidentalis*), and apple (*Malus sylvestris*) or pear trees (*Pyrus communis*) are appropriate. When planting species close to the home, select those with root systems that don't invade and interfere with water pipes, foundations, and downspouts. Medium and tall trees such as horse chestnut (*Aesculus Hippocastanum*) and mature pines, if planted a distance from the house, cast long shadows and screen late-afternoon sun. In more northerly latitudes, trees of medium to low height may also be useful on the northwest exposure, because this is where the midsummer sun sets.

Sun screening on the north side is seldom necessary, since the winter sun doesn't shine here and the midsummer sun is either not present or (in extreme northerly latitudes) at a very low angle. The majority of radiation available to northern exposures is reflected and refracted. Energy-efficient design in general suggests a minimum area of glass on the northern exposure, which reduces the impact of any plantings. However, for house designs that demand large northern window placements or for those people who simply enjoy uniform northern light, appropriate plantings can be made. Loose, open, low-crowned trees, including many fruit trees, or chest-high shrubs such as privet (*Ligustrum* species) are advised; the goal is to provide a slight windbreak without cutting off the desired light. Otherwise, wind screening is the most significant consideration on the north.

Vegetation on western exposure

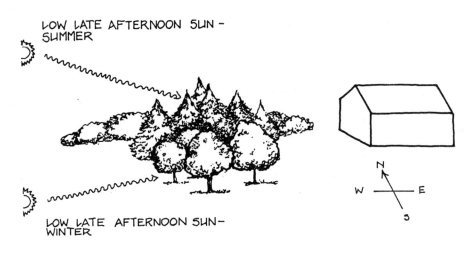

LOW LATE AFTERNOON SUN – SUMMER

LOW LATE AFTERNOON SUN – WINTER

WIND

By taming winds you can dramatically diminish your winter fuel needs by up to 30 percent. Wind blows and redistributes the sun's heat and drains off warmth created by your indoor heating system. Typically, wind is the second most important climatic consideration in energy-efficient landscape design. If your home gets heavy winds, creating windbreaks should be your first priority. A row of trees or shrubs can filter, divert, or obstruct up to 85 percent of the force of cold winds. Plants that block wind can also guide or trap drifting snow, intercept unwanted precipitation, and affect the depth of the frost line, as discussed in chapter 2.

Intelligent use of landscaping also reduces the costs of interior cooling by accentuating and guiding cooling breezes in the summer months. Such wind funnels use the Venturi effect (see chapter 2) to increase wind velocity at their narrowest point.

It's more challenging to design a landscape to control wind than to control sun because you must contend with plantings already established to use or screen sunlight. Managing both the sun and wind requires thoughtful analysis and planning.

The first step in wind control is determining the direction(s) of the prevailing winds on your site throughout the year. Use the strategies suggested in chapters 2 and 13. Peculiarities of individual location, such as the slope of the land, existing vegetation, and the positions of neighboring buildings, influence the patterns of airflow.

When summer and winter winds come from different directions, there is little problem in designing landscaping to manage both. But if both winds come from the same direction, you must choose which is more energy-efficient to control. As a general rule, if your winter heating bills are greater than summer air-conditioning bills, landscape plans should focus on using plants for winter windbreaks and insulation. Different planting strategies are used to cut cold winter winds and to enhance the cooling breezes of summer. In general, winter winds are prevented from reaching the

Ideal windbreaks—block winter winds and funnel summer breezes

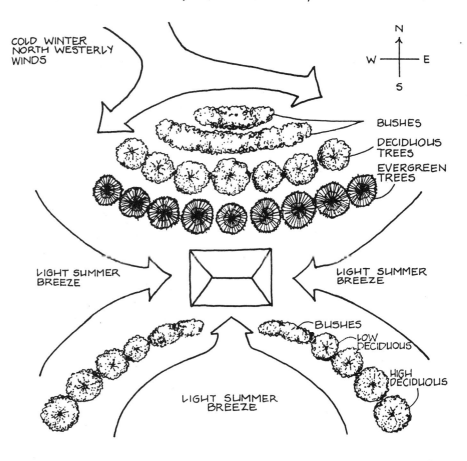

home and summer breezes are funneled toward the living area.

An all-purpose scheme for controlling cold winds is to establish a barrier of tall, dense plantings close to and upwind of your home. However, while this windbreak diverts winds over the structure, it also blocks available sunlight. If your goal is to permit sunlight to reach the home and to manage wind as well, distant, sparse windbreaks planted upwind of your home are better. They will calm winds without screening the sun.

Rows of trees and shrubs are far more desirable than small clusters; trees planted singly are nearly useless for wind control. New trees for wind control should be selected to grow rapidly to a large height, as do black locust (*Robinia Pseudoacacia*). Wind screens are always oriented perpendicular to observed wind direction rather than to compass points. But because in temperate climates landscaping to control wind is usually secondary to landscaping to control sun, we approach wind analysis in the same way we resolve sun management— that is, by compass direction.

If the prevailing winter winds blow from the east, your goal is to block the heat-dissipating gusts without shutting out all solar radiation. This is done by placing tall trees with loose foliage such as larch (*Larix* species) and locust two to five tree lengths away from the house. Ideal plantings temper wintry blasts without preventing the warmth of the low winter sun from reaching living areas. To further reduce the impact of cold gusts , place well-maintained high-crowned trees such as Norway maple (*Acer platanoides*) close to the house on the eastern side. These will further deflect wind that has already been calmed by the distant, tall plants but will not interfere with heat from the low morning sun.

Southern winter winds are trickier to control. Again, it is desirable to have a hedge of trees with sparse foliage some distance from the house to filter winds. This will buffer wind speeds for a distance up to fifteen times the trees' height. But because the low winter-afternoon sun is needed to supply warmth, wind blocks must not be so high that they obstruct sun. To determine the maximum height for such a southern windbreak on your property, use the same equation that was used to determine the maximum height for a hedge of trees that is a given distance south of the structure.

Wind controls on the north

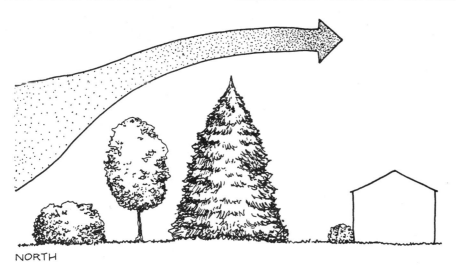

NORTH

$$\frac{\text{tangent of the angle of}}{\text{sun at winter solstice}} = \frac{\text{maximum height of barrier}}{\text{distance of wind barrier}}$$
from house

The heights and densities of most common deciduous trees are such that they should be placed two to six times their mature height from the building to be protected.

A tree very close to the house on the southern side is also desirable for deflecting winds over the structure. But it must be a well-maintained, tall specimen with a high crown, or it will block the desirable winter sun.

On the western side use a wind-blocking strategy similar to the one used on the eastern side; that is, plant tall trees with loose foliage some distance from the house, or dense species up close. Thick plantings may be used anywhere north of west; thinner, higher-canopied plantings are preferred south of west to retain warmth of the low winter sun.

Plantings to control wind on the northern side are easy to plan. Because there is no solar conflict, thick, coniferous trees close to the home are best. They give maximum shelter immediately downwind of the planting.

If cold winter winds are not a problem in your area but cooling summer breezes are needed, as in southern regions of the temperate zone, different strategies to control winds should be used. The goal here is to encourage breezes toward the building. A funnel of tall hedges that channels the prevailing winds uses the Venturi effect to accelerate breezes, dissipate heat, and provide constant natural air conditioning. As the funnel narrows, wind velocity increases, making the arrangement more effective. This breeze enhancement alters our perception of temperature. For example, at 70° F. an 18-mile-per-hour wind makes the air temperature feel like 58° F.

Elaborate wind funnels are complicated to design. Universities and other research organizations test plans by using expensive wind chambers, with tiny buildings carefully built to scale. For home analysis you can use a smoky fire in a garbage can on a windy day (if town regulations permit).

A word of caution on wind control for those who live near the seashore: By the seashore, extra efforts to funnel summer winds toward the home are usually unnecessary, since existing offshore breezes offer ample, periodic airflow. For example, in the San Francisco area from May through September the winds exceed 20 miles per hour two out of every three days. In Seattle almost every summer day has winds above 10 miles per hour. Prolonged buffeting from winds can be upsetting. The persistent, whistling mistral wind of the Mediterranean is said to drive people mad, and the hot, sandy sirocco wind out of the Sahara has similar notoriety. If cyclical breezes at your home are so strong that wind blocks are needed, but tall plant growth near the seashore is a problem, a well-anchored fence will serve as a windbreak. A louvered fence (one with slats) gives the largest area of protection downwind, even though some wind passes through it into the protected area. (See chapter 2.)

Another landscaping strategy for controlling wind is the use of berms. Such mounds of earth will deflect winds before plants grow tall enough to produce a similar effect. However, berms must also be designed with attention to the prevailing winds and outdoor living space. A poorly placed berm may improve a home's energy efficiency but create unwanted wind turbulence and gusts outside the house.

WATER

Ponds, pools, and lakes are powerful climate controllers because they store enormous amounts of heat energy. During the warmer months they evaporate water, draw energy from the air, and reduce temperature. But along with this desirable cooling effect comes an increase in humidity, which is undesirable in most temperate regions. Placid pools or ponds can also reflect unwanted heat and light into living areas and may attract insects. For these reasons, manmade reservoirs are usually not beneficial, energy-efficient additions to the landscape.

The decision to include bodies of water in your landscaping plans should be for reasons other than energy efficiency. Small ponds do have their benefits: They store water, control runoff, give animals a place to drink, and raise the water table. And of course, there's something soothing about watching a rippling pond.

Rows of trees that funnel a breeze into a living area offer much the same cooling effect as a pond, but without the drawbacks. If you want a pond anyway, place it some distance from your house, and position a few trees or shrubs to block reflected glare that may enter your home.

SPECIAL PLANTING STRATEGIES

Using Shrubs, Vines, and Groundcovers

Landscaping in temperate regions offers the greatest potential for using a wide variety of plant forms and design schemes. After planning basic sun, wind, and water management with trees and large bushes, the next step for the energy-efficient designer is to use low-growing foliage or vegetation such as shrubs, vines, and ground covers. They're excellent at tempering extremes of hot and cold. These plant materials throw cooling shade, draw heat out and away from the earth and buildings, reduce heat reflected from building materials, and insulate against excessive wind and cold. Plant species with low or small foliage such as honeysuckle (*Lonicera* species) or grapevines (*Vitis* species) often grow faster than trees and provide climate control before larger species establish themselves. They offer quick solutions to problems of excessive heat loss and buildup and can be used while grander landscaping matures. (Note: the benefit of rapid growth brings the risk of invasive growth. Such plants must be carefully tended.)

Small-scale evergreen trees and shrubs are valuable when planted next to homes because they create dead-air spaces that insulate buildings from abrupt temperature changes. Yew species and the dwarf juniper (*Juniperus chinensis* cv. "Sargentii") are ideal for this purpose.

Deciduous shrubs such as *Euonymus alata* cv. "Compacta" can shade walls from a hot summer sun and in winter will permit the sun to warm walls through bare branches. This arrangement is especially effective for western exposures.

Both deciduous and evergreen bushes can hold snow around their low-growing branches, thus offering additional wall insulation. The wall and ground near the house under the snow's protective blanket will be warmer than frigid air temperatures. The heat inside the home is trapped by the snow. Heat loss from an exposed foundation can be significant in winter, and snow around the base of home-hugging shrubs cuts heating costs. Be sure the roots of the shrubs you select do not invade and destroy building foundations or drainage tiles. If fallen leaves are left under the plants in autumn, they provide even more insulation under the snow. When they decay, they return nutrients to the soil. Fallen leaves do have one potential gardening drawback: They remain wet and cold late into spring and will retard the growth of early blooms.

A particularly effective combination windbreak and insulator is a double-row plant screen, with a row of evergreens such as yew planted behind a row of deciduous shrubs. Shrubs are less expensive to plant than pine or spruce (*Picea* species) trees and will outperform them for the first few years. Eventually, the evergreens grow taller, while the shrubs in front continue to provide depth and color. Shade-tolerant shrubs such as witch hazel (*Hamamelis virginiana*) and Japanese barberry (*Berberis Thunbergii*) are tough enough to survive as underplantings beneath taller plants, as long as they are watered and occasionally fertilized.

Because this planting strategy obstructs sunshine, it should be used only where sun is of little

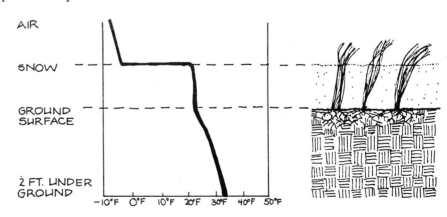

Temperature differential between air and earth insulated under snow

concern, such as on the north face of a building.

In temperate regions, deciduous vines such as Japanese wisteria (*Wisteria floribunda*), most clematis hybrids, concord grapes (*Vitis Concord*), and goldflame honeysuckle (*Lonicera Heckrottii*) reflect sun and heat away from the home, provide dense shade and a layer of insulating air between plant growth and the wall, and give a cooling effect in summer. They grow rapidly—10 to 50 feet in a single season—and offer shade benefits almost immediately to outdoor living areas or sun-struck walls. They give their cooling effect by evaporating enormous amounts of water from leaf surfaces. However, vines lower temperature at the expense of increasing humidity. Windows on walls covered by vines should be kept closed to prevent excessive humidity indoors. Vines are therefore not used in hot, humid regions or in temperate regions that lack breezes to blow away the excess moisture.

Protective effect of vines

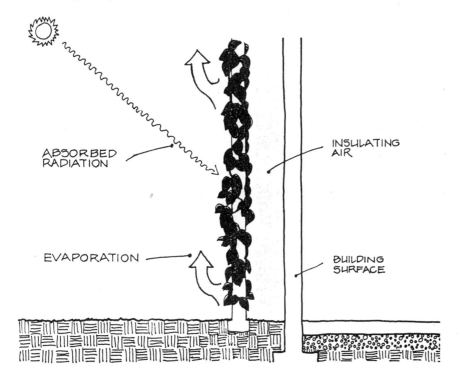

ABSORBED RADIATION

EVAPORATION

INSULATING AIR

BUILDING SURFACE

Vines have two other serious drawbacks. They can grow too rapidly, entangling and even killing adjacent trees and shrubs, and they give a junglelike appearance to a garden. Some species, such as Chinese actinidia (*Actinidia chinensis*), Hall's honeysuckle (*Lonicera japonica* cv. "Halliana"), kudzu vine (*Pueraria lobata*), glory vine (*Vitis coignetiae*), and select wisteria species, sometimes grow 50 feet in a year. Some vines may also attack mortar, wood shingles, window frames, downspouts, and gutters with a vengeance. If you don't have the time to devote to this careful tending, avoid these species.

Ground covers such as grasses, common periwinkle (*Vinca minor*), ivy (*Hedera* species), Japanese spurge (*Pachysandra terminalis*), mondo grass (*Ophiopogon japonicus*), and creeping thyme (*Thymus praecox*) are also effective controllers of microclimates in gardens. They reduce heat buildup by evaporating water, and they don't reflect or reradiate heat as walls and pavements do. Recall from chapter 2 that the ability of ground covers to temper heat depends on the species and its height. (Their ability to moderate high temperatures is even more impressive when one considers that many natural and manmade materials, such as artificial turf, asphalt, stone, and shingle, accentuate heat accumulation. It is not uncommon for an asphalt surface to be 25° F. hotter than the air temperature.)

Ground covers can be any height. A good bed of thickly planted, 1- to 3-foot-high juniper, such as carpet juniper (*Juniperus horizontalis* cv. "*Wiltonii*") or creeping juniper (*Juniperus chinensis* cv. "Procumbens") requires little maintenance and is much cooler in full sun than is a paved area. Eventually it grows taller than most weeds. Getting it started will cost a bit, but still less than paving. Usually selecting a ground cover involves a choice between increased initial investment with a promise of reduced future maintenance and less expensive ground covers that often need more maintenance. The classic American ground cover, lawn grass, is among the least expensive to establish but requires lots of energy-intensive care. In temperate climates, many ground covers are completely or almost completely self-sustaining. Some need no more than a yearly weeding—as long as they have good soil and adequate water.

Successful use of low-growing foliage for climate control depends on careful selection and maintenance. Shrubs and hedges need regular clipping; vines demand conscientious pruning; and ground covers require weeding, feeding, and trimming.

The common practice of cutting bushes to have flat tops or rounded shapes conflicts with their natural growth. Unless that style is important to you, it's a waste of energy—both human and, as usually is the case, electrical. If you want low-growing shrubs, plant low-growing varieties. Yews, for example, must be selected with care. The plant you intended to frame a door may soon block it.

Landscaping for Apartments

Urban gardeners, even those with just a small balcony, can plant an energy-efficient garden. Several square feet of rooftop or terrace is all you need for a lush container garden. Potted plants can screen sun, block unwanted wind, and deliver a welcome dose of greenery and color to the urban landscape.

Begin by measuring the area and drawing a simple diagram, noting its widest and narrowest dimensions and the locations of doors and windows. Then note the solar path over the planned

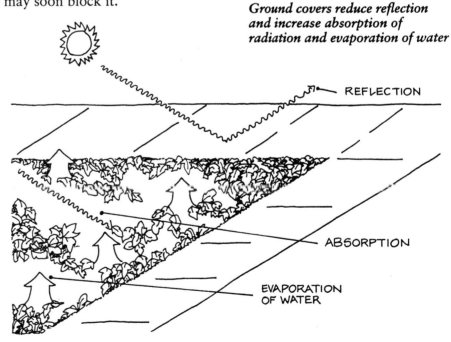

Ground covers reduce reflection and increase absorption of radiation and evaporation of water

REFLECTION

ABSORPTION

EVAPORATION OF WATER

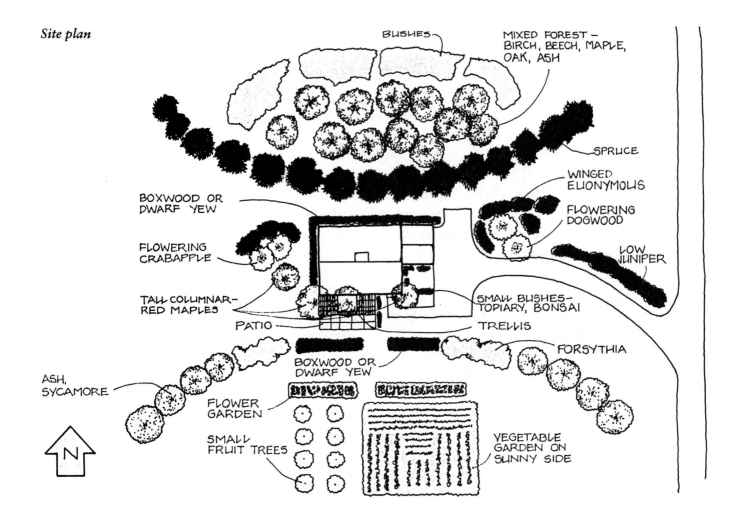

BUSHES

MIXED FOREST — BIRCH, BEECH, MAPLE, OAK, ASH

SPRUCE

WINGED EUONYMOUS

FLOWERING DOGWOOD

LOW JUNIPER

BOXWOOD OR DWARF YEW

FLOWERING CRABAPPLE

TALL COLUMNAR-RED MAPLES

PATIO

SMALL BUSHES-TOPIARY, BONSAI

TRELLIS

FORSYTHIA

ASH, SYCAMORE

BOXWOOD OR DWARF YEW

FLOWER GARDEN

SMALL FRUIT TREES

VEGETABLE GARDEN ON SUNNY SIDE

N

garden. Check the sun's strength along with its position.

What you find will determine your plant purchases. Part shade or morning sun is fine for growing begonias (*Begonia* species), a flowering crab apple tree (*Malus* species), rhododendrons (*Rhododendron* species), or Japanese maple (*Acer palmatum*). But roses, dwarf fruit trees, and rosemary (*Rosmarinus officinalis*) prefer longer hours of stronger sunlight.

Wind sometimes presents a problem in the city, especially in areas with many tall buildings. The strength and location of these gusts can vary greatly, even for different tenants in the same apartment complex. Observe where they occur, and if they seem severe, consider planting a barrier of wind-tolerant trees or shrubs. Wind-resistant species include black pine (*Pinus nigra* subsp. *Laricio*), forsythia (although they may fail to blossom in the northern reaches of the temperate region), Russian olive (*Elaeagnus angustifolia*), and privet (*Ligustrum* species). Dogwoods, laurels (*Rhododendron maximum*), and fuchsia species do not have a good tolerance for high winds and will do better in a quiet corner.

Plan to place your tubs where the plants will be seen from inside, through windows or glass doors. Where space is tight, use the corners and ends of terraces and balconies for larger specimens. If the containers are arranged in groupings of three or four, a more interesting design and an illusion of more space will result.

City gardeners are sometimes surprised to discover there are many woody plants that will grow outside in containers all year long. These are winter-hardy trees and shrubs such as flowering cherry (*Prunus* species), fire thorn (*Pyracantha coccinea*), and winged euonymus (*Euonymus alata* cv. "Compacta"). The key to successful maintenance of woody species is to provide them with as large a planter as possible. The roots of plants can use a generous amount of soil for storing water and nutrients. The soil also insulates against frost injury. Use common sense: Don't overload balconies with large tubs. Check with your building engineer for structural considerations.

Another successful city-garden strategy is landscaping with climbing deciduous vines. When planted on a western facade, they screen harsh late-afternoon summer sun and offer a dazzling, colorful display. They can be planted in tubs and trained onto wide-mesh netting secured to stakes or balcony rails. They offer maximum vertical display without taking up much ground space. Japanese wisteria (*Wisteria floribunda*) and select rose varieties can be trained into an attractive aerial bower.

THE RESULTS

In temperate regions homes and gardens with energy-efficient design are appealing to the eye and harmonize with the environment. The seasonal transitions in foliage patterns respond elastically to human energy needs: In summer they block excess radiation, and in winter they allow the penetration of sunlight. Also, the availability of a great variety of plant materials provides for continual transitions of color and texture and year-round protection from extremes of heat and cold.

Plant Suggestions

The following lists include a selection of plants appropriate to landscaping in temperate regions. Not all species can be grown throughout the temperate region. Ask your local extension agent or a nursery if a species will thrive in your area and if its particular growth rate and form are appropriate.

Tall Deciduous Trees
(growing to a height greater than 35 feet)

Acer platanoides (Norway maple)
Acer rubrum (red maple, scarlet maple, swamp maple)

Acer saccharinum (silver maple, soft maple)
Acer saccharum (sugar maple, rock maple)

Aesculus X carnea cv. "Briotii" (ruby horse chestnut)
Aesculus Hippocastanum (horse chestnut)
Betula papyrifera (canoe birch, paper birch, white birch)
Betula pendula (European white birch)
Carya ovata (shagbark hickory)
Castanea mollissima (Chinese chestnut)
Cercidiphyllum japonicum (katsura tree)
Cladrastis lutea (American yellowwood)
Cornus Nuttallii (Pacific dogwood)
Fagus sylvatica (European beech)
Fraxinus pennsylvanica (green ash)
Ginkgo biloba (ginkgo, Chinese maiden hair tree)
Gleditsia triacanthos var. *inermis* (thornless honey locust)
Koelreuteria paniculata (golden-rain tree, varnish tree)
Larix decidua (European larch)
Liquidambar Styraciflua (sweet gum)
Liriodendron Tulipifera (tulip tree)
Magnolia heptapeta (Yulan magnolia)
Morus alba (white mulberry)
Nyssa sylvatica (black tupelo, black gum, sour gum, pepperidge)
Paulownia tomentosa (empress tree, paulownia)
Platanus X acerifolia (London plane tree)
Platanus occidentalis (eastern sycamore)
Pyrus calleryana (callery pear)
Quercus alba (white oak)
Quercus coccinea (scarlet oak)
Quercus macrocarpa (mossy-cup oak)
Quercus palustris (pin oak)
Quercus phellos (willow oak)
Quercus rubra (northern red oak)
Quercus virginiana (live oak)
Robinia Pseudoacacia (locust, false acacia)
Salix alba (golden weeping willow)
Sophora japonica (Japanese pagoda tree, Chinese scholar tree)
Sorbus Aucuparia (European mountain ash, rowan tree)
Stewartia Pseudocamellia (Japanese stewartia)
Tilia americana (American linden)

Tilia cordata (little-leaf linden)
Tilia tomentosa (silver linden)
Ulmus parvifolia (Chinese elm)
Ulmus procera (English elm)
Zelkova serrata (Japanese zelkova)

Short and Medium Deciduous Trees
(growing to heights less than 35 feet)

Acer Ginnala (Amur maple)
Acer palmatum (Japanese maple)
Albizia Julibrissin (silk tree)
Amelanchier canadensis (shadblow or downy serviceberry)
Amelanchier X grandiflora (apple serviceberry)
Cercis canadensis (eastern redbud)
Chionanthus virginicus (fringe tree)
Cornus florida (flowering dogwood)
Cornus Kousa (Japanese dogwood)
Crataegus mollis (downy hawthorn)
Crataegus laevigata (English hawthorn)
Crataegus Phaenopyrum (Washington hawthorn)
Elaeagnus angustifolia (Russian olive, oleaster)
Halesia carolina (Carolina silverbell)
Laburnum X watereri, also called *Laburnum vossii* (golden chain tree)
Magnolia X soulangiana (saucer magnolia)
Magnolia stellata (star magnolia)
Malus X atrosanguinea (carmine crab apple)
Malus floribunda (showy crab apple)
Malus ioensis (prairie crab apple)
Malus X purpurea (purple crab apple)
Malus sylvestris, also known as *Pyrus malus* (apple)
Oxydendrum arboreum (sorrel tree)
Phellodendron amurense (Amur cork tree)
Prunus X blireiana (Blireiana plum, purpleleaf plum)
Prunus cerasifera (cherry plum)
Prunus serrulata (Oriental cherry)
Prunus subhirtella (Higan cherry)
Prunus virginiana (choke cherry)
Prunus yedoensis (Yoshino cherry)
Pyrus communis (pear)
Salix babylonica (Babylon weeping willow)

Sorbus decora (showy mountain ash)
Syringa reticulata var. *japonica*
   (Japanese tree lilac)

Tall Evergreen Trees

(growing to a height greater than 35 feet)

Abies concolor (white fir, concolor fir)
Calocedrus decurrens (California
   incense cedar), also called
   Libocedrus decurrens
Cedrus atlantica cv. "Glauca" (blue
   Atlas cedar)
Cedrus Deodara (Deodar cedar)
Chamaecyparis Lawsoniana (Lawson
   false cypress, Port Orford cedar)
Cryptomeria japonica (cryptomeria,
   Japanese cedar)
Magnolia grandiflora (southern
   magnolia, bull bay)
Magnolia virginiana, also called
   Magnolia glauca (sweet bay)
Picea Abies, also called *Picea excelsa*
   (Norway spruce)
Picea glauca cv. "Densata" (Black
   Hills spruce)
Picea pungens (Colorado spruce)
Pinus nigra subsp. *Laricio* (black pine)
Pinus ponderosa scopulorum (Rocky
   Mountain yellow pine)
Pinus Strobus (eastern white pine)
Pinus sylvestris (Scotch pine,
   Scots pine)
Pinus Thunbergiana (Japanese
   black pine)
Pseudotsuga Menziesii, also called
   Pseudotsuga taxifolia
Pseudotsuga Douglasii (Douglas fir)
Tsuga canadensis cultivars (Canada
   hemlock)

Short and Medium Evergreen Trees

(growing to heights less than 35 feet)

Cephalotaxus Harringtonia, also called
   Cephalotaxus drupacea (Japanese
   plum yew)
Podocarpus macrophyllus (yew
   podocarpus)
Sciadopitys verticillata (umbrella pine)
Tsuga canadensis cultivars (Canada
   hemlock)
Tsuga caroliniana (Carolina hemlock)

Deciduous Windbreaks, Hedges, or Borders

Berberis Thunbergii (Japanese barberry)
Calycanthus floridus (strawberry shrub)
Caragana arhorescens (Siberian
   pea tree)
Chaenomeles species, also called
   Cydonia (flowering quince)
Cotoneaster divaricatus (spreading
   cotoneaster)
Elaeagnus multiflora, also called
   Elaeagnus longipes (cherry elaeagnus)
Euonymus alata cv. "Compacta"
   (dwarfed winged bush, dwarf
   burning bush)
Forsythia species (forsythia)
Kolkwitzia amabilis (beauty bush)
Ligustrum amurense (Amur privet)
Ligustrum ovalifolium (California privet)
Ligustrum vulgare (prim privet)
Lonicera species (honeysuckle)
Prunus tomentosa (Manchu or
   Nanking cherry)
Salix discolor (pussy willow)
Symphoricarpos albus var. *laevigatus*,
   also called *Symphoricarpos
   racemosus* (snowberry)
Syringa vulgaris cultivars (lilacs)
Vitex Agnus-castus (chaste tree)
Weigela species (weigela)

Evergreen Windbreaks, Hedges, or Borders

Berberis Julianae (wintergreen
   barberry)
Buxus microphylla japonica (Japanese
   littleleaf boxwood)
Buxus sempervirens (common boxwood)
Camellia japonica (common camellia)
Camellia Sasanqua (sasanqua camellia)
Cotoneaster lacteus (Parney's red
   clusterberry)
Euonymus japonica (evergreen
   euonymus)
Ilex vomitoria (yaupon)
Juniperus chinensis cultivars (Chinese
   juniper)
Juniperus scopulorum cultivars (Rocky
   Mountain juniper, western red cedar)
Juniperus virginiana cultivars (eastern
   red cedar)

Kalmia latifolia (mountain laurel)
Ligustrum japonicum (Japanese privet)
Osmanthus heterophyllus, also
    Osmanthus ilicifolius (holly manthus)
Photinia serrulata (Chinese photinia)
Pieris japonica (Japanese andromeda,
    lily-of-the-valley bush)
Prunus Laurocerasus (cherry laurel,
    English laurel)
Pyracantha coccinea (fire thorn)
Taxus cuspidata (Japanese yew)
Taxus X media (intermediate yew)
Thuja occidentalis (American arborvitae,
    Douglas arborvitae)
Viburnum rhytidophyllum (leatherleaf
    viburnum)
Viburnum Tinus (laurestinus)

Deciduous Shrubs

Buddleia davidii (orange-eye
    butterfly bush)
Cornus alba cv. "Sibirica" (Siberian
    dogwood)
Cornus mas (Cornelian cherry)
Cotinus Coggygria (smoke bush)
Cotoneaster apiculatus (cranberry
    cotoneaster)
Cytisus species (broom)
Daphne Mezereum (February daphne)
Deutzia species (deutzia)
Enkianthus campanulatus (redvein
    enkianthus)
Fuchsia species (fuchsia, lady's
    eardrops)
Hamamelis virginiana (witch hazel)
Hibiscus syriacus (rose of Sharon,
    shrub althea)
Hydrangea macrophylla, also called
    Hydrangea hortensis (common bigleaf
    hydrangea, house hydrangea)
Hydrangea paniculata cv. "Grandiflora"
    (peegee hydrangea)
Paeonia suffruticosa (tree peony)
Philadelphus species (mock orange)
Potentilla fruticosa (bush cinquefoil)
Prunus glandulosa, double-flowered
    cultivars (dwarf flowering almond)
Rhododendron calendulaceum, also
    called *Azalea calendulacea*
    (flame azalea)

Rhododendron mucronulatum (Korean
    rhododendron)
Rhododendron Schlippenbachii, also
    called *Azalea Schlippenbachii*
    (royal azalea)
Rosa rugosa (rugosa rose)
Spiraea species (spirea, bridal wreath)
Tamarix ramosissima, also known as
    Tamarix pentandra (Odessa tamarisk)
Viburnum X carcephalum (fragrant
    snowball)
Viburnum plicatum, also called *Viburnum
    tomentosum sterile* (Japanese
    snowball)
Viburnum trilobum, also called *Viburnum
    americanum* (American cranberry bush)

Evergreen Shrubs

Abelia X grandiflora (glossy abelia)
Aucuba japonica (Japanese aucuba)
Chamaecyparis obtusa (Hinoki false
    cypress)
Chamaecyparis pisifera (Sawara false
    cypress)
Euonymus Fortunei (winter creeper)
Ilex X altaclarensis cv. "Wilsonii"
    (Wilson holly)
Ilex Cassine (dahoon, dahoon holly)
Ilex cornuta (Chinese holly)
Ilex crenata (Japanese holly)
Ilex opaca (American holly)
Juniperus communis (common juniper)
Juniperus conferta (shore juniper)
Juniperus sabina (savin juniper)
Leucothoe Fontanesiana, also called
    Leucothoe Catesbaei (drooping
    leucothoe)
Mahonia Aquifolium (Oregon grape
    holly)
Nandina domestica (nandina, Chinese
    sacred bamboo)
Pieris floribunda (mountain andromeda)
Pinus aristata (bristlecone pine,
    hickory pine)
Pinus Mugo, also called *Pinus montana*
    (mugo pine, Swiss mountain pine)
Rhododendron carolinianum (Carolina
    rhododendron)
Rhododendron indicum cultivars
    (Indian azalea)

Rhododendron maximum (rosebay
rhododendron, great laurel)
Skimmia japonica (Japanese skimmia)
Spartium junceum (Spanish broom)
Taxus baccata (English yew)

Deciduous Vines
Actinidia arguta (bower actinidia,
tara vine)
Actinidia chinensis (Chinese actinidia)
Campsis X Tagliabuana (trumpet vine)
Celastrus scandens (American
bittersweet)
Clematis hybrids (hybrid clematis)
Clematis montana (pink anemone
clematis)
Hydrangea anomala subsp. *petiolaris*,
also called *Hydrangea petiolaris*,
or *Hydrangea scandens* (climbing
hydrangea)
Lonicera Heckrottii (goldflame
honeysuckle)
Lonicera japonica cv. "Halliana"
(Hall's honeysuckle)
Lonicera sempervirens (trumpet
honeysuckle)
Parthenocissus quinquefolia, also called
Ampelopsis quinquefolia
(Virginia creeper, woodbine)
Parthenocissus tricuspidata, also called
Ampelopsis tricuspidata (Boston ivy,
Japanese creeper)
Polygonum aubertii (silver-fleece vine,
silver-lace vine)
Pueraria lobata, also known as *Pueraria
Thunbergiana* (kudzu)
Vitis coignetiae (glory vine)
Vitis species (grapevine species)
Wisteria floribunda (Japanese wisteria)
Wisteria sinensis, also called *Wisteria
chinensis* (Chinese wisteria)

Evergreen Vines
Akebia quinata (five-leaf akebia)
Euonymus Fortunei (common winter
creeper)
Hedera Helix (English ivy)
Lonicera sempervirens (trumpet
honeysuckle)

Ground Covers
Aegopodium Podagraria (silver-edge
bishop's weed, silver-edge goutweed)
Ajuga reptans cultivars (bugleweed,
carpet bugle)
Arctostaphylos uva-ursi (bearberry,
kinnikinnick)
Euonymus Fortunei "Coloratas" (purple
winter creeper)
Hedera Helix (English ivy)
Juniperus horizontalis cv. "Wiltonii"
(Wilton carpet juniper)
Juniperus horizontalis (creeping juniper)
Mahonia repens (creeping mahonia,
dwarf holly grape)
Ophiopogon japonicus (mondo grass)
Pachysandra terminalis (Japanese
pachysandra, Japanese spurge)
Paxistima Canbyi (Canby pachistima)
Rosmarinus officinalis cv. "Prostratus"
(rosemary)
Sedum species (stonecrop, live-forever)
Thymus praecox (mother-of-thyme)
Vinca minor (common periwinkle,
trailing myrtle, creeping myrtle)

2

Other Environmental Landscaping Considerations

CHAPTER SEVEN

Water-Efficient (Low-Maintenance) Landscaping

Less than one-half of 1 percent of the earth's water is fresh and drinkable. You'd think we'd treat the stuff with a little respect. Instead, we've been on a water-spending binge, acting as if water is free. We've dumped sewage into our rivers, crowded manicured lawns onto the desert, and literally flushed countless gallons down the toilet unnecessarily. Underground aquifers and water tables that took millions of years to form—drop by drop—are being depleted by the yard every year. That means we not only have less useable water, but to get what we've got, we have to burn more and more oil for pumping and shipping.

To make matters worse, if there is a global warming trend, as many scientists predict, we can expect more droughts at the same time the increased heat makes everything that moves or grows want to drink more. You can imagine the political troubles that could cause, not to mention high water prices.

Even if predictions of global warming are wrong, we have serious water worries; the signs of strain are already here. Droughts are increasing each year. Countries and counties are fighting over rights to water reservoirs. And worldwide sales of water have surpassed those of oil. California's state house has even entertained such harebrained schemes as towing icebergs from the North Pole and creating a transcontinental Alaskan water pipeline.

The best way to solve our water problems is to treat water like a precious commodity: Conserve it, don't waste it, keep it clean. Unfortunately, water is one of those things you don't notice until its gone. The time to save water is now—while we still have it.

For most homes, landscaping is by far the biggest user of household water. In many areas of the country, almost 50 percent of total water consumption goes to the yard. Reducing how much we spray on the yard will go a long way toward easing our water woes. And using less water makes good practical sense: It saves money and time. Creating or altering your landscape so it needs less water can dramatically lower your water bill (or reduce your electric bill if you have a well). It's possible to cut your water bill by 80 percent—and still have a beautiful landscape. In some areas of the country, that translates into savings of more than $400 a year (see pages 100-101 for a chart showing examples of savings by creating a water-efficient landscape).

GET A GOOD PLAN, STAN

Like most endeavors, the first thing to do is to come up with a good plan. A landscape design that uses water more efficiently should take into account the characteristics of your particular property as well as the needs of your plants.

Make a general survey of your yard. The plan doesn't need to be detailed yet (for full details on how to design your property for energy efficiency, aesthetics, eco-friendliness, and water-efficiency see chapter 13). A rough drawing that takes note of some water-retaining characteristics of your land will do for now.

Things to Note on Your Yard Survey

Micro Microclimates: Jot down which spots on your property get sun, shade, moisture, or wind.

Slope: As a general rule, slopes with southern and western exposures have the highest rates of water loss, especially in areas near buildings or paved surfaces. Steep slopes waste water through runoff and rapid evaporation. These spots will retain water better if terraced or covered by drought-resistant ground cover and a shade tree.

Grass: Lawns aren't evil; in fact, they have some real aesthetic and environmental benefits (see chapter 8), but the traditional American lawn is a water hog. If you live in a rainy area, then your lawn's drinking habits aren't a problem. But for most homeowners, reducing lawn size, planting drought-resistant grass, and proper maintenance will go a long way to lowering water costs.

Take a realistic look at your lawn area. Note the areas that aren't doing well and are difficult to water and maintain. Grass under heavy shade usually doesn't grow well. Typically, stretches along fences, slopes, and borders with other plants or sidewalks are trickier to water and maintain.

Patterns of usage: What part of your yard do you actually use and walk on? Where is it most important to have dramatic plants and a grass area to lounge and play on?

Your present situation: What are your plant's current water needs? Do you already have some low-water-usage plants? If so, are they planted near each other and in the best spot?

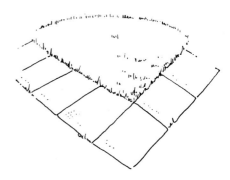

SPOIL YOUR SOIL

Perhaps the single most important factor for creating a water-efficient landscape is the makeup of your soil. Sandy soils drain too quickly and don't provide plants the nutrients they need. Clay soils repel water, resulting in runoff and thus insufficient drainage and nutrition. Ideally, your soil should be a mixture of sand, clay, and silt. (Silt is an intermediate-size particle made when sand or clay breaks down.) The most fertile balance of sand, clay, and silt is called loam.

There are three basic ways to check the makeup of your soil. You can purchase a soil-testing kit at your local nursery or garden center. You can send your soil to your local extension service. Or you can test it yourself. Fill up a quart-size glass jar with one-third soil and two-thirds water. Shake the jar and let it sit overnight. The soil should separate into sand, silt (smaller grained than sand), and clay, with some organic matter floating on top. The ideal loam contains 40 percent sand, 40 percent silt, and 20 percent clay.

If your soil isn't perfect, you have a couple of options. One choice is to work organic matter into the soil. This binds soil particles together and acts like a sponge, soaking up water and releasing it as your plants need it.

There's plenty of free organic "waste" that can be used to improve your soil: grass clippings, leaves, sawdust, hay, farm-animal manure (wait at least a few months—until it's dried out and the ammonia in it has left), or compost. If you don't have access to enough free organic material, you can pick up some peat moss at a local garden center (avoid mountain-meadow peat moss, the harvesting of which irreversibly destroys mountain-meadow ecosystems).

Shred or chop up the organic material, and mix it into your soil in the fall. This gives it time to break down before you're ready to plant. If you need to add more in the spring, use materials that have already decomposed. If you have only fresh organic matter to add, mix in a high-nitrogen fertilizer to aid in decomposition. Otherwise the decomposing organisms will use nitrogen already in the soil to break down the fresh organic matter.

Forget the Perfect Soil

If your heart says azaleas, but your soil says daylilies, you have two choices: Either spend a lot of effort (and usually money) reworking your soil, or reconsider daylilies. Conventional advice is to rework your soil to create the perfect loam. But conventional advice also results in everyone's yard looking alike. Trying to change the makeup of your soil inevitably means reworking your soil every couple of years. There are reasons why your soil is the mixture it is. Better to choose plants that will thrive in it than fight an uphill battle.

The Wormy Way

Xeriscape Gardening (an excellent book on water-efficient landscaping) recounts how an Oklahoma man with clay soil created a yard of black gold—using worms. First, he mixed some lime (his soil was too acidic) and worm delicacies (he used coffee grounds and spoiled cornmeal) into a small section of his backyard. Then he dumped in a can full of the spineless wonders. Within five years the worms had spread to every corner of his property and he had the best lawn in the neighborhood.

THE APPROPRIATE LAWN

As already noted, lawns are water hogs. But you can reduce the beasts' needs. For starters, limit the size of your lawn. For most families, 800 square feet is plenty. The lawn you do keep is usually most appreciated near decks or patios for high visual impact and accessibility. Choose a fairly level spot to avoid runoff, and try to avoid thin strips of lawn, which are difficult to water efficiently.

You can cut down your lawn's size by replacing part of it with appropriate ground covers, such as scented creeping thyme and pussy toes. You could also try a meadow lawn of wildflowers.

According to the National Xeriscape Council (Xeriscaping is a trademarked term for low-water landscaping), most lawns are over-watered. Water your lawn only when it needs it. Look for wilting or discoloration. As long as you thoroughly water your lawn within a day or two of the first sign of wilting, no damage will be done. When you do water, soak the lawn completely.

How you mow your lawn effects how much it drinks. The general rule is to cut high to encourage a deep root system. Deep roots can better tolerate drought (see our chapter on lawn care for a detailed explanation).

RESOURCES FOR WATER-EFFICIENT PLANTS

The following sources will give you extensive lists of water-efficient plants that are appropriate for your area. All are free, except where noted.

Cooperative Extension
Colorado State University
Fort Collins, CO 80523
(303) 491-6198
Ask for: Xeriscape "Service in Action" bulletins by James Feucht.

Dry Times
Organic Gardening
33 East Minor St., Emmaus, PA 18098

National Xeriscape Council
PO Box 767936, Roswell, GA 30076

South Florida Water Management District
PO Box 24680, West Palm Beach, FL 33416
(407) 686-8800; (800) 662-8876
Ask for: Xeriscape Plant Guide.

Texas Agricultural Extension Service
225 Horticultural and Forestry Building
College Station, TX 77843-2134
(409) 845-7341
Ask for: Landscape Water Conservation.

Xeriscape Gardening: Water Conservation for the American Landscape by Connie Ellefson, Tom Stephens, and Doug Welsh, ($30, Macmillan Publishing, 1992) Has extensive lists of water-efficient and drought-tolerant plants for different parts of the country.

The type of grass you choose also has a significant impact on your lawn's water needs. Unless you live in a rain forest, avoid using the ever-popular Kentucky bluegrass, which requires 35 to 40 inches of rainfall per year. Instead, use drought-tolerant grasses, such as cool-season fairway-crested wheatgrass, tall fescues, and warm-season buffalograss and blue grama grass. Also consider growing grass mixtures. *Xeriscape Gardening* points out that by planting a mixture, you avoid the problems that come with a monoculture planting: If disease hits one strain, it won't spread so easily and might not hurt the others.

The Lawn Institute has rated the following grasses in terms of their drought tolerance:

Excellent: buffalograss, blue grama, bermuda grass.

Good: fairway wheatgrass, smooth brome, western wheatgrass, fine fescue.

Fair: tall fescue, Canada bluegrass, Kentucky bluegrass, alkali-grass, perennial ryegrass, timothy, orchardgrass.

Poor: annual ryegrass, creeping bentgrass, rough bluegrass, annual bluegrass.

To find the ideal grass for your area, check with your trusty county extension agent.

GROUPING YOUR PLANTS BY WATER NEEDS

Knowing your yard's microclimates, your needs, the makeup of your soil, and how much grass you are going to keep makes it easier to know what to plant or transplant. As a rule, you should aim to use water-thrifty plants that are native or well-suited to your climate. In high-visibility and frequently used areas it's fine to splurge a little and use plantings that require more water. Heavy drinkers that you feel you can't live without should be located near the house. That's where you'll appreciate them most and where you can best take advantage of gray water (nonphosphorous water from showers and washing) and runoff from gutters, driveways, roofs, and rain catchments.

There may be some spots on your property that collect a lot of water naturally. Obviously those are good spots for heavy drinkers.

By grouping plants with similar water needs together in appropriate spots, you both reduce the maintenance they need and promote growth. You've probably already noticed that if you place a water-lover next to a plant that likes to be dry, neither will do well.

Plants with moderate water requirements can often be satisfied by runoff. Also consider placing these in a shady northern exposure. This will usually take care of all their watering needs except during very dry spells.

Drought-tolerant plants require water to help them get established, but after that they should need little or none. Locate these plants farthest from your house, on south-facing slopes and wherever sun and wind are most extreme.

Windbreaks can help to reduce drying winds. In addition to lowering heating and cooling costs, trees, tall hedges, fences, and trellises lower your water bills by reducing evaporation and transpiration.

Select Plant Varieties Carefully

You don't have to sacrifice aesthetics when selecting water-wise plants. There are thousands of plant varieties that grow well with a limited amount of water. Plants native to your area usually make good choices, since obviously they can thrive on the rainfall that normally falls in your region. Nurseries and mail-order suppliers are beginning to offer a wide variety of native water-thrifty plants. Many annuals are now being bred for garden performance rather than flower size.

For a list of drought-tolerant plants for your area, consult your local nursery or cooperative extension service and/or see the list of resources on page 94.

IRRIGATE EFFICIENTLY

If you're using appropriate plants and have designed your landscape properly, you may not need to water your property at all. Some areas, however, are so dry that you can't totally avoid some watering.

The first choice for watering is to take advantage of runoff. During a 1/4-inch rain, 150 gallons of water will fall from a 1,000-square-foot roof. You can harvest that water by extending existing downspouts to plantings. Water from steep slopes and driveways can also be directed where you need it. If these sources don't take care of all your plants' needs, you have a several options.

For most lawns, a good sprinkler is the still the easiest and most efficient way to water. Avoid overhead sprinklers that shoot water straight up into the air. On a hot, dry day, an overhead sprinkler can lose up to 50 percent of its water to evaporation. Choose a low-pressure sprinkler that has a circular pattern. Only turn the sprinkler on in the cool of the evening or early morning, and try to avoid windy conditions.

A hose and watering can are good for watering new plantings. For pinpoint watering of individual plants, use a perforated can or plastic jug sunk into the soil; this concentrates water around the root zone and lets it sink in slowly.

Trees, shrubs, flowers, and ground covers are best watered with a soaker hose. Soaker hoses are very efficient watering tools. They can use 50 percent less water than sprinklers. They deliver water directly to the root zone, so a minimum is lost to the air. And they water slowly, so little is lost to runoff. Low-volume irrigation also reduces insect problems because insects and disease like wet foliage.

A soaker hose contains thousands of tiny pores along its entire length. Water seeps through these holes, so your plants receive even watering instead of sudden bursts. You can wind the hose alongside your beds in many different configurations. A long straight run of hose works best with landscape plantings, trees, and perennial borders. A multirow or split-T design lends itself to large or rectangular garden layouts, especially raised beds.

You can lay the hose on top of the soil and cover it with a layer of mulch. Or you can bury it several inches underground. To water, you simply turn on your faucet until the soil at the root zone is moist. By attaching a timer to the system, you can even water without being home.

No matter how you choose to irrigate, it's important to do it only when it's needed. Unfortunately, that's easier said than done. The oldest and easiest method to check whether you need to water is simply to pinch some soil and feel if it's dry. If that's not scientific or accurate enough for you, consider buying a soil-moisture sensor or rain-shutoff sensor, which will shut off your automatic irrigation system if it collects rain.

HYDRO-GELS AND POLYMERS

Putting water-absorbing polymers in your soil can significantly reduce water usage and extend the time between waterings. They work by absorbing and storing enormous amounts of water—up to 400 times their weight. Plant roots grow right through the polymer "reservoirs" and tap the nourishment when they need it.

Research still hasn't determined the optimum application rates per square foot, so use with moderation (five pounds per square foot or less seems to be safe).

MULCH-O-RAMA

Mulch is a protective layer of nonliving material that covers the soil surface around plants in order to reduce weeds and conserve moisture while cooling and enriching the soil. When rain falls on bare soil, three-quarters of it is lost to evaporation and runoff. Mulch can reduce evaporation and runoff by as much as 90 percent. It also keeps the soil cooler. In hot soil, organic matter is burned up quickly, beneficial micro-organisms are less active, and roots slow their uptake of moisture and nutrients.

Put down at least two or three inches of organic mulch. This eliminates weed growth (three to five inches of mulch will almost ensure you won't have to weed) and helps slow erosion. Organic materials also restore beneficial microorganisms to the soil. These microorganisms in turn help make soil nutrients available to your plants. Wood chips, grass clippings, straw, and sawdust all work well. As they decompose and are turned into soil, they improve tilth and fertility.

Try to avoid using black plastic as a mulch. It adds nothing to the soil and tends to heat it up too much. If you have no other choice, then at least punch holes in the plastic.

CARE AND MAINTENANCE

Once you've created a low-water landscape, your grass and plants won't be ruined by a drought. Should there be a long hot dry spell that prevents you from watering your plants at all, simply leave everything alone. If you normally use fertilizer or pesticides, hold off because they just add more stress to your plants. And avoid pruning because it forces a plant to use up its reserves to make new growth.

Water-frugal landscapes require less maintenance. Designing for water efficiency means you've designed for maintenance efficiency as well. There is less lawn to mow, fewer weeds to pull, and less sprinkling to do. Of course, you'll still have to do some work on the yard, but by creating a landscape that takes nature's needs into consideration, you'll be rewarded with more free time and a larger bank account.

FURTHER READING

If you want to read more about water-efficient landscaping, check out *Xeriscape Gardening* by Connie Ellefson, Tom Stephens, and Doug Welsh (Macmillan, 1992). It is thorough, detailed, and accessible for the unitated.

WATER-THIRSTY PLANTS

Trees
Alexander magnolia (*Magnolia x. soulangiana Alexandrina*)
Aspen (*Populus tremuloides*)
Babylon weeping willow (*Salix babylonica*)
Cottonwood (*Populus deltoides*)
Flowering dogwood (*Cornus florida*)
Red maple (*Acer rubrum*)
Sugar maple (*Acer saccharum*)
Washington palm (*Washingtonia palmae*)

Shrubs
Flame azalea (*Rhododendron calendulaceum*)
Rhododendron (*Rhododendron racemosum*)
Spreading English yew (*Taxus baccata Repandens*)
Viburnum (*Viburnum plicatum*)
Yellow and red twig dogwood (*Cornus stolonifera*)

Groundcovers
Ajuga (*Ajuga reptans*)
Baby's tears (*Soleirolia soleirolii*)
Impatiens (*Impatiens wallerana*)
Myrtle (*Vinca minor*)
Pachysandra (*Pachysandra terminalis*)

Perennials
Bleeding hearts (*Dicentra spectabilis*)
Columbines (*Aquilegia x. hybrida*)
Delphinium (*Delphinium x. cultorum*)
Foxglove (*Digitalis purpurea*)
Phlox (*Phlox paniculata*)

Turf
Creeping Bentgrass (*Agrostis stolonifera*)
Dichondra (*Dichondra micrantha*)
Kentucky bluegrass (*Poa pratensis*)

Source: *Organic Gardening*

DESIGN #1: COLORADO FOOTHILLS XERISCAPE

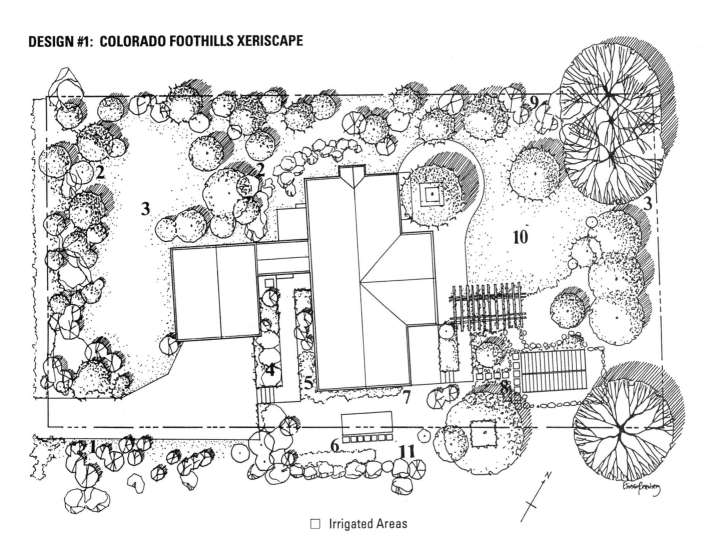

☐ Irrigated Areas

Limited Irrigation/Low Maintenance: Based on the foothills landscape in the Flatirons area of Boulder, Colorado, this yard has all low-water plantings except for the edible and experimental areas. Installation by a landscape designer cost 93 cents a square foot. This yard could be left untended for as long as a year with little appearance of neglect. The turf area is planted with Fairway crested wheatgrass which is watered with sprinklers once a week. Shaded areas have a manually operated low-volume irrigation system.

Soil in the lawn and garden was improved with 2 inches of 50 percent manure / 50 percent topsoil worked into the top 4 to 6 inches of soil. For shrub areas, 50 percent manure was worked into 50 percent soil. The front, dry perennial area was not improved. Most of the plants are thriving on a natural sandy, gravelly soil. Mulches are not used due to high winds. Surface areas are minimal, and with low water, weeds are greatly reduced.

If the foothills design is too much of a wild look for your taste, you can create a version that keeps watered areas to a minimum but has a neat manicured appearance by substituting buffalo grass for the lawn in area 3 and keeping it mowed, and use tall fescue or Kentucky bluegrass for the small lawn in area 10.

1. *Dry Perennials:* These are planted in an extremely sandy area subject to severe dry conditions from June through September. Watering every other week will produce more bloom, but most of the plants survive with no irrigation. Included are santolina. basket-of-gold, creeping phlox, white yarrow, daisies, coneflowers, penstemon, California primrose, prickly pear, iris, daffodils, and wild geranium.

2. *Semi-arid shrubs:* These include many Southwestern natives and others from places with climates similar to Boulder's. The aspen, nine-bark, Buffaloberry, and golden currant survive in the sandy soil because of runoff from the garage roof. Other shrubs are pinon pine, cowania, rock spirea, wasatch maple, gambel oak, berried mahonia, Apache plume, and various potentillas.

3. *Foothills Grasses:* These are typical of grasses naturalized in the local area, though some are not indigenous. They are crested wheatgrass, big bluestem, little bluestem, Western wheatgrass, smoothbrome, blue gamma, buffalo grass, and Canada bluegrass.

4. *Herbs:* These plants tolerate frequent dry conditions, but in this rock garden they do better with light, frequent watering. Included are creeping thyme, wooly thyme, lemon thyme, golden marjoram, oregano (*O. vulgare*), lavender, santolina, yarrow, sage (*Salvia officinalis*), and creeping mahonia.

5. *Experimentals:* Plants to be tested for drought tolerance.

6. *Edible Planting:* Vegetables are grown in tubs and a cold frame to make water and caretaking more efficient and convenient. Some are combined, such as rhubarb around the Hale Haven peach tree, for efficient watering.

7. *Ground Covers:* Drought-tolerant plants with moderate watering have been successful in this sunny, hot area that is prevented from getting natural precipitation due to the roof overhang. They are pine leaf penstemon, wooly thyme, blue veronica, Greek yarrow, hardy yellow ice plant, hardy pink ice plant, and rock soapwort.

8. *Southwest Flowers:* Nearly all are native to the Southwest including some mentioned in area 1. (dry perennials).

9. *Semimoist Shrubs:* These require partial shade and slightly more moisture than is available on most local sites. Included are Lewis' mockorange, sweet mockorange, jamesia, Rocky mountain ash, and twinberry.

10. *Lawn:* Planted in Fairway crested wheatgrass, which requires half the water that the former Kentucky bluegrass did.

11. *Lawn:* Planted in buffalo grass (Sharps Improved), which does not require irrigation. However, in hottest weather this grass looks best with about 1/2 inch of water per week. This grass benefits from light fertilization once a year and occasional mowing to trim off other cool-season grasses that may become mixed in.

IRRIGATION COSTS*	Sq. Ft.	Gallons Per Sq. Ft. Per Season**	Boulder, CO $.81/1,000 gals.	Denver, CO $.83/1,000 gals.	Santa Fe, NM $2.97/1,000 gals.
COLORADO FOOTHILLS XERISCAPE					
Fairway, crested wheatgrass lawn,	750	5	$6	$6	$20
Trees, shrubs, flowers	620				
CONVENTIONAL SUBURBAN LANDSCAPE	8,132	18	$118	$122	$435
Bluegrass lawn and trees, shrubs, flowers					

*Additional domestic water use would likely raise the total bill by as much as 50 percent. Boston, Atlanta, and Des Moines figures reflect drought conditions.
**These are Denver Water Department Figures.
Source: Reprinted with permission from *Organic Gardening*
Landscape designs by Jim Knopf, Illustrations by Elissa Rosenberg

DESIGN #2: CONVENTIONAL SUBURBAN LANDSCAPE

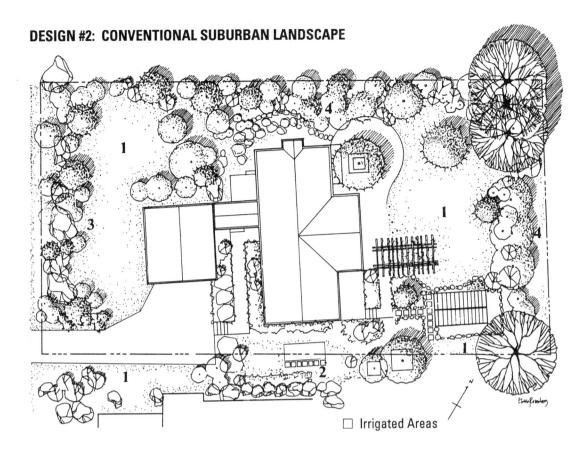

□ Irrigated Areas

Full Irrigation/High Maintenance: Design reflects typical post-World War II suburban yards from coast to coast; installation was $1.14 per square foot. The large lawn area with plantings mixed into it would require extensive, total irrigation, and would need to be mowed at least once a week five months of the year with an hour devoted to trimming. Pruning and weeding in the shrub areas would be increased from Design #1 because of the irrigation.

The intent of this design is a green, manicured look. Plants are chosen because the owner wants them, not because they are low-water. Overall irrigation is required due to large lawn area and plant groupings not done by water use. Shrubs and flower beds are mulched to hold moisture and control weeds. This design has considerably less wildlife.

1. *Lawn* **2.** *Edibles* **3.** *Shrubs* **4.** *Herbs*

Austin, TX $2.70/1,000 gals.	San Diego, CA $1.17/1,000 gals.	Phoenix, AZ $.54/1,000 gals.	Las Vegas, NV $.73/1,000 gals.	Boston, MA $3.33/1,000 gals.	Atlanta, GA $2.27/1,000 gals.	Des Moines, IA $1.82/1,000 gals.
$19	$8	$4	$5	$23	$16	$12
$395	$171	$79	$107	$487	$332	$266

CHAPTER EIGHT

Natural Lawn Care

It's time to stop trashing the lawn. We've all heard that lawns are wasteful and nonproductive. But what do you suppose is transpiring on the lawn? The grass is. What's photosynthesizing, respiring, sucking in carbon dioxide, and spewing out oxygen? The grass is. We've heard about how valuable trees are because they can convert carbon dioxide to oxygen and so lessen the greenhouse effect. Well, every tiny grass plant does the same thing. And they're four times as efficient as most trees. Multiply the 30 million grass plants that make up an acre of lawn by the 30 million acres of lawn in America, and you've got a lot of heavy breathing.

The real problem with our lawns is that Americans pour too many chemicals on them. Homeowners apply an estimated 5 to 10 pounds of pesticide per acre of lawn each year; and nearly all of the dozen or so most popular over-the-counter lawn pesticides are suspected of causing serious long-term health problems. Captan and Benomyl, for example, are carcinogens and mutagens. Dursban has caused chronic kidney damage and mutagenic effects in laboratory tests, and 2,4-D has been linked to lymphatic cancer. Federal agencies like the General Accounting Office, the investigative arm of Congress, have been cranking out studies on the perils of these pesticides, and U.S. senators at subcommittee hearings have been tsk-tsking over the testimony of homeowners who claim common lawn chemicals have triggered excruciating headaches, nausea, extreme fatigue, and other debilitating illnesses.

But the good news is that you can grow a good-looking lawn without the "help" of these or any other dangerous chemicals. The chemical-free lawn does require us to do things differently, beginning with the way we think about our lawns. For starters, we need to get away from the putting-green mentality.

Stop treating your lawn as separate from the rest of your yard. Think of it as a garden of grass. If you have weeds in your lawn, pull them out or chop them. If disease strikes, find out why and eliminate the cause. If insects move in, don't panic: Accept some damage and use safe biological controls when necessary. Fertilize lightly. Mow high and frequently, and leave the clippings on the lawn.

AVOID FERTILIZING FRENZY

Witness it each spring as soon as the snow clears: station wagons lined up at the garden center, customers hauling out bag after bag of lawn fertilizer bearing names like Turf Blaster and Ultra-Green. Back home, they dump, spread, and scatter the stuff on their lawns, then stand back and watch the grass pop.

Sure enough, the grass shoots up and turns so green it's almost blue. But weeds thrive along with the grass. Disease strikes. And the lawnmower barely has time to cool off before the grass needs cutting again. Even so, as soon as the grass begins to look the least bit pale, it's back to the garden center to load up on fertilizer again, and spread it all again, spring, summer, and fall.

For years turf experts encouraged that kind of behavior, but they've changed their tune. Finally the official word is, "Enough is enough!" Researchers have begun to realize that all that fertilizer was doing more harm than good. Massive doses are a waste of money.

"New research has led us to change the way we think about fertilizing lawns," says Eliot Roberts, director of the Lawn Institute, a trade group for the turf-grass industry. Multiple feedings of high-nitrogen fertilizer are out of style. "We've found that the grass plant is a very efficient user of nitrogen," says Mr. Roberts. Babying the grass and pouring on fertilizer reduces that natural efficiency. "The more chemicals you use, the more you disturb the natural biological processes that convert organic matter into nutrients to keep the lawn going," he says. "Some of the best lawns I've seen are never fertilized, but they have an easy time converting clippings to nutrients. Once you get heavily involved with chemical fertilizers, you're increasing the growth rate of the plant and growing it to death."

GREAT GRASSES

Growing a lawn without chemicals is easier now than it ever was before because of new vigorous, weed-beating, disease- and insect-resistant grasses.

Across the North and in the Midwest, the best grasses are named varieties of Kentucky bluegrasses (Adelphi, Fylking, Glade, and Merion), turf-type tall fescue (Clemfine, Falcon, Galway, Houndog, Mustang, and Rebel), and perennial ryegrass (Manhattan, Pennfine, Pennant, Fiesta, Diplomat, and Omega). For the humid South, plant bermudagrass (Tifway, Tiflawn, U-3, Guymon, Numex S-1), carpetgrass, centipedegrass, and zoysia. In the dry South-west, plant bermudagrass, zoysia, blue gramagrass, and buffalograss. The last two are also good for the Great Plains.

"Natural, organic-type fertilizers are the best because they are slow-acting," says Mr. Roberts. "They include slow-release nitrogen, phosphorus, and potassium. This is how you get a lawn to grow slow enough so you don't kill yourself mowing it."

To most of us, "organic fertilizers" means barnyard and manure. Not many of us are ready to spread fresh manure over our lawns. But there are plenty of other natural sources of nitrogen. You can find bags of dehydrated cow manure at just about any garden center. Most brands are deodorized and easy to handle, but at only a 1 or 2 percent nitrogen content, they're fairly expensive. Dried poultry manure is a better value, packing up to 5 percent nitrogen. One 40- or 50-pound bag of dried poultry manure will feed 1,000 square feet of lawn per year. Poultry manure is not odorless, but the smell dissipates rapidly once it has been spread. Other options include bloodmeal, cottonseed meal, fish emulsion, and mixed organic fertilizers.

For the northern lawn, a single fall fertilizing works best, not the usual three or four annual applications. In the fall, photosynthetic activity remains high, but the cool temperature slows top growth. The plants make more food than they can use. The carbohydrate level in plant tissue, shoots, and roots builds up and carries over into the spring when it can be used to help the grass get off to a good start. In the South, lawns respond best to two or three light fertilizations from late spring to early fall.

GETTING TO MOW YOU

When you use natural fertilizers, your lawn doesn't grow out of control. You will be able to mow less. However, you should mow more carefully. Mowing is the most important thing you will ever do to your lawn. Proper mowing can kill weeds, cure diseases, save water, and provide fertilizer.

If you're an average American homeowner, you spend 40 hours a year behind a lawn mower. Chances are your technique falls under one of a couple of mowing styles: You mow every week, at the same time the same way, or you wait until your backyard begins to look like a savannah and mow only when you begin to lose things in the lawn. Neither style is ideal.

What you should do is mow high and often, varying the frequency and blade height according to season. Each grass type also requires a different mowing height.

The longer the top growth, the deeper the root. A plant with deep roots will be better able to withstand drought and fight off diseases. And strong roots have more volume to store food that has been manufactured in the leaves. Simply stated, the longer the root, the healthier

DROUGHT-TOLERANT GRASSES

According to *Xeriscape Gardening*, the following warm-season and cool-season grasses are best for drought tolerance.

Warm Season: Blue gramagrass, buffalograss, bermudagrass, zoysiagrass, bahiagrass

Cool Season: Crested wheatgrass, hard fescue, chewings fescue, sheep fescue, tall fescue, red fescue.

ADJUSTING YOUR MOWER'S BLADE

During hot weather, cut your grass at the high end of the range given below. During cool weather or if your grass is growing in shade use the low end of the range as a guideline. For the last cut of the season, trim your lawn to the lowest recommended height.

GRASS	CUTTING HEIGHT
Annual ryegrass	2 - 2 1/2"
Bermudagrass	1 - 1 1/2"
Centipedegrass	1 - 1 1/2"
Fine fescue	1 1/2 - 2 1/2"
Kentucky bluegrass	2 1/2 - 3"
Perennial ryegrass	1 1/2 - 2 1/2"
St. Augustinegrass	2 - 3"
Tall fescue	2 1/2 - 3 1/2"
Zoysiagrass	1 - 1 1/2"

SOURCE: *Rodale's Illustrated Encyclopedia of Gardening and Landscape Techniques*

the grass. Every time the grass is cut, the root system is weakened to some degree. When the grass is cut severely—more than 40 percent—the roots stop growing.

In the North, two inches is usually the recommended maximum height for Kentucky bluegrass. But it will grow better if you cut it to three inches during the summer. During spring, you can cut it to 2 1/2 inches. Continue mowing at that spring height, just below maximum, until summer arrives. When temperatures reach the 80s consistently, or when more than two weeks pass without at least an inch of rain, it's time to raise the mower to three inches and reduce the frequency. In late summer as temperatures drop and rainfall increases, Northern lawn grasses will begin another growth spurt. Reduce the height by a half inch and mow more frequently.

For warm-season grasses, the principle is the same: Mow high in heat and drought because high mowing causes less stress and encourages deep root growth. But warm-season grasses do not go dormant during the summer, so you will have to mow high and mow frequently through that season. Try a maximum height of 1 inch for bermudagrass and 2 inches for carpetgrass.

By mowing high, you're reducing the stress on the grass and enabling it to compete better with weeds. You're also letting the grass shade the soil to inhibit germination and growth of weeds. And in your own, small-backyard way, you're doing your part to lessen global warming. A lawn allowed to grow to 4 inches tall, for example, fixes twice as much carbon dioxide as a 2 inch high lawn.

Should you rake up the clippings after every mowing? No. Clippings do not, as once believed, cause thatch, a tightly packed layer of organic debris that develops between the soil surface and the green growth and can keep water, sun, and air from penetrating to the soil. Clippings start breaking down soon after they hit the ground. In the

GET OUT AND PUSH

According to the Environmental Protection Agency, off-road gas machinery is a large contributor to suburban smog. Cutting a one-acre lawn with a gas-powered lawnmower creates more pollution than driving a car 50 miles. Cutting your lawn with a hand push mower eliminates air and noise pollution, allows clippings—a natural fertilizer—to be evenly spread, and trims approximately 450 calories an hour from your lunch.

process, they return a lot of nitrogen to the lawn, according to researchers at the University of Connecticut Research Station. They found that grass clippings began to decompose in one week. "And within two weeks, nitrogen from the grass clippings could be found in new grass," reports Dr. Charles R. Frink, head of the research station's soil and water department. "By the end of the third year, we estimated that one-third of the nitrogen on the plots came from grass clippings," he notes. The researchers estimated that the grass clippings contributed about 1.8 pounds of nitrogen per 1,000 square feet. "You didn't need any fancy instruments to see the difference," Dr. Frink says. "Where the clippings were left, the plots were much greener."

WEED 'EM OUT

Proper mowing and fertilizing will give your grass a leg up on weeds. Don't believe the propaganda spread by the chemical companies, that you have to use herbicides or settle for a weedy lawn. It's just not true. You can have a good-looking, virtually weedless lawn without resorting to dangerous and expensive chemicals.

What is a weed, anyway? That's up to you. If you want your backyard to resemble a golf green, then everything but bentgrass is a weed. But if you're looking for a pretty place to play ball with the kids or have a barbecue, then you can afford to stretch the definition of what is acceptable.

Society's perception of weeds changes over the years, and so does the roster of the worst weeds. A flower today may be a weed tomorrow, and vice versa. Take clover. Not too long ago, a clover lawn was a sign of prestige. The silky green petals and pastel flowers made delightful lawns, though not ones well suited for heavy traffic. Clover is soft to walk on. It mows well and smothers other so-called weeds. Clover seed was sold by the bushelful to estates, or mixed with grass seed for thick combination lawns. Until the 1950s you'd be as likely find clover in a home-lawn mix as you would bluegrass. Then a major grass-seed and chemical company launched a public-relations campaign disparaging clover. Clover is a weed! they declared. It doesn't belong in the modern lawn. Coincidentally they began selling a chemical to kill it. Their message carried the day, and now homeowners spend a lot of time and money trying to get rid of it.

It's up to you to decide how many weeds you can stand, and which ones absolutely have to go. But don't try to get rid of all of them at once. Pick the one that makes your skin crawl and your teeth grind and go after that. Get rid of it by pulling, mowing, or cutting, then get rid of the conditions that encouraged it in the first place.

In the long run, the best defense against weeds is a healthy lawn. If the lawn is growing thick and vigorously, there won't be room for

TWO WAYS TO BEAT CRABGRASS

You can virtually eradicate crabgrass with no work, no chemicals, and no weeding. Hard to believe? Studies at the University of Rhode Island showed that high mowing alone reduced crabgrass cover on a test plot to virtually nothing in five years. And high mowing combined with heavy fertilization eliminated crabgrass in just one year.

In an unfertilized plot, mowed at 1.2 inches, crabgrass cover increased from year to year, reaching a high of 54 percent in the third year, and dropping to 33 percent in the fifth year. But in an unfertilized plot mowed at 2.2 inches, the crabgrass cover steadily decreased from a high of 30 percent in the first year to 7 percent in the fifth year.

A combined program of heavy fertilization and high mowing really hastened the demise of the crabgrass. One plot received 20 pounds of nitrogen fertilizer, divided into three applications—one-half in November, one-quarter in June, and one-quarter in September. When that plot was mowed at 2.2 inches high, crabgrass coverage dropped to 8 percent the first year and continued to decline to 2 percent after five years.

weeds to elbow their way in. A lawn that's fertilized properly will start up early in the spring before cool-season weeds can germinate. A lawn that's watered correctly will resist summer stress at the time when warm-season weeds are gearing up. Mowing correctly encourages thick grass growth and shades emerging weeds. Out in the jungle, it's survival of the fittest. If the lawn is fit and well cared-for, the weeds won't stand a chance.

Weeds are symptoms of problems. They'll grow in places that grass can't handle—shady spots, compacted soil, improperly fertilized plots, areas that are too wet or too dry. Other conditions that weeds love include heavy use and mowing too closely, especially during the

dormant season. Herbicides may kill off those weeds, but they don't do anything to correct the problem. Unless those conditions are changed, the weeds will return.

You can rid a lawn of weeds without chemicals. You don't have to spend a lot of time on your hands and knees, either. There are several long-handled tools—The Weed Popper is one, the BackSaver/ Weeder another—that enable you to pull out persistent weeds, tap-root and all, without much effort.

However, whenever you pull or dig a weed, there are plenty more waiting to replace it. You have to beat them to the punch by filling in the bare patch with lawn. You can reseed, and should always have a small supply of grass seed on hand for that purpose. But resodding will fill in the spot faster. Because sod is expensive and difficult to store, you can plant your own sod nursery. Pick a spot on the edge of the lawn or garden, maybe 3 feet by 5 feet. Then sow the species of your lawn grass in the bed. Whenever you dig up a clump of weeds from the lawn, dig a clump of sod to replace it.

High mowing can shade low-growing weeds and dormant weed seeds and keep them from developing. Studies at the University of Maryland show the remarkable effects of high mowing on weed populations. Researchers counted the weeds per 100 square feet in two patches of lawn. One was mowed at 1-1/2 inches, and the other at 2-1/2 inches. After the first year there were fifteen weeds in the low-mowed areas and only one in the high-mowed area. After two years there were fifty three weeds in the low-mowed patch and only eight in the high-mowed one.

DEBUGGING

When you're raising a natural lawn, insects are never a big problem. That's because the soil is alive and the vegetation is untainted by chemicals, giving natural predators a chance to build up and battle pests.

The first step in natural lawn-insect control is learning not to overreact. You can't go running for the insecticide, even if it is organic, at the first sight of a bug. This means getting to know the enemies so that you know both what they look like and when to expect them. By keeping an eye on them, you'll be able to act before they can do a lot of damage. The point is to attack only when they're actually doing damage to your lawn.

If pests do appear, or if you've inherited a chemical lawn that you're trying to set straight, go for natural controls, either biological or physical, that wipe out every turf pest. Some are long-term remedies that control pests year after year. Others are one-shot, quick-kill solutions.

Let's take a look at some of the more common pests and how to handle them naturally:

Chinch bugs are season-long pests throughout the country. At the nymph or immature stage, when they do most of the damage, they are bright red with a white band across the back. Control: beauvaria bassianna fungus, sabadilla.

Billbugs get their name from their long snout that ends in a set of mandibles. But the adult weevils aren't the troublemakers; it's the larvae that cause most of the damage to lawns, especially Kentucky bluegrass. The grubs are small, 5/8 inch long, legless, and white with yellow-brown heads. (They look like puffed rice.) Control: rotenone and diatomaceous earth.

White grubs feast on the roots of Kentucky and annual blue-grasses, bentgrasses, and tall and fine fescues. They are the larval stage of scarab beetles, june bugs, rose and other chafers, and Asiatic and Oriental beetles, among others. Their C-shaped bodies measure from 1/4 to 3/4 inch long, and are blunt-ended and creamy white, with a hard yellow or brown head. Control: Hand pick and destroy beetles to reduce next year's grub populations. Control: Margosan-O (Neem), diatomaceous earth, predatory nematodes.

Japanese beetle grubs are 1 inch long and white with brown heads. Keeping your lawn dry will discourage the adults. Control (adults): Hand pick, or use rotenone, Safer's Japanese-beetle spray containing pyrethrum. Control (grubs): milky spore (Bacillus popillae).

Sod webworms prey on Kentucky bluegrass, bentgrass, tall and fine fescues, and zoysia. The worms are larvae of the buff-colored moth, which you'll see in late spring at dusk flying in zigzag fashion over the lawn. The moths are easy to identify by the pair of snoutlike projections on their heads and the way they fold their wings close to the body when at rest. Control: insecticidal soap, Bacillus thurengiensis, resistant grass varieties.

NOW DO NOT DISTURB

Lawn diseases become disasters only where turf is overmanaged. When chemicals are poured on the turf, they take a toll. The lush growth caused by high-nitrogen regimes makes grasses easy prey to disease. Fertilizers, herbicides, and fungicides all make their way to the soil, where they often destroy beneficial bacteria, upset the balance of the soil system, and give disease-causing fungi a chance to get the upper hand. The result: more diseases, treated with more chemicals, and an even less healthy soil. "The more chemicals you use, the more you disturb the natural biological processes that convert organic matter into nutrients to keep the lawn going," cautions Eliot Roberts of the Lawn Institute.

"Disease-causing organisms are always present in the lawn, ready to infect weakened plants when conditions become favorable, "Eliot Roberts says. The chemical approach is to try to blast the fungi out of existence. But that's a hopeless battle. "Trying to kill the fungi does little good," he explains, "because complete control is never possible." Nor is it desirable.

The soil itself can keep disease in check. In healthy soil, disease pathogens are vastly outnumbered by nonpathogenic microfauna (amoeba, nematodes, and insects) and microflora (bacteria, actino-mycetes, and fungi). They usually have the upper hand and keep the disease-causing organisms in check—unless outside intervention upsets the equilibrium.

A stress, perhaps the application of a toxic herbicide, may allow the disease organisms to surge, and they go to work on the lawn. Spots, patches, and discoloration occur. Fungicides themselves can cause other disease pathogens to get the upper hand. In effect, fungicides often force you to trade one disease for another. Technical papers show more than 90 examples of turfgrass diseases that were made more severe as a result of fungicide applications.

That's why groundskeepers are constantly applying chemicals on golf courses, and why contract lawn services are a booming business:

TWO WAYS TO BEAT DANDELIONS

Get yourself a pair of long-handled clippers, a long-handled weed fork, or a weed popper, and go after them with confidence!

It's true that dandelions are painfully persistent. Their long taproots are hard to pull, and small pieces left behind will regenerate into new weeds. But they're not indestructible. The key is to get them when they're at their weakest, when they're blooming and food reserves in the roots are at their lowest. Dig out 4 to 5 inches of the root and you have better than an 80 percent chance that any remaining root pieces won't have enough strength to send up another stalk.

A weed popper pulls out the plants, roots and all, with a stomp. A long-handled weeding fork lets you do the job while standing.

Cutting with long-handled shears is even easier, although one cut won't do it. You have to cut off all the leaves and as much of the stem as possible. You have to cut lower than a lawn mower will reach, five or six times a year. The root will keep sending up new growth until it runs out of steam.

They've created a vicious cycle. That disease spiral exists on chemically treated home lawns, too, but you can break the cycle by adding beneficial microorganisms.

Healthy, virgin, chemical-free soil is teeming with good microorganisms. Bacteria and fungi work to keep the disease-causing fungi in check by competing with them for food. But there's evidence that actinomycetes may play a more active role in fighting pathogenic fungi. These microscopic plants are known primarily as decomposers of organic matter. They're responsible for the characteristic sweet smell of freshly worked soil. Plant pathologists at Michigan State University found that applying actinomycetes found in the products Lawn Restore, Lawn Rx, and Green Magic helped lawns recover from the lawn diseases necrotic ring spot, suppressed dollar spot, and reduced fusarium blight.

Applications of manure can also increase the actinomycete level in the soil. Topdressing with other organic matter such as compost, peat humus, and topsoil will do the same. Seaweed is another good natural disease fighter; naturally occurring hormones in the seaweed act as fungal inhibitors. Studies at Clemson University showed that applications of liquid seaweed to turf reduced fusarium and dollar spot.

It's time to stop throwing pesticides—and money—at our lawn problems. Once we do, we find that those problems are quite easy to handle with a little ingenuity and elbow grease.

By WARREN SCHULTZ, former editor-in-chief of *National Gardening Magazine*.

CHAPTER NINE

Landscaping For Wildlife

Wild animals require four basics: food, water, cover, and areas for reproducing and raising their young. To create a wildlife-friendly backyard, you must provide these essentials—which vary according to the needs of the animals you want to attract. Naturally, the widest variety of habitat elements will attract the most birds and other animals. The ideal habitat would be a diverse mixture of woods, open meadow, fence rows, and wetlands.

THE ESSENTIALS

Food

The best wildlife sanctuaries supply abundant food for a variety of species year-round. Shrubs, trees, and other plants that produce food, such as acorns and nuts, berries, seeds, buds, catkins, fruit, nectar, and pollen, should be planted whenever possible. The longer the plants provide food, the better. In the Northeast, for example, mountain ash, flowering in midspring, bears fruit from August to March. Your local garden center, state nongame wildlife program, or nature center can give recommendations about the best wildlife plants for your region. (Also see pages 117-119.)

While plants are maturing, or when food supplies are scarce in the winter, you will need to be the food source. The classic wildlife food dispenser is the bird feeder, but you can also set up feeding stations for deer or other animals. The best foods for birds are sunflower, niger, and proso millet seed, cracked corn, and suet. In summer, sugar water offers a backup for hummingbirds who don't get enough nectar and insects.

Water

Animals need water for drinking and bathing. You can help them out by keeping a birdbath, small pool, or pond. An elevated birdbath will protect birds from cats and other predators and can be an elegant addition to the yard. A small pool set in the ground provides not only water for drinking and bathing, but cover and reproductive areas for small fish, frogs, insects, and reptiles. Even a dripping hose or shallow, wide-rimmed dish placed near shrubbery or other cover will be a good water source for small animals.

Your water source should be available to animals year-round. In summer heat, be sure to replace water regularly and keep birdbaths clean. Otherwise mosquito larvae can thrive and bird droppings will contaminate the water. In winter, when temperatures drop below freezing, remove ice in the morning and refill with fresh water.

Cover

Cover is anyplace that protects animals from predators and the weather. Different species have different cover requirements: rock piles or stone walls work for chipmunks and lizards, brush piles or dense shrubs for cottontails and towhees, evergreens for chickadees and pine squirrels, and water for frogs and turtles.

Cover also serves as a home base. The farther an animal must venture from cover, the more vulnerable it is to predators. So try to provide cover close to food and water. Many plants that provide food also give cover. Craig Tufts, director of the National Wildlife Federation's Backyard Habitat Program, highly recommends junipers because they feed a wide variety of birds and provide good cover for small songbirds, shrews, chipmunks, and rabbits. Densely branched shrubs and evergreens will protect an assortment of animals.

Ideally you should have a wide variety of landscape elements—from meadows and hollow logs to tall, full-grown trees—so birds and other animals can choose the cover they need.

OTHER CONSIDERATIONS

Places to Raise the Younguns

Your yard could have good food sources, cover, and water and still not support animals or birds. There must also be suitable nest sites. Birds, for instance, won't nest just anywhere. As Stephen Kress explains in *Gardening for Wildlife,* "Many birds build where three or more branches emerge from the same location on a main stem. This gives the nest maximum support. Pruning to create such nest sites may increase the chance for birds selecting your shrub(s) for their nests." Other birds prefer to nest in tree hollows. If you don't have trees with big enough cavities, you can put up a bird house or nesting shelf. These can be attached to posts, trees, or your house. Bat and squirrel boxes provide safe rearing areas when den trees aren't available. And dense plantings of shrubbery provide safe areas for small animals, such as rabbits and chipmunks. Rabbits and sparrows also like tall grass.

Salamanders, frogs, turtles, and insects like dragonflies require a body of water as a safe haven for their young. A clean stream or pond is essential to their survival.

Grow Natives

Plants native to the soils and climate of your specific area offer the best overall food sources for wildlife. They also tend to require less fertilizer, water, and pest control. And native plants usually support ten to fifty times more species of native wildlife (mostly insects, the basic wildlife food) than do exotics. Exotics also run the risk of taking over native plants and eliminating food that animals have adapted to. (See chapter 10 for guidelines for acquiring native plants.)

Cut Back Your Lawn

Lawns offer little of value to wildlife. While meadows hum and buzz with insects and birds, which love eating tall-grass seed, a mani-cured lawn is silent—or host to a roaring mower that scares animals away. The exposed green patches that dominate America's landscapes also cut animals off from wooded areas and paths of migration. As Sara Stein notes in *Noah's Garden,* "Suburbia already has more holes than a slice of imported Swiss, and the routes along solid ground are becoming more and more difficult for animals to negotiate." Ms. Stein recommends bordering your property

Border plantings can create animal pathways—even in developed areas

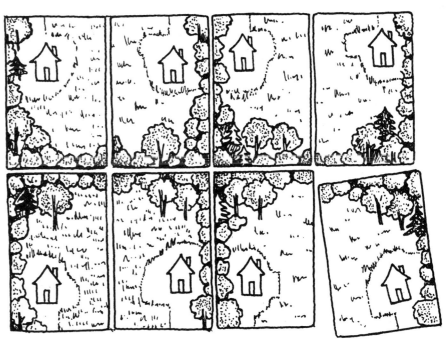

with thick plantings that will provide safe paths for animals. If your neighbors do the same thing, there will be extensive pathways that connect to large wilderness areas.

Pitch Your Pesticides; Let Predation Reign

Jeff Cox said it best in *Landscaping with Nature*: "It's cruel to lure birds and insects and mammals to your property and then use herbicides, fungicides, pesticides, and other chemicals that can poison and destroy them." Animal-friendly yards normally don't have out-of-control insect problems because there are so many natural predators, such as toads, birds, ladybugs, and spiders, to keep things in check. Should you have pest problems, try bringing in additional natural predators and remove pests by hand. If this fails, try biological controls, traps, or nonsynthetic dusts such as diatomaceous earth (a silica substance that kills soft-bodied insects such as aphids).

CREATING YOUR SANCTUARY

The first step in planning a backyard wildlife habitat is to assess your present property or garden space. Identify the habitat elements that already exist for wildlife. Plants that provide food are important to birds and small mammals. As already noted, dense shrubbery, a stand of evergreens, or a brush pile will provide cover for many animals and protection from wind and predators.

Take an inventory of everything in your yard, noting the sizes and locations of all existing plants. Make a rough drawing that shows where pathways, plants, fences, large rocks, and other objects are located (this will be used later in chapter 12, "Putting It All Together").

Try looking at your yard from an animal's point of view. Is there a dying tree in the corner of the yard you were thinking of removing? The knotholes could provide a perfect home for a family of crested fly-catchers or a colony of honeybees. Is there a pile of brush that isn't very attractive? It could be neatened up just a bit and moved under some trees, giving the protection a mother rabbit needs to safely bear and raise her young.

While assessing your yard for habitat elements, become familiar with the birds and other animals native to your region. Learn which species could use some room and board when they migrate through your area. Once you know the possibilities, you can determine which animals you want to attract and how much space you'll want to leave for them.

Some people, for example, are mostly interested in attracting butterflies. Planting beds of fragrant, brightly colored flowers—such as butterfly bush, milkweed, or cosmos—in full sunlight will draw butterflies. You may want to invite birds, chipmunks, squirrels, rabbits, and frogs. Of course, your planning and planting will vary according to how many animals you're trying to help. Read up on those animals you're most interested in attracting to learn what their needs are.

Don't think so much like an animal that you forget to plan space for yourself. A wooden bench or mossy-green spot near a small pool or shade tree will make a good place for watching the animals that visit. An arched trellis covered with the purple-flowering wisteria vine, which attracts butterflies, will create a magical spot to relax or read.

After taking an inventory of your yard and deciding what plants you want, you can work your plans for wildlife into your overall landscaping scheme (see chapter 12, "Putting It All Together"). You probably won't be able to accomplish everything at once and there may be some conflicts with other landscaping plans, but if you've taken wildlife needs into consideration, you should be able to create an environmentally friendly landscape for everyone.

Making Your Backyard Official

In 1973 the National Wildlife Federation created a program to recognize minirefuges in the backyards of concerned homeowners. To date, more than 7,500 properties have been officially certified as Backyard Wildlife Habitats.

If you own or maintain property, you are eligible to participate in the Backyard Wildlife Habitat Program. For an application and further information on gardening with wildlife, write to the National Wildlife Federation, Backyard Wildlife Habitat Program, 1400 16th Street, N.W., Washington, D.C. 20036-2266.

PLANTS RECOMMENDED BY THE NATIONAL WILDLIFE FEDERATION FOR WILDLIFE LANDSCAPING

The list below offers suggestions of plants, according to size and region, that offer food for most of the year for a variety of species. Most plants listed are native species. Be sure that moisture and light requirements match your yard's conditions.

LOW SHRUBS

Southeast
Beautyberry, *Callicarpa americana*
Saw palmetto, *Serenoa repens*
Cottoneaster, *Cotoneaster* species
Blueberry, *Vaccinium* species
Blackberry, *Rubus* species
Smooth sumac, *Rhus glabra*

Southwest
Beloperone, *Beloperone califonica*
Brittlebrush, *Encelia farinosa*
Buffaloberry, *Shepherdia rotundifolia*
Redberry buckthorn, *Rhamnus crocea*
Skunkbush, *Rhus trilobata*
Trumpetbush, *Tecoma stans*

Northwest
Salal, *Gaultheria shallon*
Manzania, *Arctosaphylos columbiana*
Mahala mat, *Ceanothus prostratus*
Evergreen huckleberry, *Vaccinium ovatum*
Rabbit brush, *Chrysothamnus nauseosus*

Rockies/Great Basin
Rabbit brush, *Chrysothamnus nauseosus*
Mormon tea, *Ephedra trifurca*
Prairie sagebrush, *Artemisia ludoviciana*
Smooth sumac, *Rhus glabra*

North/Northcentral
Beach plum, *Prunus americana*
Blueberry, *Vaccinium* species
Coralberry, *Symphoricarpos orbiculatus*
New Jersey tea, *Ceanothus americanus*
Huckleberry, *Gaylussacia* species

TALL SHRUBS
Southeast
Yaupon, *Ilex vomitoria*
Red buckeye, *Aesculus pavia*
Southern blackhaw, *Viburnum rufidulum*
Wax myrtle, *Myrica cerifera*
Hercules' club, *Aralia spinosa*

Southwest
Creosotebush, *Larrea tridentata*
Bitterbush, *Purshia tridentata*
Desertwillow, *Chilopsis linearis*
Sugar sumac, *Rhus ovata*
Serviceberry, *Amelanchier* species
Shrub live oak, *Quercus turbinella*

Northwest
Tall Oregon grape, *Berberis aquifolium*
Red currant, *Ribes sanguineum*
Serviceberry, *Amelanchier alnifolia*
Osoberry, *Osmaronia cerasiformis*
Cascara buckthorn, *Rhamnus purshiana*
Blue elderberry, *Sambucus caerulea*

Rockies/Great Basin
Golden current, *Ribes aureum*
Sand cherry, *Prunus besseyi*
Mountainmahogany, *Cercocarpus species*
Chokecherry, *Prunus virginiana*
Serviceberry, *Amelanchier canadensis*

North/Northcentral
Arrowwood viburnum, *Viburnum dentatum*
Pfitzer juniper, *Juniperus chinensis var. pfitzeriana*
Winterberry, *Ilex verticillata*
Bayberry, *Myrica pensylvanica*
Spicebush, *Lindera benzoin*
Red osier dogwood, *Cornus sericea*

SMALL TREES
Southeast
Dahoon, *Ilex cassine*
Flowering dogwood, *Cornus florida*
Serviceberry, *Amelanchier canadensis*
American holly, *Ilex opaca*
Persimmon, *Diospyros virgianiana*
Cabbage palmetto, *Sabal palmetto*

Southwest
Ironwood, *Olneya tesota*
Hackberry, *Celtis pallida*
Paloverde, *Cercidium floridum*
Velvet mesquite, *Prosopid juliflora var. velutina*
Chokecherry, *Prunus virginiana*
Madrone, *Arbutus menziesii*

Northwest
Pacific dogwood, *Cornus nuttallii*
Madrone, *Arbutus menziesii*
Mountain ash, *Sorbush sps.*
Hawthorn, *Crataegus* species
Vine maple, *Acer circinatum*

Rockies/Great Basin
Limber pine, *Pinus flexilis*
Western red birch, *Betula fontinalis*
Rocky Mountian maple, *Acer glabrum*
Utah juniper, *Juniperus osteosperma*
Rocky Mountain juniper, *Juniperus scopulorum*

North/Northcentral
Sassafrass, *Sassafras albidum*
Serviceberry, *Amelanchier canadensis*
Flowering dogwood, *Cornus florida*
Staghorn sumac, *Rhus typhina*
Nannyberry, *Viburnum lentago*

LARGE TREES (deciduous)
Southeast
Tulip poplar, *Liriodendron tulipifera*
Bald cypress, *Taxodium distichum*
Willow oak, *Quercus phellos*
Pecan, *Carya illinoensis*
Hackberry, *Celtis laevigata*

Southwest
Arizona sycamore, *Platanus wrightii*
Bigtooth maple, *Acer grandidentatum*
Gambel oak, *Quercus gambelii*
New Mexico locust, *Robinia
   neomexicana*

Northwest
Bigleaf maple, *Acer macrophyllum*
Oregon white oak, *Quercus garryana*
Red alder, *Alnus rubra*

Rockies/Great Basin
Emory oak, *Quercus emoryi*
Quaking aspen, *Populus tremuloides*
Fremont cottonwood, *Populus fremontii*

North/Northcentral
American beech, *Fagus, grandifolia*
Shagbark hickory, *Carya ovata*
Northern red oak, *Quercus borealis*
White oak, *Quercus alba*
Sugar maple, *Acer saccharum*
Blackgum, *Nyssa sylvatica*

LARGE TREES (evergreen)
Southeast
Longleaf pine, *Pinus palustris*
Live oak, *Quercus virginiana*
Southern magnolia, *Magnolia
   grandiflora*
Lohlolly pine. *Pinus taeda*
Carolina hemlock, *Tsuga caroliniana*
Eastern red cedar, *Juniperus virginiana*

Southwest
Emory oak, *Quercus emoryi*
Rocky Mountain juniper, *Juniperus
   scopulorum*
Blue spruce, *Picea pungens*
Ponderosa pine, *Pinus ponderosa*
Pinon pine, *Pinus edulis*

Northwest
Western red cedar, *Thuja plicata*
Western white pine, *Pinus monticola*
Douglas fir, *Pseudotsuga taxifolia*
Western hemlock, *Tsuga heterophylla*
Grand fir, *Abies grandis*

Rockies/Great Basin
Lodgepole pine, *Pinus controta*
Ponderosa pine, *Pinus ponderosa*
White fir, *Abies grandis*
Pinon pine, *Pinus edulis*
Douglas fir, *Pseudotsuga menziesii*
Subalpine fir, *Abies lasiocarpa*

North/Northcentral
White pine, *Pinus strobus*
Eastern hemlock, *Tsuga canadensis*
Eastern red cedar, *Juniperus virginiana*
White spruce, *Picea glauca*
Red pine, *Pinus resinosa*
Northern white cedar, *Thuja
   accodentalis*

Other Plants
Trumpet creeper, *Campis radicans*
Red maple, *Acer rubrum*
Sugar maple, *Acer saccharum*
Crab apple, *Malus* sps.
Sassafras, *Sassafras albidum*
Autumn olive, *Eleagnus ambellata*
Silky dogwood, *Cornus amomum*
Flameleaf sumac, *Rhus copallina*
Red osier dogwood, *Cornus sericea*
Elderberry, *Sambucus canadensis*
Tall Oregon grape, *Mahonia
   (Berberis) aquifolium*
Amur honeysuckle, *Lonicera maackii*
Butterflyweed, *Asclepias tuberosa*
Beebalm, *Monarda didyma*
Goldenrod, *Solidago* species

Source: *National Wildlife Federation*

LANDSCAPING FOR BUTTERFLIES

Butterflies are drawn to nectar-bearing compound flowers that are brightly colored, such as those in the daisy family—asters, marigolds, and zinnias. Old varieties, more like the original wild species, usually provide more nectar than highly hybridized and/or double flowers.

The two standout plants for attracting butterflies are butterfly weed (*Asclepias tuberosa*) and butterfly bush (*Buddleia*). Butterfly weed is an orange milkweed that prefers sandy soils but will readily naturalize in clay-based soil. Butterfly bush is a woody shrub that bears long spikes of pastel flowers resembling lilacs. Its flowers appear from late June to early frost.

BUTTERFLY CATERPILLAR FAVORITES THAT GROW THROUGHOUT MOST OF THE U.S.

Plant	Butterfly
Aster (*Aster* species)	Pearly Cresentspot
Blueberry (*Vaccinium*)	Brown Elfin
Ceanothus (*Ceanothus* species)	Spring Azure
Cherry (*Prunus*)	Red-Spotted Purple—except the West
	Two-Tailed Swallow Tail—in the West
Clover, White (*Trifolium*)	Orange Sulphur
Dogwood (*Cornus*)	Spring Azure
Hollyhock (*Alcea*)	Painted Lady
Hop Vine (*Humulus*)	Red Admiral
Mallows (*Malvaceae*)	Painted Lady
Milkweed species	Monarch Asciepias
Nasturtium (*Tropaceolaceae*)	Cabbage White
Nettle Stinging (*Urtica*)	Red Admiral
Parsley (*Petroselinum*)	Eastern Black Swallowtail
Passionflower (*Passiflora*)	Gulf Fritillary
Senna (*Cassia*)	Sulphurs
Snakeroot, Black (*Cimicifuga racemosa*)	Spring Azure
Spicebush (*Lindera benzoin*)	Spicebush Swallowtail
Thistle (*Circium*)	Painted Lady
Violet (*Viola*)	All the Fritillaries
Willow (*Salix*)	Gray Hairstreak, Viceroy, and Morning Cloak
Wisteria (*Wisteria*)	Silver-Spotted Skipper

Source: *Theme Gardens* by Barbara Damrosch (Workman)

PLANTS FOR ATTRACTING HUMMINGBIRDS

Northern Gardens

American Columbine (*Aquilegia canadensis*)

Beebalm (*Monarda didyma*)

Bugleweed (*Ajuga reptans*)

Butterfly milkweed (*Asclepias tuberosa*)

Cardinal flower (*Lobelia cardinalis*)

Coralberry (*Symphoricarpos orbiculatus*)

Fuschsia (*Fuschsia* species) vines and shrubs

Hibiscus (*Hibiscus* species especially *H. syriacus*)

Hollyhocks (*Althea* species)

Horse-chestnut (*Aesculus hippocastanum*)

Jewelweed (*Impatiens capensis* and *I. pallida*)

Larkspur (*Delphinium* species)

Madrone (*Arbutus menziesii*)

Ohio buckeye (*Aesculus glabra*)

Evening primrose (*Oenothera* species)

Siberian pea tree (*Caragana arborescens*)

Tiger lily (*Lilium tigrinum*)

Trumpet honeysuckle (*Lonicera sempervirens*)

Trumpet vine (*Campsis radicans*)

Zinnia (*Zinnia elegans*)

Southern Gardens

(*most from Northern list are also appropriate*)

Citrus tree (*Citrus* species); low trees

Coral bean (*Erythrina* species)

Fire pink (*Silene virginiana*)

Lemon bottlebrush (*Callistemon lanceolatus*)

Mimosa tree (*Albizia julibrissin*)

Red buckeye (*Aesculus pavia*)

Scarlet runner bean (*Phaseolus coccineus*)

Weigela (*Weigela* species)

Source: *Gardening for Wildlife* (Brooklyn Botanical Gardens)

CHAPTER TEN

Creating a Natural-Looking Garden with Native Plants

As enticing as it sounds, simply ignoring your landscape won't create an appealing natural-looking garden. There have been too many environmental changes in most residential areas for the "letting it go" approach to work. Too much native vegetation has been removed and replaced with imported plants. A laissez-faire approach is most likely to produce a chaotic, unpleasing mix of native and exotic plants. Recreating a natural landscape requires planning.

It's impossible to design a garden with the order, complexity, integrity, and beauty of an alluring, undisturbed natural landscape. What we can do is learn about the processes and forms that occur in the woods and try to imitate them. That's why it's so important to go into the forest and observe.

LESSONS FROM NATURE

If you're paying attention, one thing you'll note when you're in the woods is that plants often grow in communities or associations. This happens because particular conditions are just right for a certain plant species. The result is a visual harmony that comes from the right plant being in just the right spot.

Plant communities are typically identified by some of the key species in them (e.g., the oak-hickory forest, the beech-maple forest) or by their environmental characteristics (e.g., the floodplain forest, the sandy-ridge forest). Rarely is a plant community a sharply defined entity. Instead, one community usually grades almost imperceptibly into another. Still, plant communities give a framework from which to approach the design of natural-appearing gardens. Several characteristics of naturally evolved plant communities are useful as a basis for designing naturalistic gardens:

Species Composition

Start by determining the key species that occur together in a specific environment in your area; for example, what grows naturally on a dry, south-facing slope with rocky soil or on a moist, north-facing slope with deep, rich soil. Learn what the dominant species are—that is, the major plants that have the greatest influence on the community. In a forest the dominant species are typically the canopy or over-story trees. In a prairie they are the grasses.

Also note which species are most abundant (which may be different from the most dominant species). Other plant species may be critical to the visual character of the community. Perhaps one species has distinctive branching, flowering, or outstanding fall colors. Whatever it is, that character will be crucial to recreate in your natural-looking designed landscape.

Plant Distribution Patterns

After you have an understanding of the most important species in a plant community, you should observe the distribution of each species. There are two different aspects to plant distribution within a community: (a) the species' distribution relative to microclimates (Does a plant grow only at the edge of the woods, only on the interior, or both? Does a plant grow only on the upper, drier slopes, on the lower, moister slopes, or both?); and (b) the species' characteristic degree of aggregation or "clumping" (Does the species usually grow as an individual, in loose colonies, or in dense clumps?). Knowing the distribution of a species within a plant community will help when planting that species in a designed setting.

Often this information can be found in books or journals or by talking to local botanists, but nothing can replace firsthand observation (preferably with someone who is familiar with the regional vegetation).

Natural Order

In undisturbed natural landscapes, we sense a different kind of order than the simplistic, orchardlike order humans create. Natural order is subtle, found in the repetition of lines, forms, colors, and textures within a particular plant community. In a temperate North American forest, for example, a limited number of tree species will dominate the canopy level. In the Midwestern prairies, 90 percent of the vegetation is comprised of five or six grasses, with their fine textures unifying the landscape.

Variety and Diversity

The visual harmony and unity that comes from a dominant species within a specific environment is usually spiced with a variety of other plants. Even if a woodland's tree canopy is made up of a half-dozen species, the ground layer beneath probably has nine to twelve different species per square meter. And while the prairie is mainly composed of fewer than ten species, there may easily be another fifty or sixty species per acre occurring in small numbers. Additional visual variety results from assorted spacing, aging, and sizes of plants. Ephemeral qualities, such as changing flower and foliage displays, also contribute seasonal diversity.

Spaces and Edges

The shape of natural open spaces offers valuable guidance for designing spaces. Rivers provide excellent examples for garden designers. A river winds through a landscape, widening at turns or bends and disappearing behind "peninsulas" of vegetation. This creates an element of mystery, encouraging the observer to want to see what's beyond the next bend.

Enclosing vegetation usually has younger, shorter shrubs at the front edge. Also, rather than a continuous, consistent wall of enclosing vegetation, there are individuals or clumps of plants advancing into the open space, and points where the space penetrates into the enclosing vegetation. The result is a softness to nature's edges.

DESIGNING THE GARDEN USING NATURAL PRINCIPLES

The naturalistic gardens we design are simplifications and stylizations of the natural landscapes they emulate. Yet they can have the essence of nature about them, particularly over time.

The following suggestions will help you apply some of the design lessons we can learn from nature:

Site Analysis

An important first step is understanding the environmental characteristics of your landscape. For example, determine the soil type(s), sun/shade distribution, relative moisture, and existing vegetation. We need to know both the plants that are undesirable and may need to be

removed and the valued plants that will contribute to a natural-appearing landscape. A purist may want to remove all exotic species, but most of us are willing to live with some compromises.

Space Plan

The next step is to develop the spatial form of the garden. There will almost certainly be a pathway or system of open spaces in your garden. These might well emulate a river, with its gentle to sweeping curves and its partially concealed spaces. The river of space may be translated into a pathway surface or mulched area or lawn. Next, lay out zones of vegetation within different height ranges; for example, ground-layer plants below 3 feet in height; middle-story shrubs and small trees 3 to 15 feet tall; and taller canopy trees. Laying out these zones—on paper and/or on the ground—will be very helpful to provide the structure of the garden.

Plant Selection

The next step is to select the plant species for the different height zones of your plan. With an understanding of environmental conditions at your house and the needs of the native plant communities in your region, you can simply select species from the appropriate community(ies) for your property. In general, the closer you adhere to this principle, the more likely you will have a unified, harmonious landscape. But there may be situations in which exotic species are selected—such as to expand the blooming period. If you do this, avoid plants that have been known to invade surrounding natural areas and/or whose flowers will overpower the native species. Purple loosestrife (*Lythrum salicara*) is a good example of an aggressive species.

Plant Placement

Now that you have selected a palette of plants for a naturalistic garden, your next goal is to arrange those plants within their respective zones. A simple but effective approach is to delineate the different vegetation zones and then use color-coded stakes to locate individual plants within each zone. While it is unlikely that you can initially plant at the same density as nature, the same principles of distribution can be followed; for example, "drifts" of some species may flow through the zone, while other species that occur as individuals in nature may be distributed similarly in the garden. You may want mulched spaces between plants or drifts of plants to provide an environment for the natural spread of vegetation.

In the case of meadowlike or prairielike plantings, zones may be identified for different seed mixes, rather than for the placement of individual plants.

At edges, where plants meet the pathway or open spaces, the slightly undulating, irregular edges of nature may be emulated through the plants' placement.

Maintenance

Just as a natural landscape is ever-changing, so is a naturalistic garden. In the early years of a naturally designed landscape, it is particularly important to watch for intrusions or reappearances of aggressive exotic species that may take over. If exotics are kept away, the natives will eventually migrate into hospitable niches. As conditions change—and, for example, more shade develops—additional plants or seeds may need to be introduced to compensate for others being shaded out. To keep the composition, selective pruning or removal may be necessary.

The minimal upkeep will still give your landscape a designed look, but one based on the ultimate designer—nature.

By Darrel G. Morrison, dean of the School of Environmental Design at the University of Georgia.

WHERE TO GET NATIVE PLANTS

Five Commandments for Conservation-Minded Gardeners

Development, pollution, and invasion by exotic species aren't the only threats to wildnerness. Many natural areas are imperiled also by private and commercial plant collectors who dig up native species from the wild. This isn't an isolated problem. Cactus rustlers in the Sonoran Desert threaten the saguaro (*Carnegiea gigantea*). Illegal digging is decimating wild populations of Venus's flytrap (*Dionaea muscipula*), the insectivorous plant found in boggy areas of the Carolinas. Orchids of the eastern deciduous forests, such as the white fringeless orchid (*Platanthera integrilabia*), are threatened by over-collection. Part of the problem is that plants such as the native orchids are difficult to propagate. But because in most areas the nursery trade has not yet caught up with the upsurge of interest in natural landscaping, gardeners should be cautious when buying any native plant.

So what is the best way to acquire plants for your natural landscape? Here are five commandments to guide native-plant gardeners:

1 THOU SHALT NOT take a plant from the wild. It may be tempting to rationalize that taking "just this one plant" couldn't possibly make a difference. But it's almost never just one gardener or one plant. The cumulative impact of many trowels can be considerable. There is one exception to this rule—rescuing plants that would otherwise face certain obliteration by a shopping mall, suburban subdivision, or other development. Collecting small amounts of seed to germinate yourself generally doesn't endanger healthy plant populations.

2 THOU SHALT make a point of educating yourself about the propagation and cultivation requirements of the native plants you're thinking of putting in your garden. Too many of the native species sold at garden centers and by mail-order suppliers have been dug up from the wild. Plants that are difficult to propagate or slow to flower or reach marketable size are the most likely to have been collected from their native habitat and therefore most at risk. Trilliums, which typically take five years or more to go from seed to flower, are the classic example. Until nursery production of such species becomes profitable, don't buy them. Admire them in the wild instead.

3 THOU SHALT design your garden using only species that are easily propagated. Plants such as rudbeckias and cardinal flower (*Lobelia cardinalis*), which are easy to propagate and quick to mature, have most likely been propagated commercially.

4 THOU SHALT buy native species only from sources who state explicitly that their plants are nursery-propagated. If they don't volunteer the information, ask. Don't be misled by ambiguous phrases like "nursery-grown" or "field-grown," which may mean that the plant was dug from the wild and grown at the nursery for a day or week. The words to look for are "nursery-propagated." Your persistence will pay off: Nursery-propagated plants are generally healthier and better looking than those taken from the wild.

5 THOU SHALT make every attempt to use plants propagated from wild populations growing within 50 miles of your garden. Botanists are concerned also that the genetic integrity of local plant communities is compromised by the introduction of the same species from other regions. While local plants have adapted for thousands of years to the precise conditions of your area, plants of the same species from other areas have no doubt adapted to different conditions. Not just genetic integrity is at stake: Nonlocal plants may not perform as well in your garden as true natives.

By JANET MARINELLI, author of *The Naturally Elegant Home*.

The following organizations can provide you with helpful lists of nurseries selling propagated native plants:

New England Wildflower Society, Garden in the Woods, 180 Hemenway Road, Framingham, MA 01701-2699, (617) 237-4924 publishes a regularly updated booklet called Sources of Propagated Native Plants and Wildflowers, which includes species native to zones 4, 5, and 6.

For a list of nurseries offering propagated Southeastern natives, send a stamped, self-addressed envelope to: North Carolina Botanic Garden, UNC-CH, CB 3375 Totten Center, Chapel Hill, NC 27599-3375.

A list of nurseries in the West is available from: Native Plant Society of New Mexico, P.O. Box 5917, Santa Fe, NM 87502.

It's also worth checking with the native plant society in your own state as well as botanical gardens in your area.

CHAPTER ELEVEN

The Lazy Gardener's Guide to Recycling Yard Waste

Not long ago, composting was considered the quaint hobby of horticultural eccentrics who wore rumpled flannel shirts and preached the gospel of organic gardening. In those days, composting had an aura of sacredness. I should know—I started composting in the mid-1970s with a passion that bordered on religious fervor. Compost gurus like myself rapidly decomposed garden wastes in what was variously called an "aerobic," "active," or "hot" compost pile. These piles reached internal temperatures of 130° to 145° F. due to the activity of thermophilic (heat-loving) and aerobic (air-loving) bacteria. They required careful attention to the proper balance between woody (carbonaceous) and high-nitrogen materials (manures and leafy greens)—a 30-40:1 ratio to be exact—as well as the amount of moisture and air throughout the pile. More importantly, thermophilic compost piles require frequent turning—once a week or more—to "feed" the bacteria their dose of oxygen. None of this stopped me. Like many organic gardeners of that era, I made prodigious amounts of compost. Of course, I was underemployed and had plenty of time on my hands.

My near-religious fervor about composting has mellowed into a more even-handed approach toward this important part of the garden's cycle of decay and renewal. Today, instead of composting every kitchen scrap and every pruning, I separate them into different categories and treat each with the technology or technique that requires the least amount of effort.

Active composting a la 1970s is fast becoming a gardening relic. And here's the ultimate heresy: Some yard wastes need not be composted at all. There are more convenient ways to avoid throwing them away and still improve your yard. The idea is to choose the mix of options that's best for your lifestyle and budget.

MULCHING MOWERS

For many gardeners, raking, bagging, and composting the never-ending stream of lawn clippings is an occasion for some choice curses. But why bother? Letting the clippings fall where they may is good for your lawn. A human-powered push-mower works great for this and should always be the environmentalist's first choice. If your lawn is too big for a push-mower, a "new" product, the mulching mower, allows you to skip the hassle not only of composting but also of raking and bagging lawn clippings. The mulching mower was actually introduced some 30 years ago, but consumers weren't ready for it. A mulching mower has a specially designed blade and blade housing which finely chop the lawn clippings. In a mulching mower, the discharge chute that spews out the clippings is blocked off and they're blown back down into the turf where they decompose and help fertilize the lawn. Recent studies have shown that regular mowing when the grass is 1 to 1 1/2 inches taller than the cutting height may provide all the fertility your lawn requires. Not only that, but mulching mowers also save time—according to one study, seven hours over a six-month period compared to regular mowing and bagging.

Some mulching mowers, called convertible mowers, enable you to capture clippings and leaves for composting when you want them. With convertible mowers you can have it either way, bagging clippings for composting or fertilizing your lawn.

All leading manufacturers of lawnmowers now offer one or more versions of a mulching mower. The most important criterion for selecting a mulching mower is the engine's horsepower rating. These mowers need at least a 4- or 5-horsepower engine to move the blade quickly enough to achieve cutting, shredding, and mulching.

Go to a local dealer. Take different models for a test mow. Be on the lookout for clogging, bunches of clippings on top of the grass and a ragged cut. The best cut is usually made by mowers with a doughnut-shaped blade housing. Other things to consider: How convenient is it to change the blade? How easy is it to attach and release the collection bag? Is the bag hung behind the mower instead of to the side, so it's easy to mow the edges of the lawn?

For a mulching mower, you'll spend from $200 to $500; convertible mulching mowers cost $250 to more than $600.

LEAF SHREDDERS

In the fall, deciduous trees produce a flurry of compostable material throughout much of the country. Leaves make a decent mulch or wonderful rich leaf mold when fully decomposed. But the blizzard of leaves in fall can overwhelm the most dedicated gardener.

One option is to use a dedicated leaf shredder to make the volume of leaves more manageable for mulching or composting. They're designed specifically to shred leaves and nonwoody vegetable waste—not woody material, which should be shredded by a chipper.

There are several basic types of leaf shredders: leaf blowers, which can be reversed to suck and shred the leaves, and gasoline- or electrically powered leaf shredders with either a filament or metal blade—called dedicated leaf shredders. Most manufacturers claim their leaf shredders can reduce ten bags of leaves to one bag of finely chopped material, for a 10:1 ratio. But studies indicate the true ration of reduction is between 8:1 and 4:1—still helpful.

Gas-powered shredders often require frequent cleaning of the air filter. On the other hand, electric shredders need an extension cord, which can be a cumbersome bother in the landscape. Electric shredders tend to be slower than gasoline-powered models, although some slice and dice leaves as fast as the gas versions. Shredding 30 gallons of leaves can take as little as thirty to forty seconds to as long as four minutes. Always ask for a demonstration of the model you're considering to test the amount of reduction and speed. At the same time, note how much shredded material blows back out to the hopper and how much noise the shredder makes. Get names from your local dealer of people who have purchased the model you're thinking about buying. And be sure to find out how well it works with wet leaves.

Other features to consider: Is the machine designed to protect your eyes and hands? Is a safe and useful tamper for pushing leaves into the mouth of the hopper included? Do you get protective goggles? How big is the mouth of the hopper? For a leaf shredder, expect to spend from $100 to $275.

You can avoid the expense of a shredder by heaping leaves in a huge wire-mesh cylinder in some hidden corner of your yard for one or two years. In some cities, leaves are picked up free and composted; you can buy back the finished compost and avoid all the hassle of making your own. Plus, the leaves stay out of the landfill.

CHIPPERS

Woody trimmings, which take forever to break down in a compost heap, can be chipped to cover a path or to use as a mulch. Most machines both chip and shred. The chipping is usually done in a side chute where branches and limbs are inserted into a rotating disk with fixed blades that shear off chips like carrots in a food processor. Shredding is done by carefully inserting the yard waste into a hopper on top of the machine where swinging or fixed hammers shred the material. The hammer-type machines usually have a sturdy screen covering the discharge port and all the material must be shredded to the same size as the screen before exiting. Because of the screen, this type of shredder is more likely to clog and stall than a knife-blade chipper. However, unlike knife-blade chippers, you can change the size of the chips. Buying a good-quality chipper is no small investment—expect to pay at least $500 and up to $1,300. A cheaper alternative is a very slow compost pile, more like a crude heap, which will rot the woody waste if left alone long enough. Another consideration is whether you generate enough prunings to justify buying a chipper versus occasionally renting one. Remember, chippers are no fun to use— they rattle and shake, make a racket and are about the most dangerous garden tool.

The three most important considerations when buying a shredder or chipper are the engine's power, the sturdiness of the housing, and the quality of the wheels.

Chippers come with either electric or gasoline engines. The latter are up to six times faster than the best electrical versions. However, electric models are quieter and vibrate less. If you opt for a gasoline-powered shredder, select a name-brand engine with the highest horsepower you can afford.

Make sure the housing is built with heavy-gauge metal, looks and feels sturdy, and is well constructed. For example, avoid self-tapping screws in favor of nuts and bolts with lock washers. If the model has one, make sure the discharge screen covering the chipping mechanism is easy to change. Be sure it is easy to change the oil on the gas-powered models.

When testing a chipper at your local dealer, check to see if any material is thrown back out of the hopper, how well protected your hands are from the cutting mechanisms, how easy it is to get the last of the branches through the hoppers, and how safe it is to use the tamper to push material through.

Other considerations: Will the machine chip the size and type of branches found in your yard? The typical chipper ad proclaims "Takes branches up to 3 inches thick!" But these ads seldom use the word "hardwood." And some studies found that the chipper could only handle the largest diameter mentioned in the literature if the branches were straight. Take samples of the wood you'll be chipping to the dealer and do a test run. Before buying, be sure to quiz others about their experiences. If possible, rent the machine you're thinking of buying and put it through its paces.

Chipper/shredders sell from $300 to as much as $1,300. Many quality models in the $500-to-$600 price range are available.

COMPOSTING MADE EASY

After you've considered the above gizmos to determine the least time-consuming ways to manage your yard waste, it's time to consider the easiest way to compost what's left. Again, choose the least complicated options for your yard and lifestyle.

Binless Composting

With all the composting boxes, bins, and cages on the market, you'd think the eleventh commandment was: "Thou shalt not compost without a store-bought gadget." Yet the easiest way to compost is with a standing pile. Just about any pile of organic matter will eventually rot if left to its own devices. But if you're just tossing stuff in a big "passive" compost heap, you'll need a large area for the heap's wide bottom. And, as with any kind of passive composting, what you get is not as rich as carefully layered and painstakingly turned hot compost, though it certainly will improve your soil's texture.

Bins from Pallets

Resourceful gardeners discovered long ago that wooden shipping pallets make cheap and effective compost bins. The gaps between the wooden slabs help aerate the compost. Pallets are reused many times for shipping. When they're too battered to be useful any longer,

WHAT NOT TO PUT IN YOUR COMPOST PILE

- Material thicker than 1/4 inch (shred or chop large pieces to speed decomposition)
- Disease or pest-laden materials
- Plant debris carrying pesticides or herbicides
- Meat, bones, grease, or other fatty substances (these are slow to decompose and attract vermin)
- Seeds and fruit pits (attractive to rodents)
- Cat or dog manure, bird droppings (handling fresh manure and droppings and subsequent use of compost many transmit harmful parasites to humans)

SOURCE: *Rodale's Illustrated Encyclopedia of Gardening and Landscaping Techniques*

they're often available for free—but always ask the shopkeeper first. Many gardeners simply lash each pallet to the next and leave the last one loosely attached to act as a door. Other gardeners install vertical posts in all four corners of the bin to support the pallets. A pallet can also be used on the bottom of a bin to help circulate air up through the bottom of the pile.

Compost Cylinders

Large cylinders made from ranch or snow fencing are easy ways to contain large passive compost piles. In fact, any type of flexible fencing, preferably with mesh or spaces to help aerate the pile, will do. Keep the height 4 feet or less to make it easy to toss the raw materials inside the cylinder. Put a wooden or metal fence post every 2 to 3 feet around the perimeter to support the wire. Leave one end of the fencing loosely tied to a post so this flap can be opened to remove the finished compost.

Cylinders, free-standing piles, and pallet bins should be covered with a tarp to prevent the pile from getting soaked when it rains.

Designer Composters

If your taste leans toward a more expensive or ready-made composter, you have plenty of choices. Each one, of course, is advertised as the best solution to everybody's composting needs. The following discussion will help sort out the hype.

The minimum volume for active composting is about 1 cubic yard (cy) (27 cubic feet [cf] or slightly more than 22 bushels)—depending on various factors. For example, active composting at the end of November in Michigan may necessitate 3, 4, or 5 cubic yards of material to insulate enough of the pile from the cold weather to promote thermophilic activity. Passive compost piles, which don't have to heat up, can be smaller.

Many of the models listed below have no provision for protection from rain. You'll need to use a tarp, a wooden or metal lid, or plastic sheeting to cover the composter for the best results.

Simple Wire Containers

Tidier than a free-form heap, quicker than building your own bin, and able to contain a fair amount of compost, simple wire bins are perfect for the beginning composter. They're portable, economical, widely available from mail order companies, and easy to assemble. You'll find many shapes for sale—square, hexagonal, round, and pentagonal. The sizes range from 155 to 23.7 cf.

All wire bins use galvanized metal mesh made from 7- to 14-gauge wire, and some have the added protection of PVC coating. But some wire bins bend or bow out too easily. Each product is made from a different type of wire mesh; some are fairly sturdy, others are rather flimsy. The smaller the gauge number on the wire, the greater its strength. Consider how easy it is to open up the bin, to unload finished compost, and to put the bin back together.

Individual wire bins cost from $30 to $50. Some models have extra panels from $19 to $32, which allow you to expand the capacity.

Wooden Bin Kits

Wooden compost bins come in two basic styles: with sides made of solid boards or of long, thin slats that are stacked horizontally like a log cabin. For an active compost pile, purchase only a model that allows you to take all the boards out from one side, starting from the top down.

Wooden bins have some serious limitations. First, they are vulnerable to gradual decay because the composting bacteria also eat away the wooden bin itself. Models made from rot-resistant woods such as redwood or cedar are the only ones that will last. You can further slow decay by painting the wood with linseed oil or one of the new low-toxicity preservatives on the market, such as the one made by AFM. Don't use pressure-treated lumber or toxic wood preservatives, which contain arsenic, creosote, or pentachlorophenol, which can leach into your compost and contaminate your garden.

3-compartment wood composter

Second, wood warps and twists easily, especially in the log-cabin-style bin with long narrow slats. Once these warp, it is very difficult to reinsert the metal rods in the corners.

Most wooden bin kits hold from 20 to 29 cf. Prices for a wooden-slat model range from a low of about $79 to nearly $125. Solid-sided bins cost between $100 and $200.

Plastic Compost Bins

Plastic would seem to be the ultimate faux pas in an environmental garden. But compost bins made from plastic have some important advantages over wooden ones. Plastic bins don't rot, last a long time, don't warp from moisture, and are lightweight and easy to move. Some are made from 50 to 100 percent post-consumer recycled plastic. Just make sure the plastic has an ultraviolet inhibitor to protect it from sunlight.

Most models have a sliding panel near the bottom for harvesting finished compost. Check this access panel to be sure there's enough slack for easy opening and closing. Several plastic composters come with three separate sections, which can be restacked in reverse order when turning the pile.

Some-mail order catalogs tout their plastic composters with "insulating walls." These are either 1/4-inch plastic walls, double walls, or corrugated walls. The advertising copy claims such panels "promote heat retention for faster composting—even in cold weather" while a little further down maintaining that the "the ventilation system ensures rapid decomposition." Get real, guys! You can't have both excellent heat retention and air circulation, especially in cold weather.

One new plastic bin on the market is made of a plastic mesh cylinder with a solid plastic interchangeable tops and bottoms, called dishes. Because the lips of the dishes fit snugly around the cylinder and the mesh has holes only three-eighths of an inch square, these bins are rat-resistant. They're also very easy to use. The parts can be leap-frogged when turning the pile. To turn the pile inside the mesh cylinder, you simply take the top dish off, set it nearby with the lip up, undo the carriage bolts on the front of the mesh cylinder, reassemble the mesh cylinder on what used to be the top side, fill the cylinder with the partially composted material, and cover the remaining dish—which used to be the bottom dish. These models are made from 100 percent recycled plastic, come in 12 or 21 cf versions, and cost from $50 to $130.

Rotating composter

Tumbling Composters

Rotating composters spin around their long axis, and compost tumblers rotate top-to-bottom from the midpoint of their long axis. Rotating or tumbling composters have the benefits, according to the catalogs, of "compost in just twenty-one days without the back strain of hand turning." But wet or moist compost is much heavier than it looks. To compensate for this weight, rotating bins often have a limited capacity (from 7 to 11 cf). Still, some people have difficulty rotating the drum. Tumbling composters usually require squatting to either turn or harvest the compost. Some large rotating models hold up to 22 cf and have a geared drive to make the turning easier, but some people still have trouble cranking them.

Some rotating drums have lots of holes for aeration. Such composters tend to dry out the compost too quickly. And they require more attention to the proper carbon-to-nitrogen ratio.

Make sure the model you're thinking about buying is convenient to fill and empty. Some drums don't empty directly into a wheelbarrow or garden cart. Others are high enough to dump into a wheelbarrow, but the hatch is too high off the ground for easy loading.

Turning or rotating compost drums cost from $100 to nearly $400.

WHAT TO DO WITH KITCHEN WASTES

Kitchen scraps make a rich compost, but they're about the most awkward compostables to deal with. They can attract insects and rodents. If improperly disposed of, they can also smell. Most kitchen scraps can be added to hot compost piles. If you've got a passive compost heap—or no compost pile at all—the simplest way to deal with kitchen wastes is to bury them in trenches or holes through the garden with a cover of at least eight inches of soil. But this doesn't help much in small yards or where winter temperatures freeze the ground solid.

Kitchen Waste Digester

These are among the newer inventions. They're usually cone-shaped with dark green or black sides to help eat up the scraps to promote dehydration, which decreases the bulk, and bacterial digestion. Some have a plastic basket that is buried in the ground just below the cone to help fend off raccoons, mice, and rats.

Kitchen waste digesters have a few limitations: If conditions are right, bacteria and earthworms digest the wastes; if not, you get a small, slimy pile of wastes that have been decomposed anaerobically. In either case, you bury what's left when the digester is full and must be moved. The digesters are not usually free of fruit flies as manufacturer's claim. Rats sometimes chew through the plastic basket to eat the waste. The digester shouldn't be used where a high water table would flood the soil beneath the cone. In a large household, the device can fill up within four or five months. And when you move the cone to bury the rotted material, the smell can be intense if the wastes have gone anaerobic.

Worm Bins

Red worms (*Lumbricus rubellus*) have practically insatiable appetites for kitchen scraps and produce nutrient-rich worm castings. And worms can be cultured in fairly small boxes inside the house, in the basement, root cellar, garage, or even kitchen year-round.

Over the years, worms have become my preferred method of converting kitchen scraps into valuable fertilizer. I know, I know—some people need years of therapy to get beyond their aversion to slimy, snake-like things. My advice is to learn to love or at least like worms. They're one of nature's grand cultivators and decomposers. They're quite tame creatures with fascinating habits. Best of all, they produce a concentrated, highly desirable fertilizer—not just soil amendment like a passive compost pile or the various compost-in-a-black-plastic-bag techniques recommended for city gardeners.

To start, you need a two-pound coffee can's worth of worms. (Most gardening magazines have classified sections with listings of mail-order worms.) Worm bins should be kept in a cool area where temperatures stay between 55° and 75° F. Properly managed worm bins are odor-free.

By ROBERT KOURIK, author of *Designing and Maintaining Your Edible Landscape.*

CHAPTER TWELVE

An Environmental Gardener's Guide to Pest Management

Since the first seeds were gathered and deliberately planted, pests have been the bane of gardeners. Over time, we have created many of our own pest problems. By concentrating crops at one site, we've made food more accessible for pests. As a result, they reproduce more quickly. Whenever we till the soil, we create a hospitable environment for weed seeds to germinate and grow. We've imported pests from around the globe—without the natural enemies that keep them in check. More commonly, we've made pest problems worse by using pesticides indiscriminately. In fact, in the United States, on a per-acre basis, more pesticide is applied to home gardens than to farms.

We know that pesticides can cause environmental problems. What isn't so obvious is that they also cause horticultural problems. Killing the natural enemies of a pest may lead to later, more severe outbreaks of the same pest. Pesticides can also kill the natural enemies of other organisms, causing outbreaks of still more pests. Repeated pesticide use often makes the pests become resistant to the pesticides, so that ever higher doses are required. Problems—largely from pesticide use— have led to a new concept of managing pests, called "integrated pest management" or IPM.

ECOLOGICAL PEST MANAGEMENT

Integrated pest management is an ecologically based approach to pest control. Fields, gardens, or lawns aren't automatically treated with weekly or routine sprays "just in case." Even the discovery of a pest doesn't automatically trigger a control action; instead, the plants are checked regularly to make sure the pests aren't present in numbers large enough to do significant damage. IPM is a decision-making process. Using an IPM approach, you decide what causes the problem, if you need to do something, what you need to do, and when to do it.

Properly practiced, IPM includes a combination of sensible pest controls and preventive measures that minimize adverse effects to the environment while protecting the plant. IPM is an opportunity to practice backyard ecology, to understand the interaction of all living organisms in a garden environment—not just the plants.

If you find holes chewed in your tree's leaves. The villain is probably either a beetle and their larvae (grub), webworms, bagworms, or larvae of moths and sawflies (caterpillars).

HOW TO START

To start your IPM program, you need a plan. What is your objective: to have a healthy, safe, bountiful garden? To produce perfect, undamaged plants for flower shows? To nurture a variety of plant and animal species for your enjoyment? To minimize your use of pesticides? To use no pesticides at all? Your objectives will help determine which mix of management techniques is best for you. Often you'll have several conflicting objectives, and you'll need to compromise. Once you've set your priorities, there are a few basic procedures to follow:

Learn about the pests and problems associated with each crop or planting in your area. Don't wait until pests appear, as many problems can be avoided simply with proper plant selection and garden design. Different pests require different methods of control, depending on their life cycle, habits, and physiology.

Monitor your plants or crop at regular intervals to see how many pests are present and what kind of damage is being done.

Establish a threshold for damage. In agricultural IPM programs, farmers use precisely defined "economic thresholds" to determine when to treat pest populations. These are based on the value of the crop, the damage caused, and the cost of treatment. Gardeners can use a similar process for determining when and what treatment is required. Is the damage tolerable? Is it serious enough to warrant action? The action itself will depend on the degree of damage or potential damage. A few Japanese beetles may warrant hand picking, while greater numbers might justify treating the beetle grubs in the lawn while they are small and vulnerable.

Combine management strategies that complement one another. For instance, resistant plants, proper site selection, biological controls,

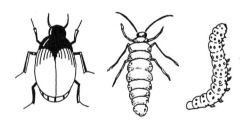

Beetle, wingless moth, caterpillar

SOURCE: **International Society of Arboriculture**

and physical barriers all reduce pest damage, but when combined or integrated, provide even greater protection. Keep in mind that a garden is a refuge for many living organisms. Most of them aren't pests, but rather useful inhabitants that enhance the garden by decomposing dead plants, pollinating, preying on pests, or providing food or shelter for other useful organisms. Select management practices least harmful to all of the organisms in your garden.

Keep notes on what you see—the level of damage, the action you take, what works and what doesn't. They will prove immensely helpful in the future.

Boring insects make tunnels in the wood of a tree as they eat through it. Trees infested with borers typically show a thinness of crown and a gradual or sudden decline in vigor. Conclusive symptoms are circular holes in the trunk or branches with frass and sometimes dripping sap, which forms a dark stain along the bark.

Borers can be eliminated by impaling them on a piece of wire. If they can't all be reached, then pour liquid into their tunnels to drown them.

SOURCE: **International Society of Arboriculture.**

CHOOSING STRATEGIES THAT WORK

The tools of IPM include cultural practices, biological controls, physical controls, traps, and chemical controls. The best courses of action will vary according to local conditions and your own objectives.

Cultural Practices

Cultural practices are growing techniques that make the garden less favorable to pests, thereby reducing the need for more expensive and disruptive controls. Practices will vary with the type of garden or planting. Some cultural controls are:

Pest-resistant species and cultivars. Look for plants without pest problems and cultivars bred specifically for pest resistance. For example, shade gardeners in the Northeast can reduce insect problems by planting witch hazel, bayberry, and other insect-resistant shrubs. (For more plants and details see "Insect-Resistant Shrubs" by R. J. Gouger in *Gardening in the Shade*, Brooklyn Botanic Garden Record, Handbook # 61.) Apple growers can significantly reduce fungicide use by selecting disease-resistant cultivars.

Light and air circulation. Choosing a site with good air circulation can reduce the need for fungicide on susceptible plants. Pruning and wide plant spacing promote air penetration and movement, further reducing disease problems. Trees around gardens or lawns can be thinned or pruned to allow more light to penetrate. On the other hand, dense plantings keep the weed population down. Apparent conflicts of this type are common in IPM, but they can be resolved by weighing the potential benefits and consequences of both actions.

Sanitation. Removing dead or infected plant parts from the garden reduces the spread of potential diseases and other pests.

Cultivation. In most garden situations, herbicides are not necessary; weeds can be controlled simply by hand cultivation. The secret is timing—one well-timed cultivation won't take any more time than spraying an herbicide but can save hours of struggle with overgrown weeds. Usually, the best time to cultivate is when weeds are small and succulent, before seeds have set. Spend some time choosing a comfortable, easy-to-use cultivator.

Biological Controls

When you introduce a pest's natural enemies into your garden or try to get them to come naturally by creating a hospitable environment, you're using a biological control. Natural enemies can be predators, parasites, or diseases. You can increase populations of natural enemies by providing them with shelter and additional food sources—nectar-producing plants, dill, coriander, caraway, and other plants in the parsley family, for example. Minimizing pesticide use also helps.

Some natural enemies, such a nematodes, ladybird beetles, and Trichogramma parasitic wasps, are available for purchase. It's important to select the right natural enemy for the specific pest and to release it under the right conditions. For example, nematodes require moist organic soils. If you purchase ladybird beetles that have just come out of hibernation, they may require a flight period before settling down to feed; and when they do settle down, it may be in someone else's yard.

Some natural enemies are general feeders, while others are more specific. Ladybird beetles feed on many soft-bodied insects, while Trichogramma wasps generally attack the eggs of moths and butterflies. Preying mantids are such general feeders that they will attack almost any insect—including pollinators and natural enemies.

The use of diseases to control insect pests is becoming increasingly effective. The bacterium *Bacillus thuringiensis*, or *B.t.*, is marketed under several trade names, including Dipel and Biobit. *B.t.* attacks specific insect groups, depending on the variety selected. *B.t.* products are available for control of caterpillars, Colorado potato beetle, elm leaf beetle, fungus gnats, and biting flies. Be sure to purchase the right strain for the pest you're trying to control. Because *B.t.* is so specific in its action it is very safe for humans and does not interfere with other management practices.

Physical Controls and Traps. Physical controls include hand picking, mulches, barriers, and even vacuum systems that suck up pests.

Mulches. In addition to conserving water, mulches are an excellent nontoxic weed control. In the home garden, plastic or fabric mulches eventually lead to disposal problems. Organic mulches that break down in the soil, contribute to the buildup of humus, and provide shelter for predators (especially spiders) are probably a better choice. Because mulches may also provide a moist habitat for slugs, clean cultivation may be the best option where slugs are a problem.

Row cover. Another multipurpose horticultural tool, spun-bonded polypropylene fabric row covers are used primarily as frost protection, growth enhancers, and season extenders. Used during pest activity periods, they can also prevent pests from infesting small fruit and vegetable crops.

Traps. You can use traps to monitor pests or to reduce pest populations. They work by using visual, odor, and sexual cues to attract insect pests.

Visual traps mimic the light waves of a host plant, but the color is more intense than that of the real thing. Thus, a yellow trap, a mimic of green foliage, is more attractive to the insect than the foliage itself. A common visual trap in the Northeast is the red sphere, which attracts apple maggot flies by mimicking a red apple. During the period when the maggot flies are in flight, the trap is larger and redder than the apples and therefore more attractive. Home gardeners can eliminate sprays against apple maggot flies by placing five red spheres in each apple tree. Other visual traps include white and blue cards, which attract different pests in different situations (for example, tarnished plant bugs are attracted to white cards, greenhouse thrips to blue cards).

Another common trap in the Northeast is the Japanese beetle trap, which is baited with sexual and floral attractants to lure beetles away from flowers and other plantings. Because these traps attract more beetles into an area, make sure you place them far enough away and downwind from plantings to avoid making the beetle infestation even worse. Generally these traps are useless in neighborhoods with large resident beetle populations. In a country setting, where the beetle population is less widespread, traps placed well away from the crop to be protected may be of some value.

You can buy traps for slugs or make them yourself using shallow pans or jar lids sunk to ground level and baited with beer. A "roof" made from a cottage cheese container can reduce evaporation and keep rain from diluting the beer.

Chemical Controls

For some pests, there is no adequate cultural, physical, or biological control; pesticides are the remaining option.

Pesticides should be selected and applied in a way that causes the least environmental disruption and the least impact on beneficial and other nontarget species. Again, combining other management techniques with the use of a pesticide will be more effective than relying on the chemical alone.

Be careful when you use any kind of pesticide. Even "organic" or naturally occurring pesticides are toxic. Insecticidal and herbicidal soaps are relatively nontoxic to humans, but they can affect a wide range of species, including beneficial insects. Whenever possible, they should be applied directly to the pest, as a spot treatment. When using soaps, look for phytotoxic reactions. Tissues of some plants react adversely to soaps, causing spotting, browning, or even plant death.

A pesticide is more effective if the application is timed to treat the most sensitive stage of the pest. Knowledge of the pest and its life cycle is therefore important. For example, nontoxic horticultural oils can smother mite eggs, while more toxic pesticides are ineffective against eggs. These oils are highly refined and under conditions of moderate temperature and low humidity can be applied to most ornamental and some vegetable crops, even in summer.

Pesticides are usually formulated specifically for specific pests on specific plants. Before using a pesticide, READ THE LABEL and make sure that it's the right pesticide for the situation.

By CRAIG HOLLINGSWORTH, extension specialist with the Massachusetts Integrated Pest Management Program, and KAREN IDOINE, a horticultural agent with Massachusetts Cooperative Extension who writes a gardening column in the *Boston Globe*.

Putting It All Together

CHAPTER THIRTEEN

Designing and Planning

"Don't include a plant unless it serves at least two or more functions."

— BILL MOLLISON,
Permaculture Pioneer

In previous chapters we have presented ideal layouts for energy-efficient landscapes and guidelines for environmentally friendly ones, but that still leaves a lot of decisions to be made: What style should your landscape be? What plants should you use? Where should the compost pile go? How about the deck? Obviously these are questions only you can answer; this chapter gives guidelines to help you answer them and then translate it all into a detailed plan.

DETERMINING WHAT YOU WANT FROM YOUR PROPERTY

Before making any changes to your property, you have to decide what you want. Forget about constraints for the moment. Take out a pencil and piece of paper and jot down all the things you'd like from your property—in addition to energy efficiency and a good environment. Some examples are: a vegetable garden, a deck, a patio, swings and a sandbox, rock walls, a pond, a tool shed, a source of firewood. The possibilities are just about endless.

After you've let yourself dream without constraints, review your list with a dose of realism. Do you really want a vegetable garden, when you hate weeding and are usually short on time? Swimming laps in your backyard sounds great, but can you afford a pool? Don't be too quick to eliminate elements of your ideal scenario, because they may be possible over time, in which case you may want to leave open space for them. But do take into consideration things like who is going to be taking care of the yard and what their gardening limits are. Will your dog dig up your flower beds? Do you need more space for cars? Can heavy machinery get in to fix your septic tank? Taking the realistic into consideration doesn't mean abandoning your dreams; it will actually help you plan more accurately for them and avoid wasting energy on projects that aren't so important. After weighing the practical, prioritize the items you have left.

You'll also want to prioritize environmental goals. There could be a conflict between letting the sun in and leaving a good tree for nesting birds. Or maybe an exotic vine is the perfect solution for shading your air conditioner, but you want to use only natives. As we've all learned by now, few things work out perfectly neatly. It's likely there will be choices and tradeoffs to be made. Fortunately, most environmental landscaping considerations work well together. For example, a small lawn with a regionally appropriate variety of grass is water-efficient, good for wildlife, easier to care for organically, and a better host to different plant species. Still, if you face choices, prioritizing will help you resolve conflicts and put your resources into what matters most for you.

Having a clear idea of what you want also makes it easier to think creatively when you run into your property's limitations.

ASSESSING YOUR PROPERTY

Start with a Map

In *Edible Landscaping*, Rosalind Creasy gives several good reasons to create a map of your property. "First, it helps you see the whole picture in one place at one time. Second, it helps avoid costly and frustrating mistakes during the installation phase. Third, it allows you to communicate your ideas and desires to others in a clear and concise manner. And finally, it greatly facilitates completion if the project must be done piece by piece over a period of time." In a word, it gives clarity.

A property survey or deed map is a good starting point because it gives an accurate representation of the property's size, shape, exact boundaries, setback lines, and rights of way. If you don't have a map, check with the previous owner, the builder, architect, or the local FHA, VA, or mortgage office. The town or county building department may also have it on file.

If you can't locate a map, don't worry. Either hire a surveyor (this is especially important if your neighbor is claiming that's his apple tree) or follow the directions below to measure it yourself. Most people can do it themselves in an hour or two.

Taking Measurements

You'll need a notebook, the longest tape measure you can get (a 100 footer is best), and a pencil. It's easiest to have another person to hold one end of the tape, but you can do it yourself by using a big nail, screwdriver, stick, or rock to hold the tape in place.

If your yard is large and you don't have a 100-foot tape measure, you will need to pace off measurements. Mark off 100 feet and count how many steps it takes you to walk. Divide that into 100, and you have your distance per pace.

Start by making a rough drawing of your house and property. Exact measurements will let you make the drawing to scale later. First, measure the property lines. Then place the house in relation to them by measuring the perpendicular distance from each corner of the house to the nearest property line. Next, measure the location of any notable features of your yard in relation to the house.

Using a carpenter's square and heavy string will help ensure the accuracy of your measurements.

If you want to measure the grade of a slope, mark a board in feet and butt it against a stake. Make sure the board is level, and then measure from the bottom of the board to the ground. If the board is 6 feet and the vertical drop 3 feet, then the grade is roughly 1:2.

The map should also include the features of your house that will interact with the outside. For example, it doesn't make sense to have your large living room window look out over your compost bin or to grow a shrub that's eventually going to block the entrance to the basement. Record the locations of windows, doors, decks, patios, garages, driveways, gutters, septic system, utility lines, wells, water lines, et cetera.

TURNING YOUR MEASUREMENTS INTO A MAP

If you have a T square, drawing board, and architect's vellum paper, great, but a pencil, ruler, and some graph paper will do. Use the

Measuring the grade of a slope.

largest scale the paper will allow. Most half-acre lots will fit on an 18-to-24-inch piece of graph paper if your scale is 1 inch equals 20 feet. For large yards you will need to reduce the scale and make a bigger sheet by taping some graph paper together.

Start by indicating north in one of the margins and drawing accurate property lines. Fill in the lines of the house and other structures. Mark off trees and other prominent features you measured on your rough sketch. If you want to be professional about it (or have a professional be able to read it), use the standard symbols that landscape architects and designers use.

Once you have an accurate drawing of your house and property, make some photocopies of it. That will let you to mark it up without ruining the original. Eventually you will want to make a new map that shows your future plans.

Filling in the Details

After your property is drawn on paper, you can start putting notes on it. The ideal way to take an inventory of your property is to observe it over the course of a year. Sun, wind, and foliage change with the seasons and should influence your plans. A perfect view of sunset in winter may be blocked in the summer. Be sure to note those features of your property that you like. It's easier and less expensive to keep something you like than to create something new.

Many of the observations you'll need to make to assess your property have been mentioned in earlier chapters. Try and note the following on your map:

Sun

• Sunny and shady spots.
• The path of the sun (where it shines on the house and/or yard at different times of the day and year).
• Prevailing shadows.

Keeping a wind chart for a few weeks will give you an accurate record of the wind's prevailing direction.

NORMAL WINDS	day	speed	weather	night	speed	weather	comments
Date 6-21	→	+	sunny	↖	+++	rain	thunder
22	→	+	sunny	↗	++	clear	
23	→	+	sunny	↘	+	cloudy	
24	↓	++	rain	↓	+	rain	
25	↖	+	cloudy	↗	++	clear	
26	→	+	sunny	↗	++	clear	
Prevailing	→	+		↗	++		

KEY   Arrows indicate the direction of the wind as related to north
        + light wind speed
        ++ moderate wind speed
        +++ strong wind
        ++++ violent wind speed

Wind

• There are several ways to determine your prevailing winds. You can note the lean of trees in your microclimate and observe the direction rain falls and snow blows—both as it comes down and by the patterns the snow makes after a few days. You can also create wind indicators by tying strips of cloth or even plastic bags to sticks 5 or 6 feet tall. Anchor the sticks on the north, south, east, and west sides of the house, and any other spot that seems particularly windy. For several weeks—preferably in all seasons, but especially during winter in the North and summer in the South—record what the wind indicators are doing. (See chart on page 152.)

• Where snow drifts in the winter and leaves collect in the fall.

Water

• Runoff patterns.

• The average amount of rainfall you receive.

Soil quality

• Testing the soil in different spots on your property is helpful.

• Damp or dry locations.

• Slopes

Plants

• Which of your existing plants are thriving or struggling.

• Where lawn grows well or poorly.

Usage

• Walkways and shortcut paths.

• The best and worst views.

• Areas where you need more privacy.

After indicating your property's microclimate and features on your map, your next major consideration is aesthetics.

PRINCIPLES OF LANDSCAPE DESIGN

Think of your yard as a whole. Everything should go together in harmony. You don't need to be professionally trained to do this, but it can help to know some basic principles of landscape design.

Start by taking special note of those properties you really like. See what they are doing right. If you're not shy, talk to the owners. Most people are happy to talk about their property—especially to an admirer. One thing you're likely to find at the properties you like is that the landscaping style is consistent with the style of the house. For example, a cottage-style garden works well with a small, quaint house. It's also likely that the same landscaping style is used throughout the whole property. A classic beginner's mistake is to create a hodgepodge of styles—rustic here, classical there, oriental in the corner. That rarely works well.

Wood Fence

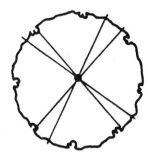
Deciduous Tree or Shrub

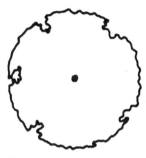
Evergreen Tree or Shrub

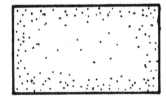
Lawn

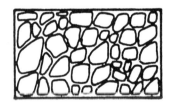
Stone

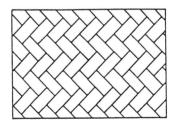
Unit Pavers

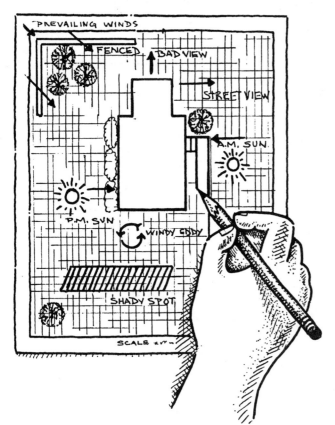

After making a detailed property map that includes the property's microclimate, it will become clear how to design for energy efficiency.

Good landscaping takes color into account. Be aware of when flowers bloom and whether they complement one another. If your house is a color other than white or gray, you'll need to take its paint shade into consideration.

Balance

Consciously or unconsciously, our brains seeks balance. You don't want to create a landscape that is so evenly balanced that it's uniform and boring. But if you have a large tree on the left of the house, something of reasonably large mass should be on the right—although it need not necessarily be a tree. You can check your house for balance by drawing a line through the center of your house (from front to back) and see if the two parts are evenly weighed.

Proportion

In *Landscape It Yourself*, Jamie Gibb points out that "You would never dominate a low ranch-type house with a towering tree, nor set 3- or 4-foot shrubs as the only ornaments for a three-story Victorian." Proportion, at its most simplistic level, requires that you pay attention to the relative sizes of the existing features of the landscape and plan from there." A common mistake novice landscapers make is not planning for future growth. Unless you're planting a dwarf variety, the trees and shrubs you plant today will be a lot bigger in a few years. Don't forget to plan for that growth.

Texture

Just as the shapes and colors of plants influence a landscape's look, so does texture. Texture refers to the size, form, density, and expressive characteristics of leaves. The delicate, lacy texture of baby's breath (*gypsophila*) creates a feeling of softness. Compare that with the gnarled trunk of an oak. If you're trying to create a soothing landscape, use plants with soft textures. If you want drama, accent, or effects that are noticeable from a distance, use coarse-textured, large-foliage plants. As a general rule, plants in a particular grouping should have a similar texture.

YOUR MAKEOVER PLAN

The Major Changes

After you've made a detailed property map that includes your property's microclimate, it will become clear how to design for energy efficiency. When you know where the prevailing winds are coming from, you know where to create a wind block or funnel. Your decisions about tempering or increasing sunlight will also become obvious. Refer back to chapter 2 and the chapter for your region for specific guidelines on how far plants need to be from your home and which ones work best. The plants and landscaping needed to make your property energy-efficient will be a major influence on what your yard will look like. But you'll still have plenty of details to add as you balance environmental concerns, your needs, and aesthetics.

Using Bubbles

The best way to initiate changes to your existing landscape map is by marking it with bubbles or circles. Think in terms of problems and solutions. Without indicating details, mark areas of the property with the desired effect and circle it. The specifics will come later. For example, you probably know where you want a boundary, but may not know whether you want a stone wall, a fence, or shrubs. Mark that section "boundary" and circle it. Later you'll decide what variety of shrub you'll use or what type of fence.

Three-Dimensional Thinking

Once you make some changes or proposed changes on paper and have consulted with any other interested parties (such as your family), walk around your property. Try to envision what your side yard will look like with a trellis and vines. You can use props like a sheet of plastic for a fence or a hose for an edge of a patio. If you want to do some realistic visualizing, take pictures of your house and property from different angles and enlarge them. Put some tracing paper over the photos and draw in your proposed changes. This will give you an excellent idea of what to expect.

Using tracing paper, superimpose a drawing of your proposed changes on a photo of your home and property. This will help you visualize your future plans.

THE FINAL PLAN

After you feel comfortable with the changes you've indicated, you'll want to draw another scale map. This time it will be of your future property. You can still be vague about structure materials and plant varieties, but it will be helpful if you know the size you want your windbreak or lawn area to be. To get more specific about plant varieties, look at the suggestions listed in earlier chapters for your region and talk to a nursery center or landscape professional.

Knowing the style you want for your property and what you want the plant to do will narrow the possibilities.

Of course, even if you call a plan your final one, you can always change it. The great thing about having a map is that you know where you're going. Even if it takes years to get there, all your work and expense will be taking you in the right direction.

DOING THE WORK

Where to Start

Do destruction work first. Then do anything that requires heavy machinery. A small mistake by a backhoe can ruin years of gardening work. Or, if you can't afford to do the big stuff yet, don't do any delicate work in that area, and leave room for trucks.

Next, plant or transplant trees. Trees need time to grow. You may want to plant fast-growing varieties near the ones you really want and remove them as your choice plants mature. This strategy can help avoid the empty look and helps get a windbreak up quickly.

Costs

Landscaping can cost $100 or $100,000 depending on what you have done and how much of it you do yourself. According to real estate appraisers, it's reasonable to spend between 10 to 15 percent of your home's value on landscaping (that does not take into account big items such as tennis courts or swimming pools). Construction materials and labor are much more expensive than plants. If you do the work yourself, you'll save a lot. You'll also save by keeping structures simple and using recycled or discarded materials—such as old telephone poles, bricks, lumber, or tires to build retaining walls (the tires can be filled with compacted soil and then covered up by soil and plantings).

CHOOSING PROFESSIONAL LANDSCAPE HELP

It's quite likely that at some point you'll need help carrying out your landscape plans. Even if you're a dedicated do-it-yourselfer, you may want to consult with a landscape designer. She or he can help you anticipate problems, solve difficult ones such as drainage, and give you confidence that you're moving in the right direction. You can even do all the work yourself but consult with a trained eye at various stages.

There are three basic types of landscape professionals: architects, designers, and contractors. Landscape architects, like building architects, are planning experts. Typically, they do mostly commercial work. Landscape designers usually do the same work as landscape architects but have less formal training and are generally more plant-oriented. Sometimes landscape designers are employed by nurseries and their fees will be absorbed if you buy enough of the nursery's plants. Landscape contractors do the actual work. They often provide design advice too. There can be much crossover among these various professionals (for example, landscape architects sometimes work on homes, and designers often do physical labor as well as planning), but these generalizations will help you know whom to try first for the help you need.

To find a good landscape designer, ask for recommendations from people whose landscapes you admire. Or call landscapers who advertise and ask for the addresses of properties they've done. Once you find at least three landscapers whose work you like, call them and have them bid on your job.

Hiring a professional doesn't mean you should forget about creating a plan—or at least a rough sketch—of your property and asking yourself a lot of questions. The exercise will clarify what you want.

For those who want to go it on their own but have scant landscaping experience, the next chapter, "Landscaping 101," presents some how-to landscaping basics.

CHAPTER FOURTEEN

Landscaping Skills 101

PLANTING A NEW TREE

Selecting a Location

Ideally, every tree should be planted in accord with some overall landscape plan that takes into consideration the effect you want to achieve, the size of the plants, and the way they are to be pruned and maintained. As a general rule, trees and shrubs should be placed so that they may develop freely without crowding one another, the house, utility lines, or other structures.

Before selecting an exact spot for a tree or shrub, determine its mature size by consulting nursery personnel, catalogs, garden books, or extension publications (the plant suggestions at the end of chapters categorize plants by approximate size—i.e., small, medium, large). Be sure to get the correct information for the specific variety of your tree. Many shrubs and round-headed trees grow about as wide as they grow tall, so if figures for width are unavailable, estimate from the ultimate height. For example, a tree that grows between 10 and 15 feet tall will commonly spread its branches about the same distance and should be planted about 7 to 8 feet (or about half its height) away from houses or other structures. Not all plants meet this standard, however, so make every effort to obtain width requirements from established sources.

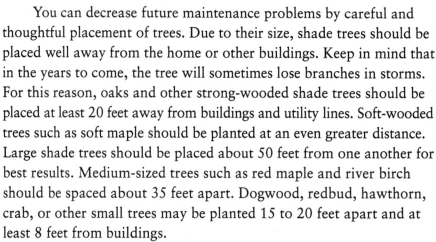

You can decrease future maintenance problems by careful and thoughtful placement of trees. Due to their size, shade trees should be placed well away from the home or other buildings. Keep in mind that in the years to come, the tree will sometimes lose branches in storms. For this reason, oaks and other strong-wooded shade trees should be placed at least 20 feet away from buildings and utility lines. Soft-wooded trees such as soft maple should be planted at an even greater distance. Large shade trees should be placed about 50 feet from one another for best results. Medium-sized trees such as red maple and river birch should be spaced about 35 feet apart. Dogwood, redbud, hawthorn, crab, or other small trees may be planted 15 to 20 feet apart and at least 8 feet from buildings.

Spacing is also a consideration for shrubs and hedges. Shrubs should be spaced about one-half of their ultimate spread from buildings. Two different varieties of shrubs should be placed at a distance approximately one-half the total spread for both plants (for example, an 8-foot shrub and a 6-foot shrub should be spaced about 7 feet apart). Hedges may be spaced closer together to form a full, dense screen. Low hedge plants (3 to 4 feet high) should be spaced approximately 18 inches apart, while tall hedge plants will need to be 3 to 4 feet apart. For advice in determining the "right tree" for the "right place," consult your garden center's staff or tree-care professional.

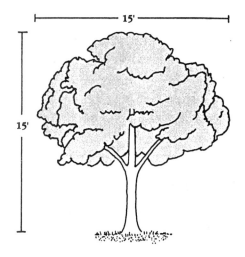

Planting the Tree

The ideal time to plant trees and shrubs is during the dormant season—fall after leafdrop or early spring before budbreak. This period of cool weather allows plants to establish roots in their new location before spring rains and summer heat stimulate new growth. However, as long as the tree has been properly cared for in the nursery or garden center, it is acceptable to plant throughout the growing season. Proper planting is essential to ensure a healthy future for new trees and shrubs.

Take time to carefully follow eight simple steps. These guidelines apply for balled and burlapped plants, specimens in plantable baskets, and plants recently removed from other containers.

Note: Always pick up the tree by the container or root ball, not by the trunk.

1 *Dig a large planting hole.* Be sure you have had all underground utilities located prior to digging. The planting hole should be dug as deep as the root ball and twice as wide. A large hole is important because as the tree begins to take hold in the ground, its roots must push through the surrounding soil. Roots will have a difficult time if the soil is rocky or compact; however, if the soil has been loosened by digging and backfilling, the roots will have room to establish well.

2 *Prune sparingly.* Examine the tree closely for injury to roots or branches. If any roots are crushed, cut them at a point just in front of the break. On the top, prune only broken branches, making sure to leave the branch collar (the swollen area where one branch meets another) intact. Begin corrective pruning after a full season of growth in the new location.

3 *Prepare the hole and soil.* While some newly transplanted trees may benefit from an application of plant food, it is best not to use fertilizer until the plant is well established. Good, rich native soil placed in the hole is usually adequate. Never apply high-nitrogen fertilizer at planting time: It may burn tender roots.

4 *Place the tree at the proper height.* To avoid damage, when setting the tree in the hole, always lift the tree by the root ball, never by the trunk. Add a sufficient amount of soil to the planting hole to bring the tree to its original growing level. This level is indicated by a dark stain on the trunk, which marks the difference between root and trunk bark. Keep in mind that on balled and burlapped trees, the point at which the burlap is tied can be much higher than the original soil line. Planting at the proper height is important because if a tree is set too deep, its roots may suffocate; on the other hand, if the tree is set too shallow, the roots may dry out in the air and sun.

5 *Fill the hole, gently but firmly.* If the tree is balled and burlapped, cut the string and remove all accessible burlap. For trees in plantable baskets, perforate the sides of the basket in four or five places and break off the top rim. Be careful not to make these punctures too big; they should allow roots to penetrate into the soil but not cause the basket to fall apart.

Fill the hole by gently firming the earth around the tree to hold it in place and to eliminate air pockets. These air pockets may cause some roots to lose contact with the soil and dry out. To avoid this problem, settle the soil with water and add soil to the hole until the tree is firmly established. Do not use your feet to tamp around the tree base: This compacts the soil and may inhibit the spread of roots. Rake a ridge of soil 2 to 4 inches high around the margin of the hole (outside the root area) to serve as a reservoir when watering.

6 *Stake the tree, if necessary.* Staking a tree can cause bark damage and cause a tree to grow too quickly for its roots, so it should be avoided where possible. However, if a tree is too tall to stand alone or has a weak root system (such as a dwarf fruit tree), it should be staked to avoid shifting during heavy rains or high winds, which can easily damage tender roots. Staking must be done very carefully with a broad, soft strapping material such as woven belt fabric or padded wire.

Drive two or three stakes into the ground just outside the perimeter of the planting hole, spacing them an equal distance apart. For each stake, attach one end of the strapping material to the tree at the lowest

STAKING AND WINDBREAK TREES
It is especially important that trees grown for permanent windbreaks develop powerful root strength naturally. Try to avoid staking them. Instead, check new plantings every few weeks. Readjust them as necessary to be sure they are straight. Mounding some extra soil or sand around the perimeter will help hold the tree in place. If the wind is so powerful that the tree(s) just won't hold without staking or if you're not up to regular monitoring, stake it loosely so the tree has some give and can develop flexible strength.

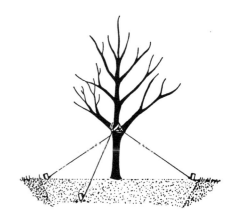

practical level to maintain it upright and fasten the other end to the stake. Remove the stakes as soon as the tree has firmly rooted itself in the soil. As a rule, the stakes should not be left in place for more than a year.

7 *Mulch the base of the tree.* Mulch by applying organic matter to the area at the base of the tree. Some good mulch materials are leaf litter, pine straw, shredded bark and twigs, peat moss, and wood chips. A 2- to 4-inch layer conserves soil moisture and protects newly planted tree roots from hot and cold temperatures. Mulch also keeps down grassy weeds that may compete with a newly planted tree for water and nutrition until the tree takes a firm hold.

8 *Water Regularly.* Since many roots were removed when the tree was dug in the nursery, regular watering is important to aid the development of a strong new root system in the new site. Keep the soil moist but not soaked, as overwatering will cause leaves to turn yellow or fall off. Water trees at least once a week, barring rain, and more frequently during hot weather. When the soil is dry 4 inches below the surface, it is time to water. Continue until midautumn, and then taper off, as this is the time for the tree to stop growing and harden for winter.

After you've completed these eight simple steps, routine care and favorable weather conditions will ensure that your new tree or shrub will grow and thrive. When questions arise, be sure to consult your tree-care or garden-center professional.

TRANSPLANTING ESTABLISHED TREES

Unless you are transplanting a very small tree or shrub, successful transplanting takes some skill and energy. Before you move a tree, be sure it's what you really want.

Preparation

First, check to see if the tree you're interested in is movable. The best candidates for transplanting will be growing by themselves in moist, well-drained soil. Trees in rocky, shallow soil or with roots that are intertwined with other tree roots make transplanting nearly impossible. Consider the size of the tree: A big tree is unlikely to take and would be extraordinarily heavy to move. The root ball for a tree with only a 1-inch trunk can weigh as much as 160 pounds. Three-to five-foot trees are easy to work with.

Early spring and fall are the best times for transplanting a tree because it's dormant. Do not dig up trees in the summer because disturbing the roots causes new growth to wilt and die.

You'll need a square-tipped nursery spade, lopping shears, burlap (or its equivalent), a wheelbarrow, and firm-soled shoes or boots. For larger trees, you'll need some rope or twine.

Root-Pruning

If the plant is large, you should prune its roots six months to a year before moving it. Root-pruning lessens the shock of transplanting by stimulating the growth of many smaller roots. Do it by cutting a circle around the base of the tree. This severs the longer roots and establishes the perimeter of the eventual root ball.

Dig your trench 6 to 8 inches wide. The trench's perimeter is determined by the plant's diameter measured a few feet above the ground. Site the trench approximately 1 foot from the center of the plant for each inch of tree diameter (i.e., a 2-inch-wide tree would need to have its trench be 24 inches from the center).

As you prune, keep your spade perpendicular. Try to cut the roots without tearing them. Use the lopping shears on the thick roots. Try not to shake the tree, so you don't loosen soil from the roots.

Backfill the trench with organic-rich soil. At the same time, remove about one-third of the top-growth. This will encourage the plant to form a more compact root system that will be better suited to transplanting. Do not fertilize during the growing season prior to transplanting.

Site your trench 1 foot from the center of the plant for each inch of tree diameter.

Moving the Tree

Whether or not you root-prune, transplant while the tree or shrub is dormant. If you have root-pruned, recut the root ball with the spade or shovel to reestablish the original pruning and sever roots missed the first time.

To separate the plant from its home, you'll need to thrust your shovel's blade between the ball and soil with sharp jabs. Keep doing this until the roots are severed all around. You may have to use the shears to separate the last, tenacious roots from the soil.

Before you remove the tree from its original home, the new hole should be dug and preparations made for moving what will most likely be a very heavy load. Depending upon the size of the tree and the distance of the move, you may want to wrap the root ball in burlap. To ball the tree, center it on a burlap square. Pull diagonal corners over the root ball, and tie them tightly.

The root ball should be keep moist. Try to put it into its new spot

TREES THAT TOLERATE ENVIRONMENTAL STRESS

D=Dry; A=Alkaline; W=Wet/Poorly Drained; S=Salt

Acer campestre (Hedge maple)-S

Acer platanoides (Norway maple)-S

Acer pseudoplatanus (Plane tree)-S

Alnus glutinosa (European alder)-W

Betula nigra (River birch)-W

Caragana arborescens (Siberian peashrub)-S

Celtis occidentalis (Common hackberry)-D

Corylus colurna (Turkish hazel)-D

Crataegus species (Hawthorn)-D

Eucommia ulmoides (Hardy rubber tree)-D

Fraxinus pennsylvanica (Green ash)-W

Ginkgo biloba (Ginkgo)-D

Koelreuteria paniculata (Goldenrain tree)-D

Nyssa sylvatica (Tupelo)-W

Platanus x acerifolia (London plane)-W

Quercus muhlenbergii (Chinkapin oak)-D

Quercus rubra (Red oak)-S

Robinia pseudoacacia (Black locust)-S

Sophora japonica (Japanese pagodatree)-D,S

Syringa reticulata (Japanese tree lilac)-D

Taxodium distichum (Bald cypress)-W

Ulmus parvifolia (lacebark elm)-D

SOURCE: *Trees: A Gardener's Guide*

as soon as possible. If the roots dry out, the tree's survival chances drop drastically.

Planting in Its New Home

Once you get the shrub or tree in its new hole, follow the directions for planting a new tree—except it shouldn't need as much water as a new planting.

MATURE TREE CARE

When one considers that the value of a healthy tree increases as it ages and that some tree species, such as oak and walnut, can live two hundred to three years, providing regular care for your trees is like putting money in the bank. Remember also that curing a problem once it develops is much more difficult, time-consuming, and costly than preventing one. An effective tree-maintenance program should include four major practices: inspection, mulching, fertilizing, and pruning.

Tree Inspection

Tree inspection will call attention to any change in the tree's health before the problem becomes too serious. By making regular inspections of mature trees (at least once a year), you can prevent or reduce the severity of future disease, insect, and environmental problems. Be sure to examine four characteristics of tree vigor: new leaves or buds, leaf size, twig growth, and crown dieback.

A reduction in the extension of shoots (new growing parts, such as buds or new leaves) or in the size of leaves is a fairly reliable cue that the tree's health has recently changed. To evaluate this, compare the growth of shoots over the past three years. Determine if there is a reduction in the tree's typical growth pattern.

Further signs of poor tree health are stem decay and crown dieback (gradual death of the upper part of the tree). These symptoms often indicate problems that began several years before. Loose bark or deformed growths, such as stem conks, are common signs of stem decay.

Any abnormalities found during this inspection should be noted and watched closely. If you are uncertain as to what should be done, report your findings to your local arborist, a tree-care professional, for advice on treatment.

Mulching

Mulching can cut down on stress by providing trees with a stable root environment that is cooler and contains more moisture than the surrounding soil. Mulch can also prevent mechanical damage by keeping machines such as lawnmowers away from the tree's base.

Further, mulch acts to reduce competition from surrounding weeds and turf.

To be most effective in all of these functions, mulch should be placed 2 to 4 inches deep and extend as far as possible from the base of the tree (at least 2 feet for young trees). When possible, mulch should extend two to three times the branch spread of the tree.

An adequate mulch layer is 2 to 4 inches of loosely packed organic material such as shredded leaves, pine straw, peat moss, or composted wood chips. Plastic should not be used because it interferes with the exchange of gases between soil and air and inhibits root growth. The thickness of the mulch layer is important; mulches 5 or 6 inches thick may inhibit gas exchange.

Fertilization

Fertilization is another important aspect of tree health care. Fertilizer is best applied in the fall or early spring, although you can fertilize any time. In addition to providing minor nutrients, fertilizers increase the amount of three major nutrients in the soil: nitrogen, phosphorous, and potassium.

Nitrogen (N) is possibly the most critical of these nutrients. It is the element most responsible for maintaining the green color in leaves and for normal twig growth. Because nitrogen is rapidly depleted from the soil, it must be replenished regularly to ensure plant health. For organic forms of nitrogen, use bloodmeal and cottonseed meal.

Phosphorous (P) assists in the maturation of tissues and stimulates root growth. It is particularly important in flower, fruit, and seed production. Fortunately, phosphorous in the soil is not depleted as rapidly as nitrogen, yet its sparsity may limit the number of plants that can thrive in a particular area. Phosphate rock, bonemeal, and fish meal are natural sources of phosphorous.

Potassium (K- also known as potash) assists in the manufacture of sugar and starches, helps tissues mature properly, and heightens the color of flowers. Plants without enough potassium may become either too succulent or too brittle. Natural sources of potash are manures, compost, plant residues, granite dust, and green sand.

Various fertilizer mixtures contain different amounts of these and other nutrients. Soil conditions, especially pH, an organic-matter content, vary greatly from region to region, thus the proper selection and use of fertilizer is a complex process. When fertilizing, remember that nitrogen can be applied directly on the soil surface, whereas phosphorous and potassium, like other insoluble nutrients, should be applied via holes in the soil. Consult your garden-center staff or a tree-care professional for advice on application and the best blend for each of your trees.

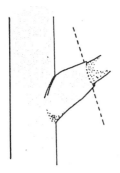

Pruning a Dead Branch
A dead branch stub that has a collar of live wood should be cut just at the outer edge of the collar (the swollen area where one branch meets another).

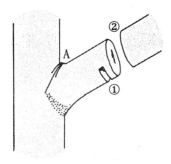

Pruning a Live Branch
Remove a large limb by making three cuts:
1. Undercut 12 to 24 inches from the branch collar (A).
2. Make a top cut all the way through the branch, within 1 inch of the undercut.

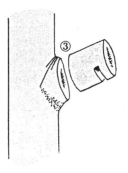

3. The final cut should be just beyond the branch collar (A).

Pruning

Pruning or trimming should be done regularly to control the tree's shape and keep damaged branches from harming other parts of the tree or surrounding structures or people. For most trees, the best time to prune is winter to early spring. Trees pruned at this time of year close their wounds more quickly. Exceptions to this are trees that have problems with disease in the spring. Oaks and honey locusts, for example, are susceptible to disease if pruned during rainy spring weather.

Pruning should always be performed sparingly: Overpruning is extremely harmful because without enough leaves, a tree cannot gather and process enough sunlight to survive.

Pruning also directs the growth pattern of a tree. Branches typically grow in the direction that the buds are pointing, and the outermost bud on a branch has the most influence on the direction of future growth. Therefore, you can control the orientation of a branch by carefully selecting the pruning cut's location. Cut so that the outermost bud on the branch is pointing in the direction that you want the branch to grow.

Once you begin a cut, always finish it. Prune limbs and branches so that you preserve the branch's collar (this often appears as a ridge of rough bark on the trunk that formed in the Y of a growing branch). The final pruning cut should be angled so that it begins in the crotch and extends down and outward at an angle opposite to the branch collar. The cut will not be flush with the trunk; rather, the base of the cut will extend out from the trunk. The purpose of cut 1 is to ensure that when cut 2 is completed, the bark does not "tear" down the remaining branch. Cut 3 finishes the job.

A healthy tree will seal on its own, so wound dressings are not necessary and may actually interfere with the process. To aid in the recovery of cuts, water and fertilize your trees well. If you are not sure about the pruning needs of a tree, contact your local tree-care professional.

Tree Removal

Sometimes, despite your greatest efforts at rejuvenation, a tree dies and must be removed. Symptoms of a thoroughly dead tree (one that has been overcome by disease or insects) include a lack of foliage in the spring and falling limbs throughout the year. Such trees will not recover and could cause considerable damage to surrounding structures if not removed promptly.

Tree removal should be handled by a reputable professional. Be sure to select someone with the necessary equipment, proven ability, and the financial responsibility to cover any damage that might occur. Because the removal of trees is a dangerous and difficult task, you can expect to pay rates ranging from less than $100 for the removal of small trees and shrubs to several hundred dollars for removal of a large tree. Before any work is done, negotiate a written contract specifying how the tree is to be removed, where the wood is to be taken, and who is liable in case of damage. A written agreement that protects the tree worker's rights as well as yours can prevent a great deal of misunderstanding and ensure that the work is done to your satisfaction. These suggestions also apply when having your trees professionally pruned.

PRUNING SHRUBS AND CREATING HEDGES

Shrubs are the workhorses of landscaping. Alone or as hedges, they block wind, direct foot traffic, create privacy, and reduce street noise. Although some species grow striking flowers and bright berries, their aesthetic role is usually to highlight a building's architectural features or to create a background for more spectacular plants.

What makes a shrub a shrub is it's multiple woody stems and limited height (generally they don't grow higher than 15 feet). This makes them flexible and trainable with appropriate pruning.

Why Prune?

To the novice landscaper, pruning may seem contrary to the laws of nature. Cutting a plant doesn't make sense. Plants evolved without any lopping shears around, so why should pruning be necessary?

Actually, nature does prune. Weak or dying branches are snapped off by wind, heavy rain, snow, and ice. The problem is that nature doesn't work carefully. Weak limbs don't always break off by themselves, or when they do fall, they don't necessarily exit gracefully. Jagged, diseased, or damaged portions of a branch may be left—threatening the life of the whole plant.

For Health

Pruning, done properly, improves the health of a plant. Besides just removing the weak links that the elements overlooked or didn't remove neatly, pruning improves plant vitality by allowing more air to circulate and sun to penetrate to the innermost leaves. This creates a more vigorous plant that is more resistant to diseases and insects.

When Transplanting

Pruning increases your shrub's chances of transplanting successfully by reducing the number of leaves the plant has to support. This creates a healthier leaf/root ratio.

For Greater Production and Revitalizing the Old

By reducing the number of branches (thinning), those branches that remain will bear thicker growth and larger flowers or fruit. Heading, or heading back, which means removing only part of a branch, causes multiple branches to grow where there was only one. Heading creates a denser, smaller shrub; thinning creates a larger, more natural-looking plant.

Old, neglected shrubs can be given another chance by cutting them back. Start by clearing away all the weak, thin shoots to open the plant up to more air and sun. What remains are older, bigger branches. Remove branches that point inward or cross other branches.

Step back and look at the new old plant. How does it look? Is more cutting back necessary? Before cutting off any major branches, have someone pull them back to give you an idea of what it will look like.

If the top part of a shrub seems hopeless, you can cut it back—even taking it all the way to the ground. As long as the plant has the strength to produce new shoots and leaves, it will have the strength to regrow what you cut off. If you're not sure whether a shrub can survive a radical haircut, head one branch back to a leafless stub to see how it responds. If new growth appears, that's a good sign that you can cut it back all the way.

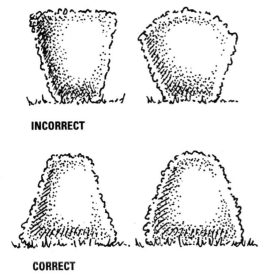

INCORRECT

CORRECT

To Shape

Most shrubs have natural forms—from columnar to weeping. If you're buying new plants, it's best to purchase the naturally occurring shape and size you want rather than trying to make them something they're not.

If you inherited shrubs that aren't the right size, pruning can shape them to fit your needs. Pruning can balance a plant that is lopsided, or it can let in the sun or breeze you need. If you want more of a barrier, head a shrub back so it will grow fuller. You can also make shapes just for the sake of making shapes—including archways or shrub sculptures. The classic shrub shaping is the hedge.

Hedges

Hedges can be formal or informal. Both can work to block wind, direct foot traffic, or create privacy. Choosing one is a matter of taste. Informal hedges are larger-leafed and more open shrubs, often grown for ornamental flowers. Because formal hedges need to be cut evenly, small-leafed, close-textured plants work best. Whether you choose a formal or informal hedge, for energy-efficient landscaping be sure the mature shrub will have the right size and foliage to do its job.

Planting Formal Hedges

Buy bare-root shrubs or ones that have been grown in gallon-size containers. Place the plants 18 to 30 inches apart, and shear off about a third of the sides and tops. Shearing forces thicker growth right down to the ground. Shape them smaller at the top than at the sides so that the bottom leaves will get proper light.

For the first two years, you will need to trim the hedge back 3 or 4 inches at least three or four times a year. Don't try to grow the hedge to your desired height the first year.

Maintaining Mature Hedges

If an already established hedge has been neglected and you want to make it a uniform size, place a string midway between the tallest and shortest shrub in the hedge. Cut branches cleanly just above side-branch junctions or just obvious dormant buds. Make slightly slanting cuts 1/4 inch above side branches or buds that remain. Allow plants below the string to grow to the height of the other plants before cutting them back. For most species, pruning once a year will be enough.

When to Prune

Shrubs that don't flower, such as evergreens, require less attention regarding the timing of your trimming. For most plants, the best time to prune is when they are dormant. As a general rule, early spring is good because you can cut off branches killed by frost or broken during the winter. It also works well for trimming deciduous shrubs because the leaves are off and you can see what you're doing. Not every plant, however, should be pruned in the spring. It depends on when the plant flowers.

Some shrubs flower on old wood and others on new wood. New wood is growth that occurs during the current growing season. It's usually light green or pink. Old wood is growth that has happened before the present growing season. Before pruning any shrub, notice when it blooms and whether it happens on old or new wood. Plants that bloom in the early spring bloom on old wood and should be pruned a week or two after the flowers drop. Pruning during the dormant season will remove the blossom buds. By waiting until after the flowers bloom you give the plants the rest of the season to grow more blossom buds for next year.

Shrubs that produce blossoms in the late spring or summer (i.e., on new wood) should be cut during their dormant season. Pruning in the very early spring encourages more new stem growth and blossoms for the upcoming season.

CHOOSING THE RIGHT BUD
Where you make your cut directs future growth.

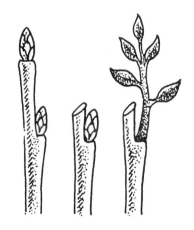

CUTTING OFF A TERMINAL BUD
The terminal bud has the most growing strength. When you cut it, the closest lateral bud becomes the new terminal bud and inherits that strength.

PRUNING TOOLS

Pruning Shears

There are several types to choose from, but stick with those that cut like scissors. Keep your shears sharp, clean, dry, and oiled.

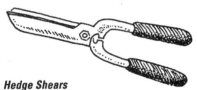

Hedge Shears

Designed to cut light new growth. Some have a notch at the base for cutting through thicker branches.

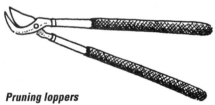

Pruning loppers

These are for pruning sturdy branches up to 1 1/2 inches in diameter.

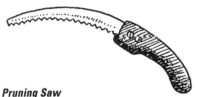

Pruning Saw

For large shrubs and thick branches that loppers can't cut off.

Where to Cut

There are two types of buds: terminal buds and lateral buds. As the names suggest, terminal buds are the last bud at the end of a branch and lateral buds are buds on the side of the branch. The placement of your cuts in relation to the terminal and lateral buds will determine the future growth of a branch.

If you cut off lateral buds or side branches, a shrub will put its energy to the terminal bud—pushing more vigorous growth in the direction the branch is going.

If you want to change the direction in which a shrub is growing, cut an eighth of an inch above a lateral bud. Choose a bud that is pointing outward, otherwise you'll force growth in toward the plant.

When you're ready to make a pruning cut, hold the branch just below where you want the cut to be. Put the cutting blade of your pruners under the branch, on an upward angle. The slant of the cut should be in the direction you want the new growth to go. Remember, there should always be a bud below where you cut, or the remaining stub will die and become susceptible to insects and diseases.

Appendices

The Zones of Plant Hardiness

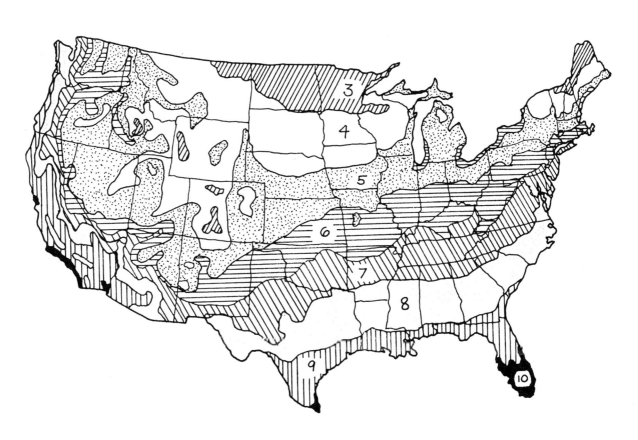

APPROXIMATE RANGE OF AVERAGE ANNUAL MINIMUM
TEMPERATURES FOR EACH ZONE

ZONE 3	-40°F	TO	-30°F
ZONE 4	-30°F	TO	-20°F
ZONE 5	-20°F	TO	-10°F
ZONE 6	-10°F	TO	0°F

ZONE 7	0°F	TO	10°F
ZONE 8	10°F	TO	20°F
ZONE 9	20°F	TO	30°F
ZONE 10	30°F	TO	40°F

The Latitudes of North America

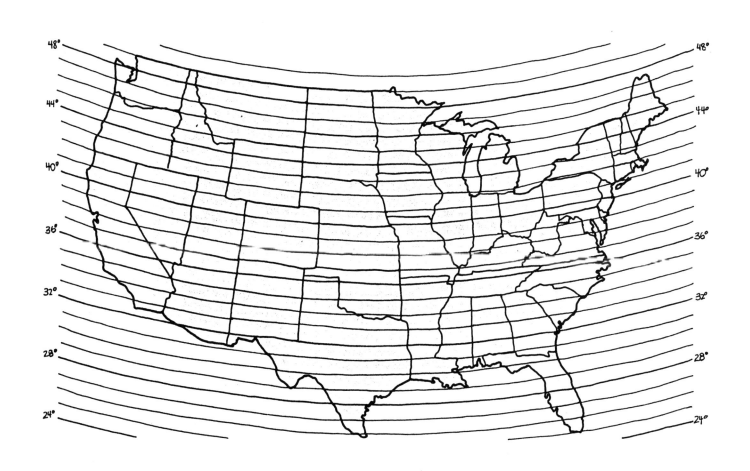

Table of Solar Angles for the U.S.

26.0 DEGREES NORTH LATITUDE

Winter solstice, December 22			Spring and Fall Equinox, March 21, Sept 24			Summer solstice, June 22		
Time	α Altitude Angle	β Bearing Angle	Time	α Altitude Angle	β Bearing Angle	Time	α Altitude Angle	β Bearing Angle
7:00 a.m.	2.23	117.51	7:00	13.26	97.07	6:00 a.m.	10.04	68.70
8:00 a.m.	13.76	125.11	8:00 a.m.	26.50	104.59	7:00 a.m.	22.82	74.03
9:00 a.m.	24.12	134.70	9:00 a.m.	39.23	114.10	8:00 a.m.	35.92	78.85
10:00 a.m.	32.66	146.98	10:00 a.m.	50.83	127.66	9:00 a.m.	49.24	83.55
11:00 a.m.	38.46	162.34	11:00 a.m.	59.88	148.94	10:00 a.m.	62.69	88.83
12:00 noon	40.55	180.00	12:00 noon	63.59	180.00	11:00 a.m.	76.14	97.39
1:00 p.m.	38.46	197.65	1:00 p.m.	59.88	211.05	12:00 noon	87.44	180.00
2:00 p.m.	32.66	213.01	2:00 p.m.	50.83	232.33	1:00 p.m.	76.14	262.60
3:00 p.m.	24.12	225.30	3:00 p.m.	39.23	245.90	2:00 p.m.	62.69	271.16
4:00 p.m.	13.76	234.88	4:00 p.m.	26.50	255.40	3:00 p.m.	49.24	276.44
5:00 p.m.	2.23	242.48	5:00 p.m.	13.26	262.93	4:00 p.m.	35.92	281.14
						5:00 p.m.	22.82	285.96
						6:00 p.m.	10.04	291.29

28.0 DEGREES NORTH LATITUDE

	Winter solstice, December 22			Spring and Fall Equinox, March 21, Sept. 24			Summer solstice, June 22	
Time	α Altitude Angle	β Bearing Angle	Time	α Altitude Angle	β Bearing Angle	Time	α Altitude Angle	β Bearing Angle
7:00 a.m.	1.31	117.57	7:00 a.m.	13.01	97.53	6:00 a.m.	10.76	69.04
8:00 a.m.	12.60	125.49	8:00 a.m.	25.98	105.54	7:00 a.m.	23.35	74.85
9:00 a.m.	22.70	135.31	9:00 a.m.	38.39	115.56	8:00 a.m.	36.28	80.28
10:00 a.m.	30.98	147.65	10:00 a.m.	49.58	129.54	9:00 a.m.	49.42	85.87
11:00 a.m.	36.56	162.80	11:00 a.m.	58.16	150.62	10:00 a.m.	62.66	92.70
12:00 noon	38.55	180.00	12:00 noon	61.59	180.00	11:00 a.m.	75.75	105.23
1:00 p.m.	36.56	197.19	1:00 p.m.	58.16	209.38	12:00 noon	85.44	180.00
2:00 p.m.	30.98	212.34	2:00 p.m.	49.58	230.45	1:00 p.m.	75.75	254.76
3:00 p.m.	22.70	224.68	3:00 p.m.	38.39	244.43	2:00 p.m.	62.66	267.29
4:00 p.m.	12.60	234.50	4:00 p.m.	25.98	254.45	3:00 p.m.	49.42	274.12
5:00 p.m.	1.31	242.42	5:00 p.m.	13.01	262.46	4:00 p.m.	36.28	279.71
						5:00 p.m.	23.35	285.14
						6:00 p.m.	10.76	290.95

30.0 DEGREES NORTH LATITUDE

	Winter solstice, December 22			Spring and Fall Equinox, March 21, Sept. 24			Summer solstice, June 22	
7:00 a.m.	0.38	117.60	7:00 a.m.	12.74	97.98	6:00 a.m.	11.47	69.41
8:00 a.m.	11.44	125.84	8:00 a.m.	25.43	106.47	7:00 a.m.	23.86	75.70
9:00 a.m.	21.27	135.87	9:00 a.m.	37.50	116.95	8:00 a.m.	36.59	81.74
10:00 a.m.	29.28	148.26	10:00 a.m.	48.28	131.29	9:00 a.m.	49.53	88.21
11:00 a.m.	34.64	163.22	11:00 a.m.	56.40	152.11	10:00 a.m.	62.50	96.54
12:00 noon	36.55	180.00	12:00 noon	59.59	180.00	11:00 a.m.	75.01	112.52
1:00 p.m.	34.64	196.77	1:00 p.m.	56.40	207.88	12:00 noon	83.44	180.00
2:00 p.m.	29.28	211.73	2:00 p.m.	48.28	228.70	1:00 p.m.	75.10	247.47
3:00 p.m.	21.27	224.12	3:00 p.m.	37.50	243.04	2:00 p.m.	62.50	263.45
4:00 p.m.	11.44	234.15	4:00 p.m.	25.43	253.52	3:00 p.m.	49.53	271.78
5:00 p.m.	0.38	242.40	5:00 p.m.	12.74	262.01	4:00 p.m.	36.59	278.25
						5:00 p.m.	23.86	284.30
						6:00 p.m.	11.47	290.58

32.0 DEGREES NORTH LATITUDE

	Winter solstice, December 22			Spring and Fall Equinox, March 21, Sept. 24			Summer solstice, June 22	
8:00 a.m.	10.26	126.15	7:00 a.m.	12.46	98.42	5:00 a.m.	0.54	62.40
9:00 a.m.	19.83	136.39	8:00 a.m.	24.85	107.37	6:00 a.m.	12.17	69.80
10:00 a.m.	27.57	148.83	9:00 a.m.	36.57	118.29	7:00 a.m.	24.34	76.56
11:00 a.m.	32.73	163.60	10:00 a.m.	46.94	132.91	8:00 a.m.	36.86	83.22
12:00 noon	34.55	180.00	11:00 a.m.	54.62	153.44	9:00 a.m.	49.55	90.55
1:00 p.m.	32.73	196.39	12:00 noon	57.59	180.00	10:00 a.m.	62.20	100.32
2:00 p.m.	27.57	211.16	1:00 p.m.	54.62	206.55	11:00 a.m.	74.23	119.09
3:00 p.m.	19.83	223.60	2:00 p.m.	46.94	227.08	12:00 noon	81.11	100.00
4:00 p.m.	10.26	233.84	3:00 p.m.	36.57	241.70	1:00 p.m.	74.23	240.90
			4:00 p.m.	24.85	252.62	2:00 p.m.	62.20	259.67
			5:00 p.m.	12.46	261.57	3:00 p.m.	49.55	269.44
						4:00 p.m.	36.86	276.77
						5:00 p.m.	24.34	283.43
						6:00 p.m.	12.17	290.19
						7:00 p.m.	0.54	297.60

34.0 DEGREES NORTH LATITUDE

Winter solstice, December 22			Spring and Fall Equinox, March 21, Sept. 24			Summer solstice, June 22		
	α Altitude	β Bearing		α Altitude	β Bearing		α Altitude	β Bearing
Time	Angle	Angle	Time	Angle	Angle	Time	Angle	Angle
8:00 a.m.	9.08	126.42	7:00 a.m.	12.15	98.86	5:00 a.m.	1.47	62.43
9:00 a.m.	18.38	136.87	8:00 a.m.	24.24	108.24	6:00 a.m.	12.85	70.22
10:00 a.m.	25.86	149.35	9:00 a.m.	35.61	119.57	7:00 a.m.	24.79	77.46
11:00 a.m.	30.81	163.95	10:00 a.m.	45.56	134.42	8:00 a.m.	37.07	84.72
12:00 noon	32.55	180.00	11:00 a.m.	52.82	154.63	9:00 a.m.	49.49	92.90
1:00 p.m.	30.81	196.05	12:00 noon	55.59	180.00	10:00 a.m.	61.78	104.00
2:00 p.m.	25.86	210.64	1:00 p.m.	52.82	205.36	11:00 a.m.	73.17	124.90
3:00 p.m.	18.38	223.12	2:00 p.m.	45.56	225.57	12:00 noon	79.44	180.00
4:00 p.m.	9.08	233.57	3:00 p.m.	35.61	240.42	1:00 p.m.	73.17	235.10
			4:00 p.m.	24.24	251.75	2:00 p.m.	61.78	255.99
			5:00 p.m.	12.15	261.14	3:00 p.m.	49.49	267.09
						4:00 p.m.	37.07	275.27
						5:00 p.m.	24.79	282.54
						6:00 p.m.	12.85	289.77
						7:00 p.m.	1.47	297.56

36.0 DEGREES NORTH LATITUDE

Winter solstice, December 22			Spring and Fall Equinox, March 21, Sept. 24			Summer solstice, June 22		
8:00 a.m.	7.88	126.66	7:00 a.m.	11.84	99.28	5:00 a.m.	2.39	62.49
9:00 a.m.	16.91	137.30	8:00 a.m.	23.60	109.08	6:00 a.m.	13.52	70.66
10:00 a.m.	24.13	149.82	9:00 a.m.	34.60	120.78	7:00 a.m.	25.21	78.37
11:00 a.m.	28.88	164.26	10:00 a.m.	44.14	135.83	8:00 a.m.	37.22	86.23
12:00 noon	30.55	180.00	11:00 a.m.	51.01	155.70	9:00 a.m.	49.35	95.23
1:00 p.m.	28.88	195.73	12:00 noon	53.59	180.00	10:00 a.m.	61.24	107.55
2:00 p.m.	24.13	210.17	1:00 p.m.	51.01	204.29	11:00 a.m.	71.95	129.95
3:00 p.m.	16.91	222.69	2:00 p.m.	44.14	224.16	12:00 noon	77.44	180.00
4:00 p.m.	7.88	233.33	3:00 p.m.	34.60	239.21	1:00 p.m.	71.95	230.04
			4:00 p.m.	23.60	250.91	2:00 p.m.	61.24	252.44
			5:00 p.m.	11.84	260.72	3:00 p.m.	49.35	264.77
						4:00 p.m.	37.22	273.76
						5:00 p.m.	25.21	281.62
						6:00 p.m.	13.52	189.33
						7:00 p.m.	2.39	297.50

38.0 DEGREES NORTH LATITUDE

Winter Solstice, December 22			Spring and Fall Equinox, March 21, Sept. 24			Summer Solstice, June 22		
8:00 a.m.	6.69	126.87	7:00 a.m.	11.51	99.68	5:00 a.m.	3.31	62.57
9:00 a.m.	15.44	137.69	8:00 a.m.	22.93	109.89	6:00 a.m.	14.18	71.13
10:00 a.m.	22.40	150.25	9:00 a.m.	33.56	121.94	7:00 a.m.	25.60	79.30
11:00 a.m.	26.96	164.55	10:00 a.m.	42.69	137.13	8:00 a.m.	37.33	87.75
12:00 noon	28.55	180.00	11:00 a.m.	49.18	156.67	9:00 a.m.	49.12	97.53
1:00 p.m.	26.96	195.45	12:00 noon	51.59	180.00	10:00 a.m.	60.58	110.94
2:00 p.m.	22.40	209.74	1:00 p.m.	49.18	203.32	11:00 a.m.	70.61	134.33
3:00 p.m.	15.44	222.30	2:00 p.m.	42.69	222.86	12:00 noon	75.44	180.00
4:00 p.m.	6.69	233.12	3:00 p.m.	33.56	238.05	1:00 p.m.	70.61	225.66
			4:00 p.m.	22.93	250.10	2:00 p.m.	60.58	249.05
			5:00 p.m.	11.51	260.31	3:00 p.m.	49.12	262.46
						4:00 p.m.	37.33	272.24
						5:00 p.m.	25.60	280.69
						6:00 p.m.	14.18	288.87
						7:00 p.m.	3.31	297.42

40.0 DEGREES NORTH LATITUDE

Winter Solstice, December 22			Spring and Fall Equinox, March 21, Sept. 24			Summer Solstice, June 22		
Time	α Altitude Angle	β Bearing Angle	Time	α Altitude Angle	β Bearing Angle	Time	α Altitude Angle	β Bearing Angle
8:00 a.m.	5.48	127.04	7:00 a.m.	11.17	100.08	5:00 a.m.	4.23	62.69
9:00 a.m.	13.95	138.05	8:00 a.m.	22.24	110.67	6:00 a.m.	14.82	71.62
10:00 a.m.	20.66	150.64	9:00 a.m.	32.48	123.04	7:00 a.m.	25.95	80.25
11:00 a.m.	25.03	164.80	10:00 a.m.	41.21	138.34	8:00 a.m.	37.38	89.28
12:00 noon	26.55	180.00	11:00 a.m.	47.34	157.54	9:00 a.m.	48.82	99.81
1:00 p.m.	25.03	195.19	12:00 noon	49.59	180.00	10:00 a.m.	59.81	114.17
2:00 p.m.	20.66	209.35	1:00 p.m.	47.34	202.45	11:00 a.m.	69.16	138.11
3:00 p.m.	13.95	221.94	2:00 p.m.	41.21	221.65	12:00 noon	73.44	180.00
4:00 p.m.	5.48	232.95	3:00 p.m.	32.48	236.95	1:00 p.m.	69.16	221.88
			4:00 p.m.	22.24	249.32	2:00 p.m.	59.81	245.82
			5:00 p.m.	11.17	259.91	3:00 p.m.	48.82	260.19
						4:00 p.m.	37.38	270.71
						5:00 p.m.	25.95	279.74
						6:00 p.m.	14.82	288.37
						7:00 p.m.	4.23	297.30

42.0 DEGREES NORTH LATITUDE

Winter solstice, December 22			Spring and Fall Equinox, March 21, Sept. 24			Summer solstice, June 22		
8:00 a.m.	4.28	127.17	7:00 a.m.	10.81	100.46	5:00 a.m.	5.15	62.84
9:00 a.m.	12.46	138.36	8:00 a.m.	21.52	111.42	6:00 a.m.	15.44	72.13
10:00 a.m.	18.91	150.99	9:00 a.m.	31.38	124.08	7:00 a.m.	26.27	81.22
11:00 a.m.	23.10	165.04	10:00 a.m.	39.70	139.46	8:00 a.m.	37.38	90.81
12:00 noon	24.55	180.00	11:00 a.m.	45.48	158.33	9:00 a.m.	48.44	102.04
1:00 p.m.	23.10	194.96	12:00 noon	47.59	180.00	10:00 a.m.	58.94	117.21
2:00 p.m.	18.91	209.00	1:00 p.m.	45.48	201.66	11:00 a.m.	67.63	141.38
3:00 p.m.	12.46	221.63	2:00 p.m.	39.70	220.53	12:00 noon	71.44	180.00
4:00 p.m.	4.28	232.82	3:00 p.m.	31.38	235.92	1:00 p.m.	67.63	218.61
			4:00 p.m.	21.52	248.57	2:00 p.m.	58.94	242.78
			5:00 p.m.	10.81	259.53	3:00 p.m.	48.44	257.96
						4:00 p.m.	37.38	269.19
						5:00 p.m.	26.27	278.77
						6:00 p.m.	15.44	287.86
						7:00 p.m.	5.15	297.15

44.0 DEGREES NORTH LATITUDE

Winter solstice, December 22			Spring and Fall Equinox, March 21, Sept. 24			Summer solstice, June 22		
8:00 a.m.	3.07	127.28	7:00 a.m.	10.44	100.83	5:00 a.m.	6.06	63.01
9:00 a.m.	10.96	138.63	8:00 a.m.	20.77	112.14	6:00 a.m.	16.04	72.67
10:00 a.m.	17.16	151.30	9:00 a.m.	30.24	125.06	7:00 a.m.	25.56	82.20
11:00 a.m.	21.16	165.24	10:00 a.m.	38.17	140.50	8:00 a.m.	37.32	92.33
12:00 noon	22.55	180.00	11:00 a.m.	43.62	159.05	9:00 a.m.	47.99	104.22
1:00 p.m.	21.16	194.75	12:00 noon	45.59	180.00	10:00 a.m.	57.98	120.07
2:00 p.m.	17.16	208.69	1:00 p.m.	43.62	200.94	11:00 a.m.	66.04	144.21
3:00 p.m.	10.96	221.36	2:00 p.m.	38.17	219.49	12:00 noon	69.44	180.00
4:00 p.m.	3.07	232.71	3:00 p.m.	30.24	234.93	1:00 p.m.	66.04	215.79
			4:00 p.m.	20.77	247.85	2:00 p.m.	57.98	239.92
			5:00 p.m.	10.44	259.16	3:00 p.m.	47.99	255.77
						4:00 p.m.	37.32	267.66
						5:00 p.m.	26.56	277.79
						6:00 p.m.	16.04	287.32
						7:00 p.m.	6.06	296.98

46.0 DEGREES NORTH LATITUDE

Winter solstice, December 22			Spring and Fall Equinox, March 21, Sept. 24			Summer solstice, June 22		
Time	α Altitude Angle	β Bearing Angle	Time	α Altitude Angle	β Bearing Angle	Time	α Altitude Angle	β Bearing Angle
8:00 a.m.	1.86	127.35	7:00 a.m.	10.06	101.19	5:00 a.m.	6.96	63.22
9:00 a.m.	9.46	138.87	8:00 a.m.	20.01	112.82	6:00 a.m.	16.63	73.23
10:00 a.m.	15.41	151.58	9:00 a.m.	29.08	125.99	7:00 a.m.	26.82	83.20
11:00 a.m.	19.23	165.43	10:00 a.m.	36.62	141.46	8:00 a.m.	37.22	93.85
12:00 noon	20.55	180.00	11:00 a.m.	41.75	159.70	9:00 a.m.	47.46	106.34
1:00 p.m.	19.23	194.56	12:00 noon	43.59	180.00	10:00 a.m.	56.94	122.75
2:00 p.m.	15.41	208.41	1:00 p.m.	41.75	200.29	11:00 a.m.	64.39	146.66
3:00 p.m.	9.46	221.12	2:00 p.m.	36.62	218.53	12:00 noon	67.44	180.00
4:00 p.m.	1.86	232.65	3:00 p.m.	29.08	234.01	1:00 p.m.	64.39	213.33
			4:00 p.m.	20.01	247.17	2:00 p.m.	56.94	237.24
			5:00 p.m.	10.06	258.81	3:00 p.m.	47.46	253.65
						4:00 p.m.	37.22	266.14
						5:00 p.m.	26.82	276.79
						6:00 p.m.	16.63	286.76
						7:00 p.m.	6.96	296.77

48.0 DEGREES NORTH LATITUDE

Winter solstice, December 22			Spring and Fall Equinox, March 21, Sept. 24			Summer solstice, June 22		
8:00 a.m.	0.64	127.38	7:00 a.m.	9.66	101.53	5:00 a.m.	7.86	63.45
9:00 a.m.	7.95	139.07	8:00 a.m.	19.22	113.48	6:00 a.m.	17.20	73.81
10:00 a.m.	13.64	151.83	9:00 a.m.	27.89	126.86	7:00 a.m.	27.03	84.21
11:00 a.m.	17.29	165.60	10:00 a.m.	35.04	142.35	8:00 a.m.	37.06	95.36
12:00 noon	18.55	180.00	11:00 a.m.	39.87	160.29	9:00 a.m.	46.86	108.40
1:00 p.m.	17.29	194.40	12:00 noon	41.59	180.00	10:00 a.m.	55.82	125.25
2:00 p.m.	13.64	208.16	1:00 p.m.	39.87	199.70	11:00 a.m.	62.70	148.81
3:00 p.m.	7.95	220.92	2:00 p.m.	35.04	217.64	12:00 noon	65.44	180.00
4:00 p.m.	0.64	232.61	3:00 p.m.	27.89	233.13	1:00 p.m.	62.70	211.18
			4:00 p.m.	19.22	246.51	2:00 p.m.	55.82	234.75
			5:00 p.m.	9.66	258.46	3:00 p.m.	46.86	251.59
						4:00 p.m.	37.06	264.63
						5:00 p.m.	27.03	275.78
						6:00 p.m.	17.20	286.18
						7:00 p.m.	7.86	296.54

50.0 DEGREES NORTH LATITUDE

Winter solstice, December 22

Time	α	β
9:00 a.m.	6.44	139.24
10:00 a.m.	11.88	152.04
11:00 a.m.	15.35	165.74
12:00 noon	16.55	180.00
1:00 p.m.	15.35	194.25
2:00 p.m.	11.88	207.95
3:00 p.m.	6.44	220.75

Spring and Fall Equinox, March 21, Sept. 24

Time	α	β
7:00 a.m.	9.26	101.85
8:00 a.m.	18.42	114.10
9:00 a.m.	26.68	127.68
10:00 a.m.	33.45	143.18
11:00 a.m.	37.98	160.83
12:00 noon	39.59	180.00
1:00 p.m.	37.98	199.17
2:00 p.m.	33.45	216.81
3:00 p.m.	26.68	232.31
4:00 p.m.	18.42	245.89
5:00 p.m.	9.26	258.14

Summer solstice, June 22

Time	α	β
4:00 a.m.	0.57	52.61
5:00 a.m.	8.75	63.71
6:00 a.m.	17.74	74.42
7:00 a.m.	27.22	85.23
8:00 a.m.	36.84	96.86
9:00 a.m.	46.20	110.39
10:00 a.m.	54.63	127.56
11:00 a.m.	60.97	150.69
12:00 noon	63.44	180.00
1:00 p.m.	60.97	209.30
2:00 p.m.	54.63	232.43
3:00 p.m.	46.20	249.60
4:00 p.m.	36.84	263.13
5:00 p.m.	27.22	274.76
6:00 p.m.	17.74	285.57
7:00 p.m.	8.75	296.28
8:00 p.m.	0.57	307.38

Table of Tangents

Angle	Tangent	Angle	Tangent	Angle	Tangent
1.00	0.017	31.00	0.601	61.00	1.804
2.00	0.035	32.00	0.625	62.00	1.881
3.00	0.052	33.00	0.649	63.00	1.963
4.00	0.070	34.00	0.675	64.00	2.050
5.00	0.087	35.00	0.700	65.00	2.145
6.00	0.105	36.00	0.727	66.00	2.246
7.00	0.123	37.00	0.754	67.00	2.356
8.00	0.141	38.00	0.781	68.00	2.475
9.00	0.158	39.00	0.810	69.00	2.605
10.00	0.176	40.00	0.839	70.00	2.747
11.00	0.194	41.00	0.869	71.00	2.904
12.00	0.213	42.00	0.900	72.00	3.078
13.00	0.231	43.00	0.933	73.00	3.271
14.00	0.249	44.00	0.966	74.00	3.487
15.00	0.268	45.00	1.000	75.00	3.732
16.00	0.287	46.00	1.036	76.00	4.011
17.00	0.306	47.00	1.072	77.00	4.331
18.00	0.325	48.00	1.111	78.00	4.705
19.00	0.344	49.00	1.150	79.00	5.145
20.00	0.364	50.00	1.192	80.00	5.671
21.00	0.384	51.00	1.235	81.00	6.314
22.00	0.404	52.00	1.280	82.00	7.115
23.00	0.424	53.00	1.327	83.00	8.144
24.00	0.445	54.00	1.376	84.00	9.514
25.00	0.466	55.00	1.428	85.00	11.430
26.00	0.488	56.00	1.483	86.00	14.300
27.00	0.510	57.00	1.540	87.00	19.081
28.00	0.532	58.00	1.600	88.00	28.635
29.00	0.554	59.00	1.664	89.00	57.286
30.00	0.577	60.00	1.732	90.00	∞

Angle	Tangent	Angle	Tangent	Angle	Tangent
91.00	−57.286	141.00	−0.810	191.00	0.194
92.00	−28.635	142.00	−0.781	192.00	0.213
93.00	−19.082	143.00	−0.754	193.00	0.231
94.00	−14.301	144.00	−0.727	194.00	0.249
95.00	−11.430	145.00	−0.700	195.00	0.268
96.00	−9.514	146.00	−0.675	196.00	0.287
97.00	−8.144	147.00	−0.649	197.00	0.306
98.00	−7.115	148.00	−0.625	198.00	0.325
99.00	−6.314	149.00	−0.601	199.00	0.344
100.00	−5.671	150.00	−0.577	200.00	0.364
101.00	−5.145	151.00	−0.554	201.00	0.384
102.00	−4.705	152.00	−0.532	202.00	0.404
103.00	−4.332	153.00	−0.510	203.00	0.424
104.00	−4.011	154.00	−0.488	204.00	0.445
105.00	−3.732	155.00	−0.466	205.00	0.466
106.00	−3.487	156.00	−0.445	206.00	0.488
107.00	−3.271	157.00	−0.424	207.00	0.510
108.00	−3.078	158.00	−0.404	208.00	0.532
109.00	−2.904	159.00	−0.384	209.00	0.554
110.00	−2.747	160.00	−0.364	210.00	0.577
111.00	−2.605	161.00	−0.344	211.00	0.601
112.00	−2.475	162.00	−0.325	212.00	0.625
113.00	−2.356	163.00	−0.306	213.00	0.649
114.00	−2.246	164.00	−0.287	214.00	0.675
115.00	−2.145	165.00	−0.268	215.00	0.700
116.00	−2.050	166.00	−0.249	216.00	0.727
117.00	−1.963	167.00	−0.231	218.00	0.781
118.00	−1.881	168.00	−0.213	219.00	0.810
119.00	−1.804	169.00	−0.194	220.00	0.839
120.00	−1.732	170.00	−0.176	221.00	0.869
121.00	−1.664	171.00	−0.158	222.00	0.900
122.00	−1.600	172.00	−0.141	223.00	0.933
123.00	−1.540	173.00	−0.123	224.00	0.966
124.00	−1.483	174.00	−0.105	225.00	1.000
125.00	−1.428	175.00	−0.087	266.00	1.036
126.00	−1.376	176.00	−0.070	227.00	1.072
127.00	−1.327	177.00	−0.052	228.00	1.111
128.00	−1.280	178.00	−0.035	229.00	1.150
129.00	−1.235	179.00	−0.017	230.00	1.192
130.00	−1.192	180.00	−0.000	231.00	1.235
131.00	−1.150	181.00	0.017	232.00	1.280
132.00	−1.111	182.00	0.035	233.00	1.327
133.00	−1.072	183.00	0.052	234.00	1.376
134.00	−1.036	184.00	0.070	235.00	1.428
135.00	−1.000	185.00	0.087	236.00	1.483
136.00	−0.966	186.00	0.105	237.00	1.540
137.00	−0.933	187.00	0.123	238.00	1.600
138.00	−0.900	188.00	0.141	239.00	1.664
139.00	−0.869	189.00	0.158	240.00	1.732
140.00	−0.839	190.00	0.176	241.00	1.804

Angle	Tangent	Angle	Tangent	Angle	Tangent
242.00	1.881	282.00	− 4.705	322.00	− 0.781
243.00	1.963	283.00	− 4.332	323.00	− 0.754
244.00	2.050	284.00	− 4.011	324.00	− 0.727
245.00	2.144	285.00	− 3.732	325.00	− 0.700
246.00	2.246	286.00	− 3.487	326.00	− 0.675
247.00	2.356	287.00	− 3.271	327.00	− 0.649
248.00	2.475	288.00	− 3.078	328.00	− 0.625
249.00	2.605	289.00	− 2.904	329.00	− 0.601
250.00	2.747	290.00	− 2.748	330.00	− 0.577
251.00	2.904	291.00	− 2.605	331.00	− 0.554
252.00	3.078	292.00	− 2.475	332.00	− 0.532
253.00	3.271	293.00	− 2.356	333.00	− 0.510
254.00	3.487	294.00	− 2.246	334.00	− 0.488
255.00	3.732	295.00	− 2.145	335.00	− 0.466
256.00	4.011	296.00	− 2.050	336.00	− 0.445
257.00	4.331	297.00	− 1.963	337.00	− 0.424
258.00	4.705	298.00	− 1.881	338.00	− 0.404
259.00	5.144	299.00	− 1.804	339.00	− 0.384
260.00	5.671	300.00	− 1.732	340.00	− 0.364
261.00	6.314	301.00	− 1.664	341.00	− 0.344
262.00	7.115	302.00	− 1.600	342.00	− 0.325
263.00	8.144	303.00	− 1.540	343.00	− 0.306
264.00	9.514	304.00	− 1.483	344.00	− 0.287
265.00	11.430	305.00	− 1.428	345.00	− 0.268
266.00	14.300	306.00	− 1.376	346.00	− 0.249
267.00	19.080	307.00	− 1.327	347.00	− 0.231
268.00	28.635	308.00	− 1.280	348.00	− 0.213
269.00	57.286	309.00	− 1.235	349.00	− 0.194
270.00	788935.938	310.00	− 1.192	350.00	− 0.176
271.00	− 57.286	311.00	− 1.150	351.00	− 0.158
272.00	− 28.635	312.00	− 1.111	352.00	− 0.141
273.00	− 19.082	313.00	− 1.072	353.00	− 0.123
274.00	− 14.301	314.00	− 1.036	354.00	− 0.105
275.00	− 11.431	315.00	− 1.000	355.00	− 0.087
276.00	− 9.515	316.00	− 0.966	356.00	− 0.070
277.00	− 8.145	317.00	− 0.933	357.00	− 0.052
278.00	− 7.116	318.00	− 0.900	358.00	− 0.035
279.00	− 6.314	319.00	− 0.869	359.00	− 0.017
280.00	− 5.671	320.00	− 0.839	360.00	− 0.000
281.00	− 5.145	321.00	− 0.810		

Table of Tree Densities

This chart describes the sun-blocking ability of various trees, which is expressed in the last two columns as percentages of visible radiation blocked by a species in full foliage.

Scientific Name	Common Name	Density	Range
Acer ginnala	Amur Maple	91	90-92
Acer platanoides	Norway Maple	90	85-94
Acer rubrum	Red Maple	83	78-92
Acer saccharinum	Silver Maple	79	72-86
Acer saccharum	Sugar Maple	84	73-97
Aesculus hippocastum	Common Horse Chestnut	85	73-91
Alnus glutinosa	European Alder	83	81-85
Amelanchier canadensis	Serviceberry	77	75-80
Betula pendula	European White Birch	81	76-86
Carya glabra	Pignut Hickory	86	82-90
Carya ovata	Shagbark Hickory	77	72-85
Catalpa speciosa	Western Catalpa	76	70-82
Cercidiphyllum japonicum	Katsura Tree	78	71-82
Corylus Colurna	Turkish Hazelnut	80	70-90
Fagus sylvatica	European Beech	88	85-93
Fraxinus pennsylvanica	Green Ash, Red Ash	80	71-90
Ginkgo biloba	Ginkgo, Maidenhair	78	75-82
Gleditsia triacanthos	Honey Locust	62	49-75
Juglans cinerea	Butternut	75	69-80
Larix decidua	European Larch	73	58-88

Scientific Name	Common Name	Density	Range
Picea pungens	Colorado Spruce	80	72-87
Pinus Strobus	White Pine	72	70-75
Populus deltoides	Cottonwood	85	80-90
Populus nigra	Lombardy Poplar	86	81-91
Populus tremuloides	Quaking Aspen	69	67-71
Pyrus communis	Common Pear	80	77-87
Quercus alba	White Oak	75	62-87
Quercus robur	English Oak	81	77-87
Quercus rubra	Northern Red Oak	81	77-88
Salix alba	White Willow, Golden Willow	84	71-93
Sophora japonica	Japanese Pagoda Tree	78	75-82
Tilia americana	Basswood	88	86-94
Tilia cordata	Small-leaved European Linden	83	73-88
Tilia tomentosa	Silver Linden	90	88-92
Zelkova serrata	Japanese Zelkova	76	70-81

TECHNICAL NOTE:

The above table shows the comparative densities of some trees commonly found in North America. These are visual densities or overall occlusion, and do not represent density of specific spectra, since foliage varies in its transmission depending on light wavelength. Values may be prorated to determine exact radiant heat gain based on percentage stem materials vs. percentage leaf material.

Lists of Plants According to Size and Form

TALL DECIDUOUS TREES (OVER THIRTY-FIVE FEET)

Name	Hardiness Zones	Growth Rate	Comments
Acer macrophyllum (big-leafed maple, California maple)	3, 4, 5, 6, 7	Variable	Globe-shaped. Chloride-tolerant. Yellow and orange fall foliage.
Acer platanoides (Norway maple)	3, 4, 5, 6, 7, 8, 9	Medium	Columnar- or globe-shaped. Grows in cities. Low maintenance. Yellow fall foliage.
Acer rubrum (red maple, scarlet maple, swamp maple)	3, 4, 5, 6, 7, 8	Fast	Globe-shaped. Sensitive to salt, nitrous oxide. Tolerant of sulfur dioxide, ozone. Red or yellow fall foliage.
Acer saccharinum (silver maple, soft maple)	3, 4, 5, 6, 7, 8	Fast	Pendulous branches. Red and yellow fall foliage. Source of commercial wood.
Acer saccharum (sugar maple, rock maple)	3, 4, 5, 6, 7, 8	Fast	Columnar- or globe-shaped. Sensitive to salt, nitrous oxide. Tolerant of sulfur dioxide, ozone. Must remove dead wood. Good fall color.
Aesculus X *carnea* cv. 'Briottii' (ruby horse chestnut)	4, 5, 6	Slow	Oval-shaped. Salt-tolerant. Must remove dead fruit and flowers. Susceptible to mildew. Red blossoms, horse chestnuts.

Betula papyrifera (canoe birch, paper birch, white birch)	2, 3, 4	Medium	Columnar-shaped. Needs dark night (i.e., won't tolerate electric night lights). Tolerant of salt, chloride. Sensitive to sulfur dioxide, 2-4-D. Must be sprayed. Resistant to birch borer. White bark.
Betula pendula (European white birch)	3, 4, 5, 6, 7, 8, 9, 10	Fast	Weeping. Prefers medium shade. Tolerant of salt, ozone, chloride. Sensitive to sulfur dioxide, 2-4-D. Subject to borers.
Bursera simaruba (gumbo-limbo, West Indian birch)	9, 10	Medium	Red, peeling bark. Good shade tree.
Carya ovata (shagbark hickory)	to zone 5	Slow	Oval-shaped. Hard wood. Salt-tolerant. Yellow fall foliage.
Castanea mollissima (Chinese chestnut)	to zone 5	Medium	Low, oval-shaped. Medium shade. Resistant to chestnut blight. Yellow flowers.
Cercidiphyllum japonicum (katsura tree)	5, 6, 7, 8, 9	Fast	Oval-shaped. Disease-free. Distinctive foliage.
Cladrastis lutea (American yellowwood)	4, 5, 6, 7, 8, 9	Medium	Globe-shaped. Sensitive to 2-4-D. Needs spray against oyster scale. Weak wood. White blossoms.
Cornus Nuttallii (Pacific dogwood, mountain dogwood)	6, 7, 8, 9	Medium	Globe-shaped, horizontal branching. Sensitive to 2-4-D. Bright red fruit, flowers.
Fagus sylvatica (European beech)	4, 5, 6, 7, 8	Slow	Globe-shaped. Needs full sun. Sensitive to fluoride. Susceptible to beech bark disease. Bronze fall foliage.
Fraxinus pennsylvanica (green ash)	3, 4, 5, 6, 7, 8, 9	Fast	Oval-shaped. Tolerant of sulfur dioxide, 2-4-D. Sensitive to fluoride, ozone. Weak wood. Yellow fall color.
Fraxinus velutina var. *glabra* (Modesto ash, Arizona ash)	5, 6, 7	Fast	Tolerant of fluorine, 2-4-D.
Ginkgo biloba (ginkgo, maidenhair tree)	5, 6, 7, 8, 9, 10	Slow	Columnar. Thrives in city. Tolerant of sulfur dioxide. Sensitive to nitrous oxide, ozone. No diseases. Yellow fall foliage. Female produces obnoxious, smelly fruit.
Gleditsia triacanthos var. *inermis* (thornless honey locust)	5, 6, 7, 8, 9	Fast	Low, globe-shaped. Grows in cities. Sensitive to ozone. Must remove pods, needs some spraying. Strong wood. Pest-resistant. Yellow fall foliage.

Jacaranda mimosifolia (green ebony)	10	Medium	Globe-shaped. Sensitive to salt. Blue, showy flowers. Fernlike leaves.
Koelreuteria paniculata (golden-rain tree, varnish tree)	5, 6, 7, 8, 9, 10	Medium	Globe- or columnar-shaped. Needs full sun. Grows in cities. Tolerant of salt. Low maintenance. Pest-free. Yellow flowers, fruit.
Larix decidua (European larch)	to zone 3	Fast	Pyramidal-shaped. Sensitive to nitrous oxide, chloride, ozone. Tolerant of PAN,* sulfur dioxide. Susceptible to insects. Yellow fall foliage.
Liquidambar Styraciflua (sweet gum)	5, 6, 7, 8, 9, 10	Medium	Pyramidal-shaped. Sensitive to ozone, chloride. Tolerant of 2-4-D. Needs no special maintenance. Pest-resistant. Good fall color.
Liriodendron Tulipifera (tulip tree)	4, 5, 6, 7, 8, 9	Fast	Oval-shaped. Needs sun. Sensitive to ozone, PAN, smog. Tolerant of sulfur dioxide. Weak wood. Resistant to gypsy moth. Yellow flowers, yellow fall foliage.
Magnolia heptapeta (Yulan magnolia)	4, 5, 6, 7, 8	Medium	Pyramidal-shaped. Prefers medium shade. White fragrant flowers.
Morus alba (white mulberry)	to zone 4	Medium	Globe-shaped. Sensitive to salt, ozone.
Nyssa sylvatica (black tupelo, black gum, sour gum, pepperidge)	5, 6, 7, 8, 9	Slow	Pyramidal-shaped. Tolerant of sulfur dioxide. Sensitive to chloride. Low maintenance. No pests. Good fall foliage.
Paulownia tomentosa (princess tree, royal paulownia, karri tree)	7, 8, 9, 10	Medium	Globe-shaped. Medium shade. Sensitive to fluoride. Lavender flowers.
Pistacia chinensis (Chinese pistachio)	6, 7, 8, 9, 10	Slow	Flowers, red fall foliage.
Platanus X acerifolia (London plane tree)	5, 6, 7, 8, 9	Fast	Globe-shaped. Needs sun. Grows in cities. Sensitive to 2-4-D. Tolerant of fluorine. Low maintenance. Resistance to anthracnose. Fruit.
Platanus occidentalis (eastern sycamore)	4, 5, 6, 7, 8, 9	Fast	Globe-shaped. Tolerant of salt, sulfur dioxide. Sensitive to ozone. Spray twice annually. Susceptible to anthracnose.
Platanus racemosa (California plane tree)	10	Fast	Globe-shaped. Sensitive to ozone. Tolerant of fluoride. Spray twice annually. Susceptible to anthracnose.

*PAN refers to peroxyacetyl nitrate.

Populus alba cv. 'Pyramidalis,' also known as Populus bolleana (Bolleana poplar)	to zone 4	Fast	Columnar-shaped. Roots likely to stop drains or cause heaving of sidewalks.
Pyrus Calleryana (Callery pear)	6, 7, 8, 9, 10	Medium	Oval-shaped. Pollution-resistant. Good street tree. Resistant to fire blight. Good fall color.
Quercus alba (white oak)	4, 5, 6, 7, 8, 9, 10	Slow	Globe-shaped with horizontal branches. Tolerant of ozone. Sensitive to salt. Low maintenance. Susceptible to scale.
Quercus coccinea (scarlet oak)	4, 5, 6, 7, 8	Slow	Globe-shaped. Needs full sun. Grows in cities. Good fall color.
Quercus macrocarpa (mossy-cup oak, bur oak)	4, 5, 6, 7, 8, 9	Slow	Globe-shaped. Sensitive to salt.
Quercus nigra (water oak)	6, 7, 8, 9, 10	Slow	Globe-shaped.
Quercus palustris (pin oak, Spanish oak)	5, 6, 7, 8, 9, 10	Slow	Pyramidal-shaped. Needs full sun. Sensitive to salt, ozone. Susceptible to horned oak gall. Red fall foliage.
Quercus phellos (willow oak)	6, 7, 8, 9	Medium	Pyramidal-shaped. Grows in cities. Low maintenance. No pests. Yellow fall foliage.
Quercus rubra (northern oak)	5, 6, 7, 8	Slow	Globe-shaped. Grows in cities. Susceptible to oak wilt. Good fall color.
Quercus virginiana (live oak, southern live oak)	7, 8, 9, 10	Medium	Upright. Needs full sun. Tolerates salt spray. Sensitive to ozone. Low maintenance.
Robinia Pseudoacacia (black locust, false acacia, yellow locust)	to zone 3	Fast	Columnar-shaped. Tolerant of sulfur dioxide, salt, fluoride. Sensitive to ozone, nitrous oxide. Needs treatment for borers. Weak wood. White flowers.
Salix alba (golden weeping willow)	to zone 2	Fast	Weeping. Tolerant of salt. Sensitive to sulfur dioxide, ozone. Weak wood. Yellow fall color.
Sophora japonica (Japanese pagoda tree, Chinese scholar tree)	5, 6, 7, 8, 9, 10	Medium	Globe-shaped. Grows in cities. Resistant to salt. Needs pruning to maintain shape. Susceptible to twig blight. Flowers.
Sorbus Aucuparia (European mountain ash, rowan tree)	3, 4, 5, 6, 7, 8	Slow	High, globe-shaped. Tolerant of fluoride, ozone. Sensitive to sulfur dioxide. Susceptible to borers, fire blight. White flowers, orange-red fruit.

Name	Hardiness Zones	Growth Rate	Comments
Stewartia Pseudocamellia (Japanese stewartia)	8, 9, 10	Fast	Oval-shaped. Needs sun to medium shade.
Taxodium distichum (swamp cypress)	5, 6, 7, 8, 9, 10	Medium	Columnar-shaped. Needs sun. Reddish brown fall foliage.
Tilia americana (American linden, basswood)	3, 4, 5, 6, 7, 8	Medium	Pyramidal. Sensitive to salt, ozone, nitrous oxide. Tolerant of fluoride. Susceptible to Japanese beetle. Fragrant blooms.
Tilia cordata (little leaf linden)	4, 5, 6, 7, 8	Medium	Pyramidal-shaped. Grows in cities. Tolerant of fluoride. Must be sprayed and pruned. Susceptible to Japanese beetle. Fragrant blooms.
Tilia tomentosa (silver linden)	4, 5, 6, 7, 8	Medium	Pyramidal-shaped. Fragrant blooms.
Ulmus parvifolia (Chinese elm)	6, 7, 8	Fast	Globe-shaped. Tolerates salt. Sensitive to ozone, sulfur dioxide, 2-4-D. Less susceptible to Dutch elm disease.
Ulmus procera (English elm)	to zone 6	Fast	Propagated by suckers. Popular tree in Northeast.
Zelkova serrata (Japanese zelkova)	5, 6, 7, 8, 9, 10	Medium	Globe-shaped. Grows in cities. Susceptible to Dutch elm disease, beetles. Yellow fall foliage.

SHORT DECIDUOUS TREES (UNDER THIRTY-FIVE FEET)

Name	Hardiness Zones	Growth Rate	Comments
Acer Ginnala (Amur maple)	3, 4, 5, 6, 7, 8	Slow	Globe-shaped. Sensitive to salt. Good fall color.
Acer palmatum (Japanese maple)	6, 7, 8, 9	Slow	Low, globe-shaped. Prefers medium shade. Sensitive to nitrous oxide, salt. No special maintenance required. Red foliage on some cultivars.
Albizia Julibrissin (silk tree, mimosa tree)	7, 8, 9, 10	Fast	Horizontal branching. Needs sun. Grows in cities. Sensitive to salt.
Amelanchier canadensis (downy serviceberry)	5, 6, 7, 8	Medium	Globe-shaped. Grows in shade. Salt sensitive. White blossoms, red fall foliage.
Amelanchier X grandiflora (apple serviceberry)	3, 4, 5, 6, 7, 8	Medium	Globe-shaped. Grows in shade. Sensitive to salt. Red flowers.

Amelanchier canadensis (shadblow, serviceberry)	to zone 4	Medium	Showy, early spring bloom. Edible fruit.
Bauhinia variegata (Buddhist bauhinia, mountain ebony, orchid tree)	9, 10	Medium	Globe-shaped. Needs full sun. White flowers.
Cercidium floridum (palo verde)	7, 8, 9, 10	Medium	Globe-shaped. Yellow flowers.
Cercis canadensis (eastern redbud)	5, 6, 7, 8, 9	Medium	Globe-shaped. Grows in shade. Sensitive to 2-4-D. Pink flowers. Colored fall foliage.
Chilopsis linearis (desert willow)	8, 9, 10	Medium	Prefers full sun. May need watering. White-to-pink fragrant flowers.
Chionanthus virginicus (fringe tree)	5, 6, 7, 8, 9	Medium	Globe-shaped. Prefers full sun. White flowers, yellow fall color.
Cornus florida (flowering dogwood)	5, 6, 7, 8	Medium	Globe-shaped, horizontal branching. Grows in shade. Tolerant of sulfur dioxide. Sensitive to 2-4-D. Susceptible to dogwood borer. Flowers, bright-red fruit.
Cornus Kousa (Chinese dogwood)	5, 6, 7, 8, 9	Medium	Globe-shaped. Sensitive to 2-4-D. Flowers, fruit, distinctive foliage.
Crataegus laevigata, also known as *Crataegus Oxycantha* (English hawthorn)	5, 6, 7, 8	Slow	Low, globe-shaped. Sensitive to salt. Flowers, distinctive foliage.
Crataegus mollis (downy hawthorn)	4, 5	Medium	Low, globe-shaped. Sensitive to salt. White flowers, red fruit, useful for jellies.
Crataegus Phaenopyrum (Washington hawthorn)	5, 6, 7, 8	Medium	Low, globe-shaped. Grows in cities. Sensitive to salt. Weak wood. Susceptible to borers, scale. White flowers, red fruit.
Delonix regia (poinciana regia poinciana tree, royal flame)	10	Medium	Weeping, scarlet, showy flowers.
Elaeagnus angustifolia (Russian olive, oleaster, silver berry)	3, 4, 5, 6, 7, 8, 9	Fast	Irregular-shape. Prefers full sun. Tolerant of fluoride, chloride. Grows in cities. Pest-free. Distinctive foliage.
Halesia carolina (Carolina silverbell, wild olive, shittim wood, opposum wood)	5, 6, 7, 8, 9, 10	Medium	Globe-shaped. Flowers, attractive fruit.

Koelreuteria elegans (Chinese flame tree, flame-gold)	9, 10	Medium	Globe-shaped. Needs sun. Flowers, orange seed pods.
Laburnum X *Watereri*, also known as *Laburnum* X *Vossii* (golden chain tree)	5, 6, 7, 8, 9	Fast	Globe-shaped. Medium shade. Yellow flowers.
Lagerstroemia indica (crape myrtle)	7, 8, 9	Medium to fast	Globe-shaped. Needs full sun. Needs watering. Susceptible to mildew. Flowers.
Magnolia X *Loebneri* cv. 'Merrill' (Merrill magnolia)	4, 5, 6, 7, 8	Medium	Pyramidal-shaped. Prefers medium shade. White flowers.
Magnolia X *Soulangiana* (saucer magnolia)	5, 6, 7, 8, 9, 10	Medium	Globe-shaped. Prefers full shade. Grows in cities. Requires selective pruning. Susceptible to magnolia scale. Attractive flowers.
Magnolia stellata (star magnolia)	5, 6, 7, 8, 9, 10	Medium	Globe-shaped. Prefers medium shade. Grows in cities. Requires selective pruning. Susceptible to borers, scale. Fragrant flowers.
Malus X *atrosanguinea* (Carmine crab apple)	4, 5, 6, 7, 8	Medium	Globe-shaped. Semisensitive to salt. Flowers, fruit.
Malus baccata (Siberian crab apple)	2, 3, 4, 5, 6, 7	Medium	Globe-shaped. Semisensitive to salt. Flowers, fruit.
Malus floribunda (showy crab apple)	5, 6, 7, 8	Medium	Low, globe-shaped. Semisensitive to salt. Susceptible to borers, scale. Flowers, fruit.
Malus ioensis (Prairie crab apple, wild crab apple)	2, 3, 4, 5, 6, 7, 8	Medium	Globe-shaped. Semisensitive to salt. Susceptible to borers, scale. Flowers, fruit.
Malus X *purpurea* (purple crab apple)	4, 5, 6, 7, 8	Medium	Globe-shaped. Semisensitive to salt. Susceptible to borers, scale. Flowers, fruit.
Morus alba (white mulberry)	to zone 4	Medium	Globe-shaped. Sensitive to salt.
Oxydendrum arboreum (sorrel tree, sourwood)	5, 6, 7, 8, 9	Slow	Globe-shaped. Takes sun or shade. Grows in cities. Tolerant of sulfur dioxide. Low maintenance. Flowers, distinctive foliage.
Parkinsonia aculeata (Jerusalem thorn)	10	Medium	Yellow color. Yellow flowers.
Phellodendron amurense (Amur cork tree)	4, 5, 6, 7	Fast	Globe-shaped. Grows in cities. Insect-free. Yellow fall foliage.

Prosopis glandulosa (honey mesquite)	7, 8, 9	Medium	Weeping. Susceptible to boring mollusk. Flowers.
Prunus X *blireiana* (blireiana plum, purple leaf plum)	5, 6, 7, 8, 9	Fast	Low, globe-shaped. White flowers, purple leaves.
Prunus cerasifera (cherry plum)	4, 5, 6	Fast	Low, globe-shaped. Tolerant of fluoride. Light-pink flowers, fruit.
Prunus dulcis (almond tree)	7, 8, 9	Fast	Low, globe-shaped. Sensitive to salt. White flowers. Many cultivars grown commercially in California.
Prunus serrulata (Oriental cherry)	6, 7, 8	Fast	Low, globe-shaped. Tolerant of fluoride. Flowers.
Prunus subhirtella (Higan cherry)	6, 7, 8, 9	Fast	Low, globe-shaped. Semisensitive to fluorine. Sensitive to smog. Flowers.
Prunus virginiana (chokecherry)	2, 3, 4, 5, 6, 7, 8	Fast	Low, globe-shaped. Tolerant of salt.
Prunus yedoensis (Yoshino cherry, Japanese flowering cherry)	6, 7, 8, 9	Fast	Low, globe-shaped. Semisensitive to fluoride. Flowers.
Pyrus communis (pear tree)	to zone 5	Medium	Oval-shaped. Sensitive to sulfur dioxide, nitrous oxide. Needs spraying. Subject to scale and fire blight. White flowers.
Salix babylonica (Babylon weepng willow)	to zone 5	Fast	Weeping. Full sun. Tolerant of salt. Sensitive to sulfur dioxide, ozone. Weak wood. Needs pruning. Yellow fall foliage.
Sapium sebiferum (Chinese tallow tree)	to zone 4	Medium	Good street tree.
Sorbus americana (American mountain ash, dogberry, missey-moosey)	to zone 2	Medium to slow	Shrubby. Hardy. Thrives in dry soils.
Sorbus decora (showy mountain ash)	2, 3, 4, 5, 6	Fast	Globe-shaped. Tolerant of salt.
Syringa reticulata var. *japonica* (Japanese tree lilac)	4, 5, 6, 7, 8	Medium	Globe-shaped. Prefers full sun. Tolerant of salt. Fruit, flowers.
Ulmus pumila (dwarf elm, Siberian elm)	3, 4, 5, 6, 7, 8	Fast	Globe-shaped. Sensitive to ozone, sulfur dioxide, 2-4-D. Tolerates salt Weak wood. Less susceptible to Dutch elm disease.

EVERGREEN TREES OVER THIRTY-FIVE FEET

Name	Hardiness Zones	Growth Rate	Comments
Abies balsamea (balsam fir)	to zone 3	Medium	Does not thrive where growing season is hot or where air is polluted.
Abies concolor (white fir, concolor fir)	4, 5, 6, 7, 8, 9	Fast	Pyramidal-shaped. Semisensitive to ozone, sulfur dioxide. Grows in cities.
Araucaria heterophylla (Norfolk Island pine)	10	Medium	Pyramidal-shaped.
Calocedrus decurrens, also known as *Libocedrus decurrens* (California incense cedar)	6, 7, 8, 9, 10	Slow	Semisensitive to ozone.
Casuarina equisetifolia (horsetail tree, South Sea ironwood)	9, 10	Fast	Pyramidal-shaped. Resistant to salt.
Cedrus atlantica cv. 'Glauca' (blue atlas cedar)	to zone 4	Medium	Pyramidal-shaped. Low maintenance. Stark effect.
Cedrus Deodara (deodar cedar)	7, 8	Slow to Medium	Pyramidal-shaped. Low maintenance.
Ceratonia Siliqua (carob tree)	10	Slow	Globe-shaped. Low maintenance. Disease-free.
Chamaecyparis Lawsoniana (Lawson cypress, Port Orford cedar)	6, 7	Fast	Pyramidal-shaped. Prefers full sun. Sensitive to salt. Prized for many ornamental forms.
Cryptomeria japonica (Japanese cedar)	7, 8	Fast	Pyramidal-shaped. Thrives in fertile, moist soil and clean air.
Cupressus arizonica (Arizona cypress)	6, 7, 8, 9	Medium to Slow	Pyramidal-shaped.
Cupressus sempervirens (Italian cypress)	8, 9	Medium to Slow	Pyramidal-shaped.
Eucalyptus polyanthemos (red box gum, silver dollar tree, Australian beech)	9, 10	Fast	Globe-shaped.
Eucalyptus rudis (desert gum)	9, 10	Fast	Globe-shaped.

Ficus benjamina (weeping fig, Java fig, weeping Chinese banyan, Benjamin fig, small-leafed rubber plant)	8, 9, 10	Medium	Weeping. Prefers full sun. Pest-resistant. Fruit.
Grevillea robusta (silk oak)	10	Fast	Columnar-shaped. Thrives in full sun or full shade. Decorative street tree. Weak wood. Pest-resistant. Orange flowers.
Magnolia grandiflora (Southern magnolia, bull bay)	7, 8, 9, 10	Medium	Pyramidal-shaped. Prefers full sun. Grows in cities. Low maintenance. Flowers, fruit, distinctive foliage.
Picea Abies cultivars, also known as *Picea excelsa* (Norway spruce)	3, 4, 5, 6	Fast	Pyramidal-shaped. Prefers medium shade. Sensitive to salt. Susceptible to spruce gall aphids, mites. Cones.
Picea glauca cv. 'Densata' (Black Hills spruce, white spruce)	3, 4, 5	Slow	Pyramidal with drooping branchlets. Tolerant of PAN, sulfur dioxide, salt. Susceptible to red spider mites, aphids.
Picea pungens (Colorado blue spruce)	3, 4, 5, 6	Medium	Pyramidal-shaped. Tolerant of ozone, PAN. Sensitive to nitrous oxide. Susceptible to mites, aphids, canker.
Pinus banksiana (jackpine, gray pine, scrub pine)	2, 3, 4, 5, 6, 7, 8	Medium	Prefers full sun. Irregular-shaped. Sensitive to ozone. Tolerant of sulfur.
Pinus canariensis (Canary Island pine)	8, 9, 10	Fast	Pyramidal-shaped.
Pinus caribaea (slash pine, swamp pine, Cuban pine)	9, 10	Fast	Pyramidal-shaped.
Pinus nigra subsp. *Laricio* (black pine, Austrian pine)	4, 5, 6, 7, 8	Medium	Pyramidal-shaped. Prefers full sun. Grows in cities. Sensitive to salt, sulfur dioxide. Water heavily at first. Susceptible to pine needle scale.
Pinus ponderosa var. *scopulorium* (Rocky Mountain yellow pine)	6, 7, 8, 9	Medium	Pyramidal-shaped. Prefers full sun. Sensitive to sulfur dioxide, fluoride, ozone.
Pinus resinosa (red pine, Norway pine)	2, 3, 4, 5, 6, 7, 8	Medium	Pyramidal-shaped. Needs full sun. Tolerant of ozone. Susceptible to pine needle scale.
Pinus Strobus (eastern white pine)	3, 4, 5, 6, 7	Fast	Pyramidal-shaped with horizontal branching. Prefers full sun to medium shade. Sensitive to salt, ozone, sodium dioxide. Water heavily at first. Susceptible to white pine weevil.

Name	Hardiness Zones	Growth Rate	Comments
Pinus sylvestris (Scotch pine, Scots pine)	3, 4, 5, 6	Fast	Pyramidal-shaped. Prefers full sun. Sensitive to salt, ozone. Weak wood. Susceptible to pine needle scale. Red bark.
Pinus Thunbergiana (Japanese black pine)	to zone 5	Slow	Irregular-shaped. Good seashore evergreen. Low maintenance.
Pseudotsuga Menziesii, also known as *Pseudotsuga taxifolia, Pseudotsuga Douglasii* (Douglas fir)	to zone 4	Fast	Pyramidal-shaped. Prefers full sun. Tolerant of PAN, ozone. Sensitive to sulfur dioxide. Low maintenance. Weak wood. Cones.
Quercus agrifolia (California live oak, California field oak)	9	Slow to Medium	Horizontal branching. Sensitive to ozone. Prefers semiarid conditions.
Quercus Suber (cork oak)	8, 9, 10	Medium	Globe-shaped. Thick bark offers commercial cork. Sensitive to ozone.
Quercus virginiana (live oak, southern live oak)	7, 8, 9, 10	Rapid	Rounded in form. Prefers full sun. Sensitive to ozone. Tolerates salt spray. Low maintenance. Excellent shade or street tree.
Tsuga canadensis (Canadian hemlock)	3, 4, 5, 6, 7, 8	Medium	Pyramidal-shaped. Prefers medium shade. Does not thrive in city. Sensitive to salt. Must be watered. Susceptible to spruce mites.
Ulmus parvifolia, also known as *Ulmus sempervirens* (Chinese evergreen elm)	6, 7, 8	Fast	Globe-shaped. Sensitive ozone, sulfur dioxide, 2-4-D. Tolerant of salt. Less susceptible to Dutch elm disease.

EVERGREEN TREES UNDER THIRTY-FIVE FEET

Name	Hardiness Zones	Growth Rate	Comments
Agonis flexuosa (willow myrtle)	9, 10	Medium	White flowers.
Bauhinia Blakeana (Hong Kong orchid tree)	9, 10	Medium	Columnar-shaped. Showy pink flowers.
Brassaia actinophylla, also known as *Schefflera actinophylla* (Australia umbrella tree, Queensland umbrella tree, octopus tree)	9, 10	Medium	Prefers full sun. Red flowers.

Callistemon viminalis (weeping bottlebrush)	9, 10	Medium	Weeping habit. Needs pruning. Red flowers.
Cephalotaxus Harringtonia, also known as *Cephalotaxus drupacea* (Japanese plum yew, Harrington plum yew)	to zone 6	Medium	Male cones in clusters.
Cinnamomum Camphora (camphor tree)	8, 9, 10	Medium	Good for row plantings along street. Insect-resistant. Yellow flowers.
Citrus species (orange, lemon, lime, and grapefruit trees)	10	Variable	Globe-shaped. Prefers full sun. Sensitive to ozone, nitrous oxide, fluoride. Tolerant of sulfur dioxide. Fruit, fragrant flowers.
Litchi chinensis (lychee, litchi nut)	10	Medium	Requires abundant moisture. Edible fresh or dried fruit.
Magnolia virginiana also known as *Magnolia glauca* (sweet bay)	5, 6, 7, 8, 9	Slow to Medium	Globe-shaped. Grows in shade. Weak wood. White flowers.
Manilkara Zapota, also known as *Achras sapota* (saspodilla, nispero, chicozapote)	10	Medium	Attractive ornamental. Produces chicle, original base for chewing gum. Fruit.
Olea europaea (common olive)	9, 10	Slow	Globe-shaped. Prefers full sun. Low maintenance. Fruit.
Picea abies cultivars (Norway spruce)	2, 3, 4, 5, 6	Fast	Pyramidal-shaped. Prefers medium shade. Semisensitive to salt. Susceptible to spruce gall aphids, mites.
Pinus halepensis (Aleppo pine)	8, 9, 10	Medium	Pyramidal-shaped. Resistant to salt. Yields turpentine.
Pittosporum phillyraeoides (weeping pittosporum, narrow-leafed pittosporum)	9, 10	Medium	Weeping. Sensitive to fluoride, nitrous oxide. Flowers.
Pittosporum rhombifolium (diamond leaf pittosporum, Queensland pittosporum)	9, 10	Medium	Oval-shaped. Sensitive to nitrous oxide, fluoride. Yellow fruits, ornamental flowers.
Podocarpus macrophyllus (Yew podocarpus, southern yew, Japanese yew)	8, 9, 10	Medium	Grows in shade.

Name	Hardiness Zones	Growth Rate	Comments
Psidium littorale var. *longipes* (strawberry guava)	10	Medium	Sensitive to salt. White flowers, fruit.
Pyrus Kawakamii (evergreen pear)	9, 10	Medium	Semisensitive to salt. Flowers, distinctive foliage.
Schinus terebinthifolius (Brazilian pepper tree)	10	Fast	Weeping. Very ornamental. Much used for wreaths at Christmas. Red berries, flowers.
Sciadopitys verticillata (umbrella pine)	to zone 6	Slow	Horizontal branching, pyramidal-shaped. Prefers shade. Sensitive to pollution.
Tsuga canadensis (Canada hemlock)	3, 4, 5, 6, 7, 8	Medium	Pyramidal-shaped. Prefers shade. Sensitive to salt. Does not thrive in cities.
Tsuga caroliniana (Carolina hemlock)	to zone 4	Medium	Pyramidal-shaped. Prefers shade. Dense foliage. Grows in cities. Susceptible to spruce mites.
Yucca brevifolia (Joshua tree)	5, 6, 7, 8, 9	Slow to Medium	Irregular-shaped. Requires full sun. Good drainage, sandy loam, and open exposure are preferred. Flowers.

PALM TREES OVER THIRTY-FIVE FEET

Name	Hardiness Zones	Growth Rate	Comments
Arecastrum Romanzoffianum, also known as *Cocos plumosa* (Queen palm)	9, 10	Fast	Low maintenance.
Heterospathe elata (Sagisi palm)	10	Fast	Red-brown leaves.
Veitchia Winin	10	Fast	Leaves growing nine feet long.
Washingtonia filifera (Washington palm, desert fan, petticoat palm)	9, 10	Fast	"Petticoat" of hanging leaves at trunk. Must be watered.
Washingtonia robusta (Mexican Washington palm, thread palm.	9, 10	Fast	Trunk clothed in ragged shag. Tolerant of salt. Must be watered. Vulnerable to insects.

PALM TREES UNDER THIRTY-FIVE FEET

Name	Hardiness Zones	Growth Rate	Comments
Acoelorraphe Wrightii (Everglade palm)	9, 10	Slow	Useful cluster palm for landscapes in full sun or shade, with roots in water or in dry areas of sand or limestone with a high water table.
Brahea dulcis (rock palm)	10	Slow	Leaves grow to five feet. Susceptible to palm weevil.
Chamaerops humilis (European fan palm, Mediterranean fan palm)	9, 10	Slow	One of hardier palms. Forms clumps. Tolerant of salt. Must be watered. Weak wood.
Chrysalidocarpus lutescens, also known as *Areca lutescens* (butterfly palm, yellow palm, bamboo palm, Areca palm, cane palm)	9, 10	Medium to Fast	Globe-shaped. White fragrant flowers.
Livistona chinensis (Chinese fountain palm, Chinese fan palm)	9, 10	Fast	Globe-shaped. One of hardier palms.
Phoenix reclinata (Senegal date palm)	9, 10	Medium to Slow	Useful for large hedges and screens because of attractive clustering habit. Tolerant of salt.
Phoenix Roebelenii (dwarf date palm, pigmy date palm)	9, 10	Slow	Elegant pot plant. Prefers medium shade. Tolerant of salt.
Ptychosperma Macarthurii (Macarthur palm)	10	Fast	Columnar-shaped. Prefers medium shade. Suited to small garden or tub culture. White flowers.
Rhapidophyllum hystrix (needle palm, porcupine palm, blue palmetto)	7, 8, 9, 10	Slow	Hardiest of palms, withstanding −6°F. Prefers full shade to medium sun. Must be watered.
Rhapis excelsa, also known as *Rhapis flabelliformis* (lady palm)	9, 10	Slow	Grows in clumps or hedges. Prefers full sun to medium shade.
Sabal Etonia (scrub palmetto)	9, 10	Slow	Trunk mostly subterranean. Tolerant of salt.
Sabel Palmetto (cabbage palmetto, blue palmetto)	9, 10	Slow	Tolerant of salt. Low maintenance.

Name	Hardiness Zones	Growth Rate	Comments
Trachycarpus Fortunei, also known as *Trachycarpus excelsus, Chamaerops excelsa* (windmill palm, hemp palm)	8, 9, 10	Slow	High, globe-shaped. Trunk covered with black, hairlike fiber. Tolerant of salt. Pest-free. White to yellow flowers.

DECIDUOUS WINDBREAKS, HEDGES, OR BORDERS

Name	Hardiness Zones	Growth Rate	Comments
Berberis Thunbergii (Japanese barberry)	5, 6, 7, 8, 9	Fast	Grows in shade. Tolerant of 2-4-D. Should be pruned. Bright-red berries, fall color.
Calycanthus floridus (strawberry shrub, Carolina allspice)	5, 6, 7	Medium	Large, fragrant flowers.
Caragana arborescens (Siberian pea tree)	2, 3, 4, 5	Medium	Requires full sun, sandy soil. Tolerant of salt. Showy, yellow flowers.
Caryopteris species (bluebeard)	3, 4, 5, 6, 7, 8	Medium	Prefers sun. Needs pruning. Attractive flowers.
Chaenomeles species, also known as *Cydonia* (flowering quince)	4, 5, 6, 7, 8, 9	Medium	Attractive ornamental. Sensitive to salt. Needs pruning. Susceptible to fire blight, borers, scale. Flowers.
Cotoneaster divaricatus (spreading cotoneaster)	5, 6, 7, 8	Medium	Pink flowers, red fruit.
Elaeagnus angustifolia (wild olive, Russian olive, silverberry)	3, 4, 5, 6, 7, 8, 9	Fast	Prefers full sun. Tolerant of fluoride, chloride, salt. Grows in cities. Pest-free. Distinctive foliage.
Elaeagnus commutata (silverberry)	to zone 2	Medium	Fragrant flowers, fruit.
Elaeagnus multiflora, also known as *Elaeagnus longipes* (cherry elaeagnus)	to zone 5	Medium	Prefers well-drained soil and sunny location. Fragrant flowers, orange fruit.
Euonymus alata cv. 'Compacta' (dwarf winged bush, dwarf burning bush)	5, 6, 7, 8	Fast	Prefers full sun. Grows in cities. Red fall foliage.

Forsythia species (forsythia, golden bells)	5, 6, 7, 8	Fast	Requires full sun. Grows in cities. Needs pruning. Yellow flowers.
Hydrangea macrophylla, also known as *Hydrangea hortensis* (common big leaf hydrangea, house hydrangea, French hydrangea, hortensia)	6, 7, 8, 9, 10	Medium	Blooms in full sun or partial shade. Needs pruning.
Kolkwitzia amabilis (beauty bush)	6, 7, 8, 9	Medium	Needs full sun. Sensitive to salt. Flowers.
Ligustrum amurense (Amur privet)	4, 5, 6, 7, 8, 9, 10	Fast	Sensitive to salt, fluoride, nitrous oxide. Tolerant of ozone.
Ligustrum ovalifolium (California privet)	6, 7, 8, 9, 10	Fast	Sensitive to salt, fluoride, nitrous oxide.
Ligustrum vulgare (prim privet, common privet)	5, 6	Fast	Sensitive to salt, fluoride, nitrous oxide.
Lonicera species (honeysuckle)	4, 5, 6, 7, 8, 9	Fast	Prefers sun to medium shade. Tolerant of ozone, salt. Fragrant flowers.
Prunus tomentosa (Manchu or Nanking cherry)	3, 4, 5	Medium	Semisensitive to fluoride. One of earliest flowering shrubs. Susceptible to borers, blight scale. Red tasty fruit, white flowers.
Salix discolor (pussy willow)	to zone 2	Fast	Sensitive to sulfur dioxide, ozone. Tolerant of salt.
Spiraea species (spirea, bridal wreath)	5, 6, 7, 8, 9	Fast	Thrives in sun or shade. Requires plenty moisture. Sensitive to salt. White flowers.
Symphoricarpos albus var. *laevigatus,* also known as *Symphoricarpos racemosus* (snowberry)	to zone 3	Medium	Prefers full sun. Tolerant of ozone. Susceptible to disease. Ornamental fruits, pink flowers.
Symphoricarpos orbiculatus (Indian current, coralberry)	to zone 3	Medium	White flowers. Coral red fruit.
Syringa vulgaris cultivars (lilacs)	3, 4, 5, 6, 7	Medium	Prefers full sun. Tolerant of salt, 2-4-D. Sensitive to ozone. Susceptible to lilac borer. Fragrant flowers.
Tamarix parviflora (Tamarisk, salt cedar)	8, 9, 10	Medium	Prefers sun. Tolerant of salt. Pink flowers.
Vitex Agnus-castus (chaste tree, hemptree, wild pepper)	7, 8, 9, 10	Medium	Prefers sun. Aromatic shrub. Must be pruned. Lavender flowers.

| Weigela species (weigela) | 6, 7 | Medium | Thrives in sun to medium shade. Sensitive to 2-4-D. Low maintenance. Showy flowers. |

EVERGREEN WINDBREAKS, HEDGES, OR BORDERS

Name	Hardiness Zones	Growth Rate	Comments
Berberis Julianae (wintergreen barberry)	5, 6, 7, 8	Medium	Thrives in medium sun to medium shade. Sensitive to salt. Yellow flowers.
Berberis X mentorensis (Mentor barberry)	5, 6, 7, 8	Medium	Sensitive to salt. Red berries
Buxus microphylla japonica (Japanese littleleaf boxwood)	6, 7, 8, 9	Slow	Thrives in medium shade. Yellow flowers.
Buxus sempervirens (common boxwood)	6, 7, 8, 9	Slow	Grows in shade. Needs special care. Susceptible to leaf miner.
Camellia japonica (common camellia)	7, 8, 9, 10	Slow	Grows in medium shade. Sensitive to fluoride. Must be fertilized. More than 2,000 cultivars. Beautiful flowers.
Camellia Sasanqua (sasanqua camellia)	7, 8, 9, 10	Medium	Needs full sun. Sensitive to fluoride. Must be fertilized. White to red flowers.
Coccoloba Uvifera (sea grape, shore grape)	9, 10	Slow	Does best in rich, sandy soil. Tolerant of salt. Fruit and flowers.
Codiaeum, variegatum cultivars (croton)	9, 10	Medium	Grows best in full sun. Tolerant of fluoride, nitrous oxide. White flowers, bright foliage.
Cotoneaster lacteus (Parney's red clusterberry)	to zone 6	Medium	Prefers full sun.
Elaeagnus pungens (thorny elaeagnus, silverberry)	7, 8, 9, 10	Medium	Grows in shade. Silvery foliage.
Eriobotrya japonica (loquat, Japanese plum)	8, 9, 10	Medium	Sensitive to salt. Bronze foliage, flowers, fruit.
Eugenia foetida (Spanish stopper)	9, 10	Medium	Easily propagated. White flowers.
Euonymus japonica (evergreen euonymus, spindle tree)	6, 7, 8, 9	Medium	Many cultivars. Fruit, flowers.

Feijoa Sellowiana (pineapple guava)	9, 10	Medium	Needs pruning. Edible fruit.
Gardenia jasminoides (gardenia, cape jasmine)	8, 9, 10	Medium	Needs medium shade. Sensitive to fluoride, nitrous oxide. Fragrant flowers.
Hibiscus Rosa-sinensis (Chinese hibiscus, rose of China)	9, 10	Fast	Sensitive to fluoride, nitrous oxide. Flowers.
Ilex opaca cultivars (American holly)	6, 7, 8, 9	Variable	Sensitive to salt. Tolerant of ozone. Red fruit.
Ilex vomitoria (yaupon, cassina)	7, 8, 9	Medium	Stiffly branched. Dried leaves give bitter tea.
Ixora coccinea (flame-of-the-woods, jungle geranium, ixora)	9, 10	Medium	Sensitive to fluoride, nitrous oxide. Bright colored flowers, attractive foliage.
Jasminum humile cv. 'Revolutum' (Italian jasmine)	to zone 7	Fast	Needs sun. Large and fragrant flowers.
Juniperus chinensis cultivars (Chinese juniper)	4, 5, 6, 7, 8, 9, 10	Slow	Needs full sun. Tolerant of fluoride, sulfur dioxide. Susceptible to juniper scale, mites. Fruits.
Juniperus scopulorum cultivars (Rocky Mountain juniper, western red cedar)	to zone 4	Medium	Needs full sun. Tolerant of fluoride, sulfur dioxide. Susceptible to red spider mites. Fruit.
Juniperus virginiana cultivars (eastern red cedar)	to zone 3	Variable	Needs full sun. Tolerant of fluoride, sulfur dioxide. Susceptible to red spider mites. Fruit.
Kalmia latifolia (mountain laurel, calico bush)	4, 5, 6, 7, 8, 9, 10	Medium	Thrives in full shade. Tolerant of ozone. Susceptible to lace bug. Pink and white flowers.
Ligustrum japonicum cultivars (Japanese privet, wax leaf privet)	7, 8, 9, 10	Medium	Semisensitive to fluoride, nitrous oxide.
Lonicera nitida (box honeysuckle)	to zone 7	Medium	Thrives in sun to medium shade. Tolerant of ozone, salt. Flowers.
Myrtus communis cultivars (myrtle, Greek myrtle)	9, 10	Medium	Needs pruning. Berries, fragrant, white flowers.
Nerium Oleander (oleander, rose bay)	7, 8, 9, 10	Fast	Needs full sun. Sensitive to fluoride, nitrous oxide. Needs some watering. All plant parts are very poisonous. Many colors, flowers.

Opuntia littoralis (prickly pear, tuna cactus)	6, 7, 8, 9, 10	Medium	Needs sun. Easily propagated from cuttings placed directly in sandy, well-drained soil. Requires little water. Showy flowers.
Osmanthus heterophyllus, also known as *Osmanthus ilicifolius* (holly osmanthus, holly olive, false holly)	7, 8, 9, 10	Slow to Medium	Thrives in medium shade.
Photinia serrulata (Chinese photinia)	7, 8, 9, 10	Medium	Needs sun. Bronze foliage, red fruit.
Pieris japonica (Japanese andromeda, lily-of-the-valley bush)	6, 7, 8, 9	Slow	Needs medium shade. White flowers.
Pittosporum Tobira (Japanese pittosporum)	8, 9, 10	Medium	Semisensitive to fluoride, nitrous oxide. Susceptible to lace bug, leaf spot. Fragrant flowers. Useful for seaside plantings.
Prunus caroliniana (Carolina cherry laurel, wild orange, mock orange)	7, 8, 9, 10	Medium	Semisensitive to fluoride. Attractive foliage.
Prunus Laurocerasus cultivars (cherry laurel, English laurel)	7, 8, 9	variable	Thrives in medium shade. Susceptible to blight, borer, scale. Orange fruit.
Pyracantha coccinea (fire thorn)	6, 7, 8, 9, 10	Medium	Tolerant of salt. Susceptible to borers, scale. Berries, flowers.
Taxus cuspidata (Japanese yew)	5, 6, 7, 8, 9	Slow	Thrives in sun or shade. Semisensitive to 2-4-D. Susceptible to taxus weevil. Many cultivars.
Taxus X media cultivars (yew)	to zone 5	Slow	Branches olive green and spreading. Otherwise similar to *T. cuspidata*.
Thevetia peruviana, also known as *Thevetia nereifolia* (yellow oleander, bestill tree)	9, 10	Medium	Thrives in rich, sandy soil. Yellow fragrant flowers.
Thuja occidentalis (American arborvitae, Douglas arborvitae, white cedar)	3, 4, 5, 6, 7, 8, 9	Medium	Tolerant of sulfur dioxide, ozone, chloride. Sensitive to ethylene. Susceptible to leaf miner, bagworm. Gold fall foliage.
Viburnum odoratissimum (sweet viburnum)	8, 9, 10	Variable	White, fragrant flowers.
Viburnum rhytidophyllum (leatherleaf viburnum)	6, 7, 8	Slow	Unusual foliage. Fruits.

| Viburnum Tinus (laurustinus) | to zone 7 | Medium | White flowers. |

DECIDUOUS SHRUBS

Name	Hardiness Zones	Growth Rate	Comments
Buddleia Davidii (orange eye butterfly bush, summer lilac)	5, 6, 7	Medium	Thrives in sun. Needs some pruning. Orange, fragrant flowers.
Calycanthus floridus (Carolina allspice, pineapple shrub, strawberry shrub)	to zone 5	Medium	Large, fragrant, reddish-brown flowers.
Cornus alba cv. 'Sibirica' (Siberian dogwood)	3, 4	Medium to Fast	Sensitive to 2-4-D. Must be pruned. Flowers, red stems
Cornus mas (cornelian cherry, sorbet)	to zone 5	Medium	Thrives in full sun or full shade. Tolerant of fluoride. Sensitive to 2-4-D. Yellow flowers, red fruit.
Cotinus Coggygria (smokebush)	to zone 5	Medium	Leaves purplish. Pest-resistant.
Cotoneaster apiculatus (cranberry cotoneaster)	to zone 5	Medium	Prefers sunny location in well-drained soil. Pink flowers, red fruit.
Cotoneaster divaricatus (spreading cotoneaster)	5, 6, 7, 8	Medium	Pink flowers, red fruit.
Crataegus monogyna (English hawthorn)	4, 5, 6, 7, 8	Slow	Sensitive to salt. Flowers.
Cytisus species (broom)	5, 6, 7, 8, 9, 10	Slow	Needs sun. Grows in cities. Good fall color, flowers.
Daphne Mezereum (February daphne)	4, 5, 6, 7, 8	Slow	Thrives in medium shade. Susceptible to twig blight. Pink fragrant flowers.
Deutzia species (deutzia)	5, 6, 7, 8	Medium	Needs sun. Sensitive to fluoride. White flowers.
Enkianthus campanulatus (redvein enkianthus, Chinese bellflower)	5, 6, 7	Medium	Thrives in full sun to medium shade. Member of heath family. Yellow flowers, good fall color.
Fuchsia species (lady's eardrops)	to zone 6	Medium	Pendulous, colorful summer flowers.
Fouquieria splendens (Ocotillo, coach whip, vine cactus)	7, 8, 9, 10	Medium	Needs sun. Protected by law. Scarlet flowers.

Hamamelis virginiana (witch hazel)	to zone 5	Fast	Grows in shade. Tolerant of salt. Susceptible to horned gall. Yellow, fragrant flowers.
Hibiscus syriacus (rose of Sharon, shrub althea)	5, 6, 7, 8, 9, 10	Medium	Needs full sun. Hardy species. Should not be pruned. Small pinkish, mauve flowers.
Hydrangea macrophylla, also called *Hydrangea hortensis* (common big leaf hydrangea, house hydrangea)	to zone 6	Medium to Fast	Showy flowers. Requires rich, porous soil. Prefers full sun.
Hydrangea paniculata cv. 'Grandiflora' (peegee hydrangea)	4, 5, 6, 7	Medium	White flowers.
Paeonia suffruticosa (tree peony)	to zone 5	Medium	Needs full sun to medium shade. Showy flowers.
Parkinsonia aculeata (Jerusalem thorn, Mexican palo verde)	10	Medium	Yellow flowers.
Philadelphus species (mock orange)	4, 5, 6, 7, 8, 9	Fast	Thrives in sun or shade. Tolerant of salt. Sensitive to ozone. Needs some pruning. Susceptible to leaf miner. White flowers.
Potentilla fruticosa (bush cinquefoil)	2, 3, 4, 5, 6, 7, 8, 9	Fast	Grows in shade. Yellow flowers, good fall color.
Prunus glandulosa (flowering almond)	to zone 4	Medium	Sensitive to salt. Susceptible to borers, tent caterpillars. White or pink flowers.
Rhododendron calendulaceum, also known as *Azalea calendulacea* (flame azalea)	5, 6, 7, 8, 9	Medium	Needs sun to medium shade. Sensitive to salt, ozone. Flowers.
Rhododendron mucronulatum (Korean rhododendron)	5, 6, 7, 8, 9	Medium	Needs sun to medium shade. Sensitive to salt, ozone. Flowers.
Rhododendron Schlippenbachii, also known as *Azalea schlippenbachii* (Royal azalea)	5, 6, 7, 8, 9	Medium	Needs sun to medium shade. Sensitive to salt, ozone. Flowers.
Rosa rugosa (rugosa rose, Japanese rose)	2, 3, 4, 5, 6, 7, 8	Medium	Sensitive to fluoride, salt. Tolerant of sulfur dioxide. Needs pruning. Pink or white flowers.
Spiraea latifolia (meadowsweet)	5, 6, 7, 8, 9	Fast	Thrives in sun or shade. Sensitive to salt.

Name	Hardiness Zones	Growth Rate	Comments
Tamarix ramosissima, also known as *Tamarix odessana* (Odessa tamarisk, five stamen tamarisk)	8, 9, 10	Medium	Tolerant of salt. Useful along coast and in arid Southwest.
Viburnum X carcephalum (fragrant snowball, autumn foliage brilliant)	5, 6, 7, 8	Medium	Grows in medium shade. Good fall color, fragrant flowers.
Viburnum plicatum, also known as *Viburnum tomentosum* (Japanese snowball)	5, 6, 7, 8	Medium	Red fall foliage, white flowers.
Viburnum trilobum, also known as *Viburnum americanum* (American cranberry bush)	to zone 2	Medium	White flowers, scarlet fruit.

EVERGREEN SHRUBS

Name	Hardiness Zones	Growth Rate	Comments
Abelia X grandiflora (glossy abelia)	6, 7, 8, 9, 10	Medium	Grows in shade. Flowers.
Agave attenuata (foxtail agave, century plant)	9, 10	Slow	Needs sun. Flowers bloom every seven to fifteen years.
Agave Vilmoriniania (century plant)	9, 10	Slow	Needs sun. Erect twenty-foot column of flowers. Dies after flowering, producing hundreds of young plants.
Atriplex species (saltbush, orach)	to zone 6	Variable	Often occur in saline soils. Grown as ornamentals or for forage in desert regions.
Aucuba japonica (Japanese aucuba, Japanese laurel)	8, 9, 10	Medium	Thrives in partly shaded location in moist, well-drained soil. Fruit.
Brunfelsia pauciflora calycina (yesterday, today, and tomorrow)	9, 10	Medium	Needs full sun to medium shade. Flowers.
Callistemon citrinus, also known as *Callistemon lanceolatus* (crimson bottlebrush)	9, 10	Medium	Needs sun. Needs heavy pruning. Crimson flowers.

Carissa grandiflora (natal plum)	9, 10	Fast	Needs full sun. Tolerant of salt. Edible fruit.
Ceanothus species (deciduous or evergreen) (ceanothus, California lilac, wild lilac)	8, 9, 10	Medium to Fast	Needs full sun. Low maintenance. Blue or white flowers.
Chamaecyparis obtusa (Hinoki false cypress)	5, 6, 7	Slow	Needs medium shade.
Chamaecyparis pisifera (Sawara false cypress)	to zone 5	Slow	Needs medium shade.
Cotoneaster dammeri, also known as *Cotoneaster humifusus* (bearberry cotoneaster)	5, 6, 7, 8, 9, 10	Slow to Medium	Thrives in full sun or full shade. Susceptible to borers, scale. White flowers, scarlet berries.
Cotoneaster horizontalis (rock spray, rock cotoneaster)	4, 5, 6, 7, 8	Medium	Needs full sun to full shade. Susceptible to borers, scale. Scarlet berries.
Cotoneaster lacteus (cotoneaster)	to zone 6	Medium	White flowers in large clusters. Showy fruits.
Eriogonum giganteum St. Catherine's lace	9, 10	Medium	Leaves in rosettes. White-woolly flowers. Requires sun and well-drained soil.
Euonymus Fortunei (winter creeper)	5, 6, 7, 8, 9	Slow to Medium	Thrives in full sun or full shade. Needs some trimming and weeding.
Euphorbia pulcherrima (poinsettia)	8, 9, 10	Fast	Needs sun to partial shade. Sensitive to 2-4-D, ozone, sulfur dioxide. Attractive flowers. Many cultivars.
Fatsia japonica, also known as *Aralia japonica*, *Aralia sieboldii* (Japanese fatsia, paper plant)	8, 9, 10	Medium	Bold foliage.
Ilex X altaclarensis cv. 'Wilsonii' (Wilson holly)	6, 7, 8, 9	Medium to Fast	Vigorous tree with leathery leaves. Attractive fruit.
Ilex Aquifolium cultivars (English holly)	6, 7, 8, 9	Slow	Prefers medium shade. Sensitive to sulfur dioxide. Semisensitive to fluoride. Red fruit.
Ilex Cassine (dahoon, dahoon holly)	7, 8, 9, 10	Medium	Flowers, fruit.
Ilex cornuta (Chinese holly)	7, 8, 9, 10	Medium	Tolerant of chloride, mercury.

Ilex crenata cultivars (Japanese holly)	6, 7, 8, 9	Medium	Needs medium shade. Sensitive to ethylene.
Juniperus communis (common juniper)	to zone 2	Slow	Prefers full sun. Tolerant of fluoride, sulfur dioxide. Susceptible to insect pests. Fruit.
Juniperus conferta (shore juniper)	5, 6, 7, 8, 9, 10	Medium	Thrives in full sun or medium shade. Tolerant of salt.
Juniperus procumbens (Japanese garden juniper)	to zone 2	Slow	Prefers full sun. Tolerant of fluoride, sulfur dioxide.
Juniperus sabina (savin juniper)	5, 6, 7, 8, 9, 10	Medium	Thrives in full sun or medium shade. Tolerant of fluoride, sulfur dioxide. Must remove dead branches. Susceptible to juniper twig blight.
Justicia Brandegeana, also known as *Beloperone guttata* (shrimp plant)	8, 9, 10	Fast	Prefers medium shade. Must be pruned. Attractive, abundant flowers.
Laurus nobilis (sweet bay)	8, 9, 10	Medium	Aromatic.
Lemaireocereus Thurberi (organpipe cactus)	8, 9, 10	Medium	Needs sun. White flowers, red fruit.
Leptospermum scoparium (tea tree)	9, 10	Medium to Fast	Needs medium shade. White, pink flowers.
Leucothoe Fontanesiana, also known as *Leucothoe Catesbaei* (drooping leucothoe)	5, 6, 7, 8, 9	Medium to Slow	Prefers medium shade. Needs some pruning. White flowers, red fall color.
Mahonia Aquifolium (Oregon holly grape)	5, 6, 7, 8, 9	Medium	Prefers medium shade. Susceptible to foliar burn. Flowers, edible fruit.
Myrtis communis (Greek myrtle)	9	Medium	Dense foliage, strongly scented when crushed.
Nandina domestica (nandina, Chinese sacred bamboo)	7, 8, 9, 10	Medium	Thrives in sun or medium shade. Red fall and winter foliage.
Nolina Parryi (beargrass)	8, 9, 10	Medium	Needs sun. Should be watered. Flowers.
Pieris floribunda (mountain andromeda)	4, 5, 6, 7, 8, 9	Medium	Requires moist peaty or sandy soil and partial shade. Flowers.
Pinus aristata (bristlecone pine, hickory pine)	to zone 5	Medium	Prefers full sun. Sensitive to smog.
Pinus Mugo, also known as *Pinus montana* (mugo pine, Swiss mountain pine)	3, 4, 5, 6, 7, 8	Slow	Thrives in full sun to medium shade. Tolerant of sulphur dioxide. Sensitive to fluoride. Susceptible to pine needle scale.

Name	Hardiness Zones	Growth Rate	Comments
Platycladus orientalis (Oriental arborvitae)	to zone 5	Slow	Tolerant of ozone. Susceptible to leaf miner, bugworm.
Rhododendron carolinanum (carolina rhododendron)	5, 6, 7, 8, 9	Medium	Prefers medium shade. Sensitive to salt, ozone. Pink flowers.
Rhododendrum indicum cultivars (Indian azalea)	5, 6, 7, 8, 9	Medium	Thrives in sun or medium shade. Sensitive to ozone, salt. Flowers.
Rhododendron maximum (rosebay rhododendron, great laurel)	5, 6, 7, 8, 9	Medium	Thrives in sun to medium shade. Sensitive to ozone, salt. Flowers.
Skimmia japonica (Japanese skimmia)	8, 9	Medium	Thrives in sun or shade. Fragrant flowers, attractive fruit.
Spartium junceum (Spanish broom)	8, 9, 10	Fast	Needs full sun. Tolerates salt. Needs pruning. Fragrant yellow flowers.
Taxus baccata (English yew)	4, 5, 6, 7	Slow	Thrives in sun or shade. Sensitive to salt. Susceptible to taxus weevil.
Tetrapanax papyriferus, also known as *Fatsia papyrifera* (rice paper plant)	8, 9, 10	Medium	Source of rice paper.
Tibouchina Urvilleana, also known as *Tibouchina semidecandra* and *Pleroma grandiflora* (glory bush, princess flower)	8, 9, 10	Medium	Thrives in full sun or medium shade. Purple flowers.
Yucca Whipplei (candle of the Lord)	8, 9, 10	Slow	Requires sun. Extremely persistent after fires, sprouts leaves. Spectacular blooms.

DECIDUOUS VINES

Name	Hardiness Zones	Growth Rate	Comments
Actinidia arguta (bower actinidia, tara vine)	5, 6, 7, 8, 9, 10	Fast	Thrives in full sun or medium shade. Fruits, fragrant flowers.
Actinidia chinensis (chinese actinidia, kiwi fruit)	7, 8, 9, 10	Fast	Thrives in full sun or medium shade. Needs some support. Fruits.
Antigonon leptopus (coral vine)	9, 10	Fast	Needs full sun. Must prune dead sections. Flowers.
Campsis X Tagliabuana (trumpet vine)	5, 6, 7, 8, 9, 10	Fast	Needs full sun. Flowers.

Celastrus scandens (American bittersweet)	3, 4, 5, 6, 7, 8	Fast	Thrives in full sun or medium shade. Needs pruning. Fruits.
Clematis hybrids (hybrid clematis)	6, 7, 8, 9, 10	Fast to Medium	Thrives in full sun or medium shade. Needs some pruning. Showy flowers.
Clematis montana (pink anenome clematis)	6, 7, 8, 9, 10	Fast to Medium	Needs full sun to medium shade. Needs some pruning. Flowers.
Dolichos Lablab (hyacinth bean)	7, 8	Fast	Thrives in full sun to medium shade. Pest-free. Flowers.
Humulus japonicus, also known as *Humulus scandens* (Japanese hop)	3, 4, 5, 6, 7, 8, 9, 10	Fast	Thrives in full sun to medium shade.
Hydrangea anomala subsp. *petiolaris*, also known as *Hydrangea petiolaris* or *Hydrangea scandens* (climbing hydrangea)	5, 6, 7, 8, 9, 10	Fast	Needs full sun to medium shade. Flowers.
Ipomoea alba, also known as *Ipomoea bona-nox* and *Calonyction aculeatum* (moonflower)	6, 7, 8, 9, 10	Fast	Thrives in full sun to medium shade. Flowers.
Lonicera Heckrottii (goldflame honeysuckle)	5, 6, 7, 8, 9, 10	Fast	Thrives in full sun to medium shade. Needs trimming. White to yellow fragrant flowers.
Lonicera japonica cv. 'Halliana' (Hall's honeysuckle)	4, 5, 6, 7, 8, 9, 10	Fast	Thrives in full sun to medium shade. Tolerant of ozone, salt. Needs trimming. White to yellow fragrant flowers.
Lonicera sempervirens cultivars (trumpet honeysuckle)	4, 5, 6, 7, 8, 9, 10	Fast	Thrives in full sun to medium shade. Tolerant of ozone, salt. Needs trimming. Flowers, fruits.
Lycium halimifolium (matrimony vine)	6, 7, 8, 9, 10	Fast	Prefers full sun. Fruits. Useful for dry, poor soils.
Macfadyena unguis-cati, also known as *Bignonia tweediana* (cat's claw vine)	8, 9, 10	Fast	Needs full sun to medium shade. Needs watering. Flowers.
Parthenocissus quinquefolia, also known as *Ampelopsis quinquefolia* (Virginia creeper)	3, 4, 5, 6, 7, 8, 9, 10	Fast	Thrives in full sun to medium shade. Tolerant of salt. Sensitive to ozone. Colored, fall foliage.
Parthenocissus tricuspidata, also known as *Ampelopsis tricuspidata* (Boston ivy, Japanese creeper)	5, 6, 7, 8, 9, 10	Fast	Thrives in full sun to medium shade. Sensitive to ozone. Needs heavy trimming. Colored fall foliage.

Name	Hardiness Zones	Growth Rate	Comments
Polygonum Aubertii (silver fleece vine, silver lace vine)	5, 6, 7	Fast	Needs full sun. Flowers, fruits.
Pueraria lobata, also known as *Pueraria Thunbergiana* (kudzu)	3, 4, 5, 6, 7, 8, 9, 10	Very Fast	Needs full sun. Grows extremely fast. Flowers.
Vitis coignetiae (glory vine)	5, 6, 7, 8, 9	Fast	Needs full sun. Fruits.
Vitis riparia (riverbank grape)	3, 4, 5, 6, 7, 8, 9	Fast	Needs full sun. Sensitive to ozone, fluoride, sulfur dioxide. Needs pruning, fertilization. Fruits.
Vitis species (grapevine species)	3, 4, 5, 6, 7, 8, 9	Fast	Prefers full sun. Sensitive to ozone, fluoride, sulfur dioxide. Needs pruning, fertilization. Fruits.
Wisteria floribunda cultivars (Japanese wisteria)	6, 7, 8, 9, 10	Fast	Needs full sun. Needs pruning. Pendant clusters of flowers.
Wisteria sinensis, also known as *Wisteria chinensis* (Chinese wisteria)	6, 7, 8, 9, 10	Fast	Needs full sun. Needs pruning. Flowers.

EVERGREEN VINES

Name	Hardiness Zones	Growth Rate	Comments
Akebia quinata (five-leaf akebia)	4, 5, 6, 7, 8, 9, 10	Fast	Thrives in full sun to medium shade. Fragrant flowers (not showy). Half-evergreen.
Bignonia capreolata, also known as *Anisostichus capreolatus, Doxantha capreolata* (cross vine)	to zone 6	Fast	Needs sun. flowers.
Bougainvillea hybrids (bougainvillea)	9, 10	Fast	Needs sun. Sensitive to fluoride, nitrous oxide, ozone. Tolerant of salt. Scarlet or purple flowers.
Euonymus Fortunei (common winter creeper)	6, 7, 8, 9	Medium	Thrives in full sun or full shade. Needs trimming and weeding.
Ficus pumila (creeping fig)	9, 10	Fast to Medium	Thrives in full sun to medium shade.

Gelsemium sempervirens (evening trumpet flower, Carolina jasmine)	9, 10	Medium	Thrives in full sun or medium shade. Must be watered, thinned. Disease free. Flowers. Poisonous.
Hedera canariensis (Algerian ivy)	8, 9, 10	Fast	Needs full sun to medium shade. Trim annually. Water.
Hedera Helix (English ivy)	5, 6, 7, 8, 9, 10	Fast	Thrives in full sun or full shade. Sensitive to salt. Trim annually. Water.
Justicia Brandegeana, also known as Beloperone guttata (shrimp plant)	8, 9, 10	Fast	Thrives in full sun or medium shade. Must be pruned. Flowers.
Lantana montevidensis (lantana)	9, 10	Fast	Needs full sun. Needs cutting and thinning. Fragrant lavender flowers.
Lonicera sempervirens (trumpet honeysuckle)	5, 6, 7, 8, 9, 10	Fast	Thrives in full sun to medium shade. Tolerant of ozone, sale. Needs cutting. Flowers, fruits.
Thunbergia grandiflora (skyflower, blue trumpet vine, clock vine)	8, 9, 10	Fast	Needs full sun. Needs pruning. Susceptible to yellowing. Flowers.
Trachelospermum jasminoides, also known as Rhynchospermum jasminoides (star jasmine, Confederate jasmine)	6, 7, 8, 9, 10	Slow	Needs full sun or medium shade. Sensitive to salt. Needs cutting, feeding, weeding. Fragrant, small white flowers.

GROUND COVERS

Name	Hardiness Zones	Growth Rate	Comments
Aegopodium Podagraria (silver-edge bishop's weed, silver-edge goutweed)	to zone 3	Fast	Thrives in sun or medium shade. Flowers.
Ajuga reptans (bugleweed, carpet bugle)	4, 5, 6, 7, 8, 9, 10	Fast	Thrives in full sun or medium shade. Some feeding, trimming, watering needed. Blue flowers.
Androsace sarmentosa (rock jasmine)	to zone 2	Medium	Must be watered. Flowers.
Antennaria dioica (everlasting, pussy's toes)	2, 3, 4, 5, 6, 7, 8, 9, 10	Medium	Adapted to poor soil. Flowers.

Arctostaphylos uva-ursi (bearberry, kinnikinnick)	3, 4, 5, 6, 7, 8, 9, 10	Slow	Thrives in full sun to medium shade. Needs watering, needs good drainage.
Asparagus Sprengeri (Sprenger asparagus)	9, 10	Slow to Medium	Thrives in full sun or medium shade. Needs feeding, trimming. Fragrant pink flowers, fruits.
Baccharis pilularis (dwarf coyote bush, chaparral broom)	to zone 7	Fast	Thrives in full sun to medium shade. Needs little water, some feeding. Profuse flowers.
Bougainvillea species (bougainvillea)	9, 10	Fast	Needs sun. Sensitive to fluoride, nitrous oxide, ozone. Tolerant of salt. Needs minimal watering. Scarlet, purple, yellow flowers.
Ceanothus gloriosus (Point Reyes ceanothus)	7, 8, 9, 10	Fast to Medium	Needs full sun. Low maintenance. Lavender-blue flowers.
Ceanothus griseus var. *horizontalis* (Carmel creeper)	7, 8, 9, 10	Medium to Fast	Needs full sun. Low maintenance. Blue flowers.
Ceanothus thyrsiflorus var. *repens* (creeping blue blossom)	7, 8, 9, 10	Medium to Fast	Needs full sun. Low maintenance. Blue flowers.
Convolvulus mauritanicus (ground morning glory)	6, 7, 8, 9, 10	Medium to Fast	Needs full sun. Needs light trimming. Lavender-blue flowers.
Dichondra micrantha (dichondra)	10	Medium to Fast	Cultivated as substitute for lawn grass. Creeping herb.
Echinocereus Engelmannii (Hedgehog cactus)	9, 10	Slow	Thrives in sun or medium shade. Plants are not long-lasting. Hot pink flowers.
Euonymus Fortunei (winter creeper)	5, 6, 7, 8	Slow to Medium	Thrives in full sun or full shade. Needs trimming and weeding. Purple foliage in winter.
Hedera Helix (English ivy)	5, 6, 7, 8, 9, 10	Fast	Thrives in full sun or full shade. Sensitive to salt. Trim annually, water. Many cultivars. Berries.
Juniperus chinensis cultivars (Chinese juniper)	4, 5, 6, 7, 8, 9, 10	Slow	Needs full sun. Tolerant of fluoride, sulfur dioxide. Susceptible to juniper scale, mites. Fruit.
Juniperus horizontalis cv. 'Wiltonii' (Wilton carpet juniper)	5, 6, 7, 8, 9, 10	Medium	Needs full sun. Semisensitive to salt. Susceptible to mites. Purple fall foliage.
Juniperus prostrata (creeping juniper)	5, 6, 7, 8, 9, 10	Medium	Prefers full sun. Semisensitive to salt.
Mahonia repens (creeping mahonia, dwarf holly grape, Oregon grape)	3, 4, 5, 6, 7, 8, 9	Slow to Medium	Thrives in medium to full shade. Small yellow flowers, blackfruits.

Ophiopogon japonicus (mondo grass)	7, 8, 9, 10	Slow	Thrives in full sun or full shade. Light-lavender flowers.
Osteospermum fruticosum (trailing African daisy)	9, 10	Medium	Needs full sun. Colorful flowers.
Pachysandra terminalis (Japanese pachysandra)	5, 6, 7, 8	Fast	Thrives in medium or full shade. Keep weeded and watered. Small white flowers, white berries.
Paxistima Canbyi (canby paxistima)	4, 5, 6, 7	Slow to Medium	Thrives in full sun or medium shade.
Pilea microphylla (artillery fern)	8, 9, 10	Medium	Prefers medium shade. Must be watered.
Rosmarinus officinalis cv. 'Prostratus' (dwarf rosemary)	6, 7, 8, 9	Slow	Needs full sun. Tolerant of salt. Needs feeding and thinning out. Light-blue flowers.
Saxifraga species (rock foil)	to zone 2	Fast	Thrives in sun to medium shade. Needs watering. Good for rock gardens.
Sedum species (stonecrop, live-forever)	to zone 2	Fast	Thrives in full sun to medium shade. Succulents found from North Temperate Zone through Tropics.
Thymus praecox subsp. *arcticus* (mother-of-thyme)	to zone 2	Fast	Thrives in sun to medium shade. Low maintenance. Flowers.
Thymus serpyllum (creeping thyme)	to zone 2	Fast	Thrives in full sun to medium shade. Small, purplish-white flowers.
Vinca minor (common periwinkle, trailing myrtle, creeping myrtle)	4, 5, 6, 7, 8, 9, 10	Fast	Thrives in medium to full shade. Needs feeding, watering, cutting. Susceptible to twig blight. Small flowers.
Wedelia trilobata (wedelia)	10	Medium	Yellow flowers.
Zebrina pendula (wandering Jew)	10	Fast	Thrives in sun to medium shade. Purple underside to leaves.

Bibliography

AIA Research Corporation. *Regional Guidelines for Building Passive Energy Conserving Homes.* U.S. Department of Housing and Urban Development in cooperation with the U.S. Department of Energy, November 1978.

American Society of Heating, Refrigerating and Air-Conditioning Engineers: *Handbook of Fundamentals.* Menasha, Wis.: George Banta and Company, 1974.

Aronin, Jeffrey. *Climate and Architecture.* New York: Reinhold, 1953.

Ball, Jeff. *Garden Problem Solver: Vegetables, Fruits, and Herbs.* Emmaus, Penn.: Rodale Press, 1988.

Benson, L. *The Cacti of Areona.* Tucson: University of Arizona Press, 1969.

Calvert, Floyd. *Energy Utilization in Buildings.* Washington, D.C.: University Press of America, 1977.

Cook, Alan. *Pruning Technique.* Brooklyn, N.Y.: Brooklyn Botanical Gardens, 1991.

Cox, Jeff. *Landscaping with Nature: Using Nature's Designs to Plan Your Yard.* Emmaus, Penn.: Rodale Press, 1990.

Cravens, R. H. *Vines.* Alexandria, Va.: Time-Life Books, 1979.

Creasy, Rosalind, *The Complete Book of Edible Landscaping With Food-Bearing Plants and Resource-Saving Techniques.* San Francisco: Sierra Club Books, 1982.

Crockett, J. U. *Landscape Gardening.* Alexandria, Va.: Time-Life Books, 1971.

Crowther, Richard. *Sun, Earth: How to Use Solar and Climatic Energies.* New York: Charles Scribner's Sons, 1978.

Culjat, Boris. *Climate and the Built Environment in the North.* Stockholm: Avdelningen for Arkitektur, KTH, 1975.

Damrosch, Barbara. *Theme Gardens.* New York: Workman Publishing, 1982.

Deering, Robert B. "Effect of Living Shade on House Temperatures." *Journal of Forestry*, Vol. 54, 1956.

Ellefson, Connie; Stephens, Tom; and Welsh, Doug. *Xeriscape Gardening: Water Conservation for the American Landscape.* New York: Macmillan, 1992.

Ellis, Barbara, ed. *Rodale's Illustrated Encyclopedia of Gardening and Landscaping.* Emmaus, Penn.: Rodale Press, 1990.

Erskine, Ralph. "The Challenge of the High Latitudes." *RAIC Journal*, January 1964.

Erley, Duncan, and Jaffe, Martin. *Site Planning for Solar Access: A Guidebook for Residential Developers.* Chicago: American Planning Association.

Federer, C. A. "Trees and Forests in Urbanized Environment." Amherst, Mass.: Cooperative Extension Service, University of Massachusetts, U.S. Department of Agriculture, March 1971.

Feltwell, John. *The Naturalist's Garden.* Topsfield, Mass.: Salem House, 1992.

Ferrara, Mike. "Plant a Low-Maintenance Lawn." *Organic Gardening*, February 1993.

———. "Grow a Great Lawn Naturally." *Organic Gardening*, February 1993.

Fitch, James Marston. *American Building: Historical Forces That Shaped It.* New York: Houghton Mifflin, 1948.

———."Primitive Architecture and Climate." *Scientific American*, Vol. 203, No. 6, 1960.

Flemer, William III. "The Role of Plants in Today's Energy Conservation." *American Nurseryman*, Vol. 139, LXXXIX (9), 1974.

Foster, Ruth S. *Landscaping That Saves Energy Dollars.* New York: David McKay, 1978.

Fry, Maxwell, and Drew, Jane. *Tropical Architecture in the Dry and Humid Zones*. New York: Reinhold, 1964.

Geiger, Rudolph. *The Climate Near the Ground*. Cambridge, Mass.: Harvard University Press, 1965.

Geise, William. "Great Insulation from Little Acorns Grows," *Kiplinger's Changing Times*, October 1988.

Gibb, Jamie. *Landscape It Yourself*. New York: Harper & Row, 1988.

Givoni, B. *Man, Climate and Architecture*. London: Building Research Station, Technion, (&) Applied Science Publishers, Ltd.

Goodland, Robert. "Buildings and the Environment." Carey Arboretum of the New York Botanical Garden, 1976.

Griffin, C. W. *Energy Conservation in Buildings*. Construction Specifications Institute, Washington, D.C., 1974.

Hammond, J.; Hunt, M.; Cramer, R.; and Neubauer, L. *A Strategy for Energy Conservation*. Energy Conservation Ordinance Project, Davis, Calif.: Living Systems, 1974.

Hill, Lewis. "Spring Pruning." *Country Journal*, February 1984.

Innes, Clive. *Cacti and Succulents*. London: Ward Lock Limited, 1977.

International Society of Arboriculture. "Benefits of Trees." Bulletin, 1991.

———. "Insect and Disease Problems." Bulletin, 1991.

———. "Mature Tree Care." Bulletin, 1991.

———. "New Tree Planting." Bulletin, 1991.

———. "Tree Selection." Bulletin, 1991.

Kiplinger's Changing Times, "Plant Equity." *Kiplinger's Changing Times*, 1986.

Knox, Gerald, ed. *Better Homes and Gardens Step By Step Landscaping*. Des Moines, Iowa: Meredith Corp., 1991.

Kourik, Robert. *Designing and Maintaining Your Edible Landscape*. Santa Rosa, Calif.: Metamorphic Press, 1986.

Kramer, Paul J., and Kozlowski, Theodore T. *Physiology of Trees*. New York: McGraw-Hill, 1960.

Lake, Daniel. "Transplanting Trees." *Country Journal*, September/October 1991.

Lawn Institute. Bulletins 1-8 on Lawn Care and Seeds, 1991.

Ledin, B., ed. "Cultivated Palms." *American Horticulture*, January 1961.

Leckie, Masters, and Whitehouse, Young. *Other Homes and Garbage: Designs for Self Sufficient Living*. San Francisco: Sierra Club Books, 1975.

Lipkis, Andy and Kate. *The Simple Act of Planting a Tree*. Los Angeles: Jeremy Tarcher, 1990.

Lovins, Amory. "Institutional Inefficiency." *In Context*, No. 35, Spring 1993.

Marinelli, Janet. "Gardens for the 21st Century." *Nature Conservancy*, May/June 1993.

Marinelli, Janet, ed. *The Environmental Gardener*. Brooklyn, N.Y.: Brooklyn Botanical Gardens, 1992.

Marinelli, Janet, and Kourik, Robert. *The Naturally Elegant Home: Environmental Style*. Boston: Little, Brown, 1992.

Martin, Kent. "Dry Times." *Organic Gardening*, Vol. 35, No. 11, November 1988.

Mass Design, Architects and Planners. *Solar Heated Houses for New England and Other North Temperate Climates*.

Mathews, F. Schuyler. *Field Book of American Trees and Shrubs*. New York: G. P. Putnam's Sons, eighteenth impression.

Mathias, M., ed. *Color for the Landscape*. California Arboretum Foundation, Inc., 1973.

Mattern, Vicki, ed. "The O.G. Guide to Perfect Pruning," *Organic Gardening*. February 1993.

McClenon, C., and Robinette, G. O. *Landscape Planning for Energy Conservation*. Environmental Design Press, 1977.

McDonald, Elvin, "How Many Trees Have You Planted or 'Hugged' Lately?" *Plants and Garden News*, Vol. 5, No. 2.

McPherson, E., Gregory. *Energy-Conserving Site Design*. Washington, D.C.: American Society of Landscape Architects, 1984.

Molen, Ronald. *House Plus Environment*. Salt Lake, Utah: Olympus Press, 1974.

Moll, Gary, and Ebenreck, Sara. *Shading Our Cities*. Washington, D.C.: Island Press, 1989.

Moll, Gary, and Young, Stanley. *Growing Greener Cities*. Los Angeles: Living Planet Press, 1992.

Moore, Jr., Harold. *The Major Groups of Palms and Their Distribution*. Bailey Hortorium, 1973.

National Bureau of Standards. *Window Design Strategies to Conserve Energy*. 003-003-01794-9, Government Printing Office, Washington, D.C.

National Wildlife Federation. "Backyard Wildlife Habitat."
Washington, D.C.: National Wildlife Federation, 1990.

National Wildlife Federation. *Gardening for Wildlife: A Complete Guide to Attracting and Enjoying the Fascinating Creatures in Your Backyard*. Washington, D.C.: National Wildlife Federation, 1974.

National Wildlife Federation. "Invite Wildlife to Your Backyard." Washington, D.C.: *National Wildlife Magazine*, 1989.

Olgyay, Victor. *Design with Climate: Bioclimatic Approach to Architectural Regionalism*. Princeton, N.J.: Princeton University Press, 1963.

Packard, Robert T., ed. *Architectural Graphic Standards*. New York: John Wiley & Sons, 1981.

Pennisi, Elizabeth. "Going Native: A Gardener's Guide." *National Wildlife*, April/May 1990.

Pleasant, Barbara. "Translating Permaculture." *Organic Gardening*, April 1990.

Polunin, O., and Huxley, A. *Flowers of the Mediterranean*. Boston: Houghton Mifflin Co., 1966.

Progressive Architecture. *Energy Conscious Design*. Stamford, Conn.: Reinhold Publishing, April 1979, April 1980.

Ransom, W. H. *Solar Radiation: Thermal Effects on Building Materials*. Tropical Building Studies No. 3, Building Research Station, London, 1962.

"Regional Guidelines for Building Passive Energy Conserving Homes." U.S. Department of Housing and Urban Development in cooperation with U.S. Department of Energy, 1978.

Reich, Lee. "How Green a Lawn?" *Upriver/Downriver*, July/August 1991.

Robinette, Gary. *Plants, People and Environmental Quality: A Study of Plants and Their Environmental Function*. Washington, D.C.: U.S. Department of Interior, National Park Service, 1972.

Rothchild, John. *Stop Burning Money: The Intelligent Homeowner's Guide to Household Energy Savings*. New York: Random House, 1981.

Rudofsky, Bernard. *Architecture Without Architects*. New York: Doubleday, 1969.

Russell, Dick. "A Garden of Earthly Designs," *Amicus Journal*, Summer 1993.

Sandia Laboratories. *Passive Solar Buildings: A Compilation of Data and Results*. No. 87185, Albuquerque, N.M., 1978.

Schiler, Marc. "Foliage Effects on Computer Simulation of Building Energy Load Calculations." Ph. D. thesis, Cornell University, 1979.

Shurcliff, William A. *Solar Heated Buildings of North America.* Harrisville, N.H.: Brick Publishing Co.

Stites, J., and Mower, R. G. "Rock Gardens." Ithaca, N.Y.: New York State College of Agriculture and Life Sciences, Cornell University, 1979.

Soil Conservation Society of America. Natural Vegetation Committee, Arizona Chapter; *Landscaping with Native Arizona Plants.* Tucson: University of Arizona Press, 1973.

Stein, Sara. *Noah's Garden: Restoring the Ecology of Our Own Backyards.* Boston: Houghton Mifflin, 1993.

Symposium on Design for Tropical Living; *Proceedings,* Durban, South Africa, 1957.

Taylor, Sally. *Gardening for Wildlife.* Brooklyn, N.Y.: Brooklyn Botanical Gardens, 1987.

Tufts, Craig. *The Backyard Naturalist.* Washington, D.C.: National Wildlife Federation, 1988.

University of Minnesota. *Earth Sheltered Housing Design.* New York: Van Nostrand Reinhold Co., 1978.

U.S. Department of Energy. *Options for Passive Energy Conservation in Site Design.* Springfield, Va.: U.S. Department of Commerce.

Walsh, J.W.T. *The Science of Daylight.* London: Pitman Publishing Corp., 1961.

Watson, Donald, and Bertrand, Alain. "Indigenous Architecture as a Basis of House Design in Developing Countries." *Habitat,* Vol. 1, Nos. 3/4, 1976.

Weniger, Del. *Cacti of the Southwest.* Berlin, Texas: University of Texas Press, 1970.

Williamson, J. F. *Lawns and Groundcovers.* Menlo Park, Calif.: Sunset Books, 1975.

Woodruff, N. P. "Shelterbelt and Surface Barrier Effects on Wind Velocities, Evaporation, House Heating, Snowdrifting." Manhattan, Ks.: Kansas Agricultural Experimental Station, Technical Bulletin 77.

Zuk, Janet. *Trees: A Gardener's Guide.* Brooklyn, N.Y.: Brooklyn Botanical Gardens, 1992.

Index

Italicized page references indicate
illustrations.

using without creating excessive
humidity, 80

Water, 28–30, 91–92
    assessing on your property, 153
    in cool climates, 38–39
    in hot, arid climates, 48, 49–50
    in hot, humid climates, 62–63
    and humidity, 28
    and plants, 30
    in temperate climates, 78
    and temperature, 15, 28–30
    for wildlife, 114
    see also Water-efficient landscaping
Water-efficient landscaping, 1, 2, 91–101
    irrigation, 96–97
    and lawns, 94–95
    maintenance, 98
    makeover plan, 99–101
    planning for, 92–93, 95–96, 99–101
    savings, 2, 92, 100–101
    and soil, 93–94, 97–98
Weeds, 107–109, 97, 98
White Grubs, 109
Wildlife:
    cover, 114
    food, 113
    landscaping for, 113–121
    using native plants for, 115
    and pesticides, 116
    planning landscape for, 116–117
    plants for, 113, 117–121
    landscaping for migration paths,
    115, 115–116
    water for, 114
Windbreaks, 10, 62, 75
    for cooling, 26
    directing snow, 25
    and fences, 26–27, 78, 96
    financial benefits, 2, 10
    and precipitation, 24–25
    importance of planting perpendicular
    to wind, 21, 36
    openings in, 24, 25
    placement to avoid blocking sun, 77
    plants for, 24, 25, 26–27
    planting a, 26–27
    planning, 27–28, 36–38
    size, 26
    for temperate climates, 75–78
    for warmth, 34, 35–38, 75
    and water efficiency, 96
    and wind velocity, 24–25
    see also Venturi effect
Wind chart, *152*, 153
Wind-chill factor, 16–17
Wind, 16–17, 22–28, 29
    blocking with plants, 10, 23–26
    blocking with fence, 26–27, 78, *96*
    chart, *152*, 153

    accentuating cooling winds, 26
    in cool climates, 33–34, 35–38
    determining direction, 27–28, 77,
    152, 153
    funnels, 77
    in hot, arid climates, 45, 49
    in hot, humid climates, 62
    regional winds, 29
    in temperate climates, 75–78
    in urban areas, 33–34
    velocity, 16–17, 24–25
    and water efficiency, 96
    see also Windbreaks, Wind-chill
    factor
Wood chips, 97, 134–135
Worms:
    for improving soil, 94
    for composting, 139–140

Xeriscaping, 94
    see also Water-efficient landscaping
Xeriscape Gardening, 94, 95, 98

Yards, total in U.S., 1

ORDERING INFORMATION

Additional copies of *Energy-Efficient and Environmental Landscaping* can be ordered for $17.95 plus $3 shipping.

For bulk purchases and discount schedule contact:
Appropriate Solutions Press
Dover Road Box 39
South Newfane, Vermont 05351
(802) 348-7441